SUBLIME VIRTUE

SUBLIME
VIRTUE

SUBLIME VIRTUE

'Sainthood', as Rendered Problematic
by a Dozen Novelists

ANDREW SHANKS

DARTON·LONGMAN+TODD

INTELLIGENT ◆ INSPIRATIONAL ◆ INCLUSIVE
SPIRITUAL BOOKS

First published in 2024 by
Darton, Longman and Todd Ltd
Unit 1, The Exchange
6 Scarbrook Road
Croydon CR0 1UH

ISBN: 978-1-915412-28-7

A catalogue record for this book is available from the British Library.

Printed and bound in Great Britain by Ashford Colour Press

Contents

A.

Herd. Gang.
Mob. Saint.

CHAPTER ONE

Sublime Virtue/ Beautiful Virtue

What does it mean to say of something that it's 'sublime'? Is it simply the same as to say that it's 'magnificently beautiful'? Or is it, rather, to say that in a certain sense the phenomenon in question is so magnificent as to *exceed* beauty altogether?

The way the terms 'sublime' and 'beautiful' are used in common parlance, they generally seem to designate contrasting intensities of the same. But when Edmund Burke for instance, in 1757, published *A Philosophical Enquiry into the Origin of our Ideas of the Sublime and the Beautiful*, he was interested in what he saw as the fundamental *opposition* between these two 'ideas'. And subsequently a series of German philosophers – Kant, Schiller, Hegel, Schopenhauer – likewise pondered the differences between *das Erhabene* (the sublime) and *das Schöne* (the beautiful) as constituting the polar ends of a spectrum.

∾

This spectrum isn't only aesthetic in nature. It's also, by extension, ethical and religious.

At the simplest level, it's aesthetic. To contemplate a beautiful landscape, say, is to take a straightforwardly contented delight in the sense of inner calm it conjures up. The scene may be solitary or it may be lively. It may be homely or it may be exotic. But, whatever its character, a purely beautiful landscape, as such, always feels *safe*. The pleasure one takes in a sublime landscape, on the other hand, essentially differs, in that it's qualified by thrilling associated thoughts of *danger* to oneself. One sees tremendous waterfalls for instance, and can't help but imagine oneself swept, helpless, over them. One sees great mountains, dizzying rock-faces, tempest-tossed sea, and again one imagines oneself tumbling, out of control. One sees a vast desert prospect, and imagines oneself wandering, lost, within it. One sees a volcano erupting, and imagines being caught out by it. There's pleasure here in the sensation of being a sheltered observer, not in actual fact exposed to the danger one can so easily picture. Yet, the more vivid one's awareness of the danger, the more the pleasure is heightened. It isn't, strictly speaking, the beauty of the world which inspires dare-devil spirits to embrace physical risk; seeking to test, and to overcome, great peril. No, what such people are responding to is the call of the sublime, in nature.

Now, however, let's move on from the purely physical, to the spiritual. Again, there's a basic distinction to be drawn between two species of *virtue*. There's beautiful virtue, and there's sublime virtue.

To the thoughtful observer, beautiful virtue is just charming. So, it contributes, quite unequivocally, to the smoothly-functioning organic coherence of society. For it's that which springs from a proper recognition of, in the great philosopher F. H. Bradley's phrase, 'my station and its duties'. Such virtue is highly contagious: the virtuous individual's peers being inspired by his, or her, beautiful example, so far as possible to go and do likewise.

In the case of sublime virtue, though, matters are more complicated. Unlike beautiful virtue, sublime virtue both attracts and, at the same time, repels. It attracts inasmuch as it bears compelling witness to a sheer depth of moral wisdom which decisively transcends, and calls into question, any established consensus. But it also repels: its dissident intensity inevitably tends to be found alarming, perhaps even frightening, by those who sense the radicality of its challenge to themselves. There's always something polemical about sublime virtue: an incorrigibly *disruptive* full-frontal confrontation with the thoughtless conformism of herd-morality; with the cunning amorality of gangs; with the thoughtless amorality of mobs. Sublime virtue is sublime by virtue of the courage which such a conflictual attitude demands. Hence, it represents a sort of integrity more awe-inspiring than directly contagious. Encountering it, ordinary everyday honesty is humbled. Such honesty is moved to confess its own hypocrisy, inasmuch as sublime virtue is clearly of universal authority, an example for all to follow. And yet the fact is that, for the most part, one doesn't *dare* do so.

∾

I want to argue that both species of virtue are properly sacred.

But some religious traditions identify the sacred very much more with the beautiful than with the sublime; and some accord the highest value to the sublime.

The *Analects* of Confucius is a classic example of the former tendency. For it's a text primarily concerned with the beautiful virtue of the *junzi*, the ideal administrator: a gentleman of the utmost probity, never power-grabbing, never bullying, but absolutely dedicated to the common good. The *junzi*'s role in life is compared to that of 'a sacrificial vase of jade' (*Analects* 5. 4). In other words: he renders himself a component of beautiful sacred ritual; subsumes himself entirely into that task. Thus, the original Confucian ideal is of a beautiful bureaucratic order, envisaged as a sort of vast dance, where no one wants to step out of line, precisely lest they spoil the beauty of the overall proceedings.

Or again I think of Ancient Greek city-state religion, the way it's idealised in the poetry of Hölderlin, the philosophic prose of Hegel. For Hegel, this is the paradigmatic 'religion of art': a culture in which the sacred was purely and simply *identified* with the beauty of glorious architectural, sculptural, painterly, musical and dramatic art; the stuff of lovely festivals, celebrating the beautiful virtues constitutive of good citizenship in general.

Of course, all religious cultures involve a large element of beauty in their liturgy, and associated art. But others by contrast mix that element of beauty together with other elements belonging more towards the other pole, governed by the sublime. The regular depiction of the Buddha, for instance, shows him as an embodiment of beautiful serenity. Yet, this is a beauty understood to involve a sublime discipline of self-abnegation. And one finds something, at any rate, of the same duality in the sages of Taoist China; or of Greco-Roman Stoicism.

For religious sublimity *at maximum sheer impassioned intensity*, however, there's required something more. *God* needs to enter the fray. That's to say: the God of the prophets; God confronting all earthly authorities, and utterly outbidding their claims. If the confrontational imperatives of sublime virtue are to be registered at full poetic blast, they need to be voiced by God; God-recognised and duly honoured in the most subversive terms.

Granted: the *corruption* of corrupt God-religion is, by nature, more dangerous than the corruption of corrupt purely beautiful, non-theistic, or God-anonymising, religion. For, whilst the latter may still be co-opted into tribal, *inter*-religious gang-and-mob political violence, at least it doesn't so readily degenerate into that particular sort of *intra*-religious violence which derives from God-invoking zealotry, or fanaticism; where co-religionist is pitted against co-religionist, in God's name. I though, for my sins, am a Christian priest. And what therefore concerns me in the present work is just the highest ethical ideal of Abrahamic (Jewish/Christian/Islamic) God-religion as a whole: the proper nature of 'the saint', in that broad, but also quite specific, cultural context.

Thus: sublimely prophetic religion may be said to bifurcate into corrupt *ideo*-logy of the zealot, versus authentic *theo*-logy, celebrating a truly thoughtful ideal of sainthood. And this is a book about what it might take to rescue theology, so defined, from mere sacred ideology, as decisively as possible; even whilst still staying with the full, primal intensity of the sublime, which zealotry corrupts.[1]

12

Christianity especially has, over the centuries, developed a rich literature of hagiography; lives of the saints. First, it was tales of martyrdom. Then, it was accounts of great ascetics. Bishop Athanasius of Alexandria's *Life of Antony*, written in honour of the desert-dwelling Egyptian hermit who became the 'Father of Monasticism', was immensely influential in helping to establish the genre. The *Life of Antony* dates from around the year 360; shortly after the saint's death. And since then, all sorts of other notable figures in Church history have received hagiographical treatment: bishops, monastic reformers, missionaries, scholars, visionaries, royal patrons. To some extent or other, all the figures so honoured have indeed been represented as exemplars of sublime virtue.

But alas, that isn't the only criterion for sainthood at work in this literature. If only it was! A Church *wholly* dedicated to the cultivation of true sublime virtue, alone: wouldn't that be the kingdom of God arriving on earth?

The trouble with traditional hagiography, I'd argue, is that it gets so caught up into the corporate egoism, and evangelistic impatience, of the Church, instead. There are, I think, three inter-connected layers to the problem:

- In this literature, 'saints' are remembered as miracle-workers. That, though, tends to distract from, and to dissolve, the commemoration of their sublime virtue. For, the sublimity of sublime virtue consists both in its exceptional nature, and also in in the acutely challenging fact that it's, nevertheless, achieved by people who are otherwise *like us*. Yet in traditional hagiography the miracle-working of 'saints' has the effect of distancing them from us: it appears to be a sort of superpower, a gift of God which we others – through no fault of our own – just haven't received.

- Again, inasmuch as traditional hagiography is part of the propagandistic self-promotion of the ecclesiastical institution, the memory of these 'saints'' sublime virtue tends to be more or less occluded by the memory of their services rendered to that institution. So, they tend to be celebrated – not so much for any sublime stand they may have made against the folly of the herd as such, the gang as such, the mob as such – but, rather, for heroically upholding the cause of the Church. And if the herd, the gang, the mob professes a basic loyalty to the Church – well then, it may seem, never mind!

- And then, at its best, traditional hagiography is precisely a project for framing a representation of sublime virtue in beauty. But to the extent that it's infected with evangelistic impatience, it naturally aims at kitsch-beauty; beauty of the most generally accessible, because sentimental and self-indulgent, kind. In which case the element here of remembered sublimity – as opposed to beauty – straight away evaporates. For sublimity is purely and simply incompatible with kitsch.

What follows, therefore, is a book about the necessary re-conceptualisation of 'sainthood'; lifting the concept of 'the saint', once and for all, beyond the confines of its representation in traditional hagiography; imaginatively connecting in quite a different, fresh way with the actual reality of sublime virtue.

∾

In order to accomplish the transformation in question, it seems to me that, first of all, we surely need quite another, *secular* species of literature; by way of a matrix.

But look! That other, secular species of literature already, to a prolific extent, does exist.

Biography, memoir, poetry: all of these may contribute.

Above all, however, I want to explore the immense potential, for imaginatively appreciating the sublime virtue of the saint, intrinsic to the *modern novel*.

And, in particular, I'm interested in what one might call 'sacramental' novels.

A sacrament is definable as a theistically framed spiritual transaction which, in the old scholastic formula, 'effects what it signifies'. It interprets divine grace – this is what it 'signifies'. And by, so to speak, immersing oneself in it, one may actually receive something of that grace – this is its 'effect'. Sublime virtue is the work of divine grace, above all as awakening empathy for others. In the words of Jesus, welding together passages from *Deuteronomy* and *Leviticus*:

> You shall love the Lord your God out of the whole of your heart and in the whole of your soul and in the whole of your strength and in the whole of your mind, and your neighbour as yourself. (*Luke* 10:27, David Bentley Hart's version; and c.f. *Matthew* 22:37, 39, *Mark* 12:30—31)

A 'sacramental novel' on the one hand gives us, to admire, examples of empathy escalated to the level of sublime virtue, no less. It 'signifies' that admiration; whilst, on the other hand, it 'effects' empathy, the admired quality; stimulating the reader to empathise with the characters evoked, and hence also with anyone, in real life, akin to them. Of course, all significantly humane novels attempt to stimulate empathy. But a 'sacramental novel' does so with especial gravitas, due to its sacramentality.

Here, then, I discuss the work of a dozen – for my purposes, I think, very interesting – modern 'sacramental novelists', as such. A sort of informal canon ...

---

1. Some Christian thinkers have actually wanted to banish the 'modern' or 'postmodern' distinction between the sublime and the beautiful, from theology. See for example David Bentley Hart, *The Beauty of the Infinite:*

The Aesthetic of Christian Truth (Grand Rapids, Michigan: Eerdmans, 2003), pp. 43—93. This is a reaction against the use of the distinction by 'postmodern' French atheists and anti-theologians; in the first instance, J.-F. Lyotard.

But why, after all, surrender potentially helpful terminology, just because others use it for other purposes than one's own?

CHAPTER TWO

George Eliot:
Middlemarch

'Don't preach at me! Don't nag! Enough already, now, of your excessive moralising!'

When this is the reaction to some bludgeoning expression of mere herd-morality, or fashionable political correctness, as such, that's one thing. But it isn't always so. For one may very well also recoil, in just this way, from that quite opposite sort of phenomenon, the sublimity of sublime virtue, as celebrated in a 'sacramental' novel. Which is quite another matter.

Nor indeed is such a recoil necessarily unthinking, unsophisticated. Thus, consider for example F. R. Leavis's critique of *Middlemarch*.

∾

Leavis famously begins his magisterial study of *The Great Tradition* by declaring George Eliot to be – alongside Jane Austen, Henry James and Joseph Conrad – one of the four chief classic novelists of English literature.[1] He admires *Middlemarch* in particular, as her greatest work. But he argues that it nevertheless has one major 'weakness'. And that's precisely the portrayal of the young, saintly heroine, Dorothea Brooke, right at the heart of it.[2]

Middlemarch is a prime illustration of what I mean by a 'sacramental' novel. It doesn't matter, in this regard, that Eliot herself was an atheist; a post-Christian admirer of Ludwig

Feuerbach who translated Feuerbach's pioneering anti-theological polemic, *The Essence of Christianity*, into English. Like Feuerbach before her, she remains deeply Christian in her atheism. So, her humanist ethical ideal, as set out above all in *Middlemarch*, is still altogether sublime. Notwithstanding its polemical mutation – renaming the divine as 'Humanity' – it still belongs very much within the general domain of Abrahamic religious tradition.

First published in 1871 – 72, *Middlemarch* describes events in a small provincial town of the English midlands, some forty years earlier. All the characters in the world described are, as a matter of course, Christian. The saintly Dorothea Brooke belongs to the congregation of her Church of England parish church. In good Anglican fashion, she seems quite indifferent to matters theological. And yet, much to the alarm of those around her, she's sublimely resistant to the ethical banality of her world. Although she doesn't use the term, she scorns its prevailing herd-morality.

Before Dorothea has even appeared on the scene, Eliot signals, in a 'Preface', her intention to describe a saint; albeit one excluded by circumstance from any great engagement in public affairs, and hence from actual historic fame. By way of contrast, here, she evokes the historic fame of Saint Teresa of Avila. As a member of a religious order – one in evident need of reform – Teresa did indeed have just the sort of scope for moral action which Dorothea lacks. An opportunity which she, eventually, seized with gusto. But what Eliot, first and foremost, sets out to evoke is the ultimate waste of potential, in the lives of so many free-spirited women like Dorothea, where no such scope has been provided.

~

This, though, isn't what interests Leavis. On the contrary: he describes the characterisation of Dorothea as a curious '*enclave of immaturity*' in Eliot's otherwise so profoundly mature work.[3] 'Maturity' is a recurrent term in his critical writing, not only with regard to Eliot. He generally leaves it undefined. But here it

18

seems to mean, precisely, a proper moral temperance; restraint of the impulse to idealise. Leavis (himself a notoriously intemperate man, albeit in another more acerbic way!) absolutely disapproves of what he sees as Eliot's quite *in*-temperate idealisation of Dorothea's sublime virtue. It is, he thinks, all too typical of a tendency to be observed in other novels of hers: notably, her intemperate idealisation of the heroes Adam Bede, Felix Holt, Daniel Deronda; and her idealising self-projection into the heroines Maggie Tulliver and Romola.

His development of the critique is admirably trenchant.

> We have the danger-signal [he writes] in the very outset, in the brief Prelude, with its reference to St Theresa ... [This] is a dangerous theme for George Eliot, and we recognize a far from reassuring accent.[4]

The opening couple of chapters serve to introduce Dorothea's puritanical ardour in quite ironical fashion, as she is shown being somewhat thoughtlessly irritable with her sister; and we are also shown the provincial nature of her mentality. Leavis is happy enough with this. But unfortunately, he thinks, the irony then rather lapses. The trouble he sees foreshadowed in the Prelude already begins to re-surface in Chapter 3, as Dorothea begins to consider the possibility of marriage to the elderly, dry-as-dust scholar Mr Casaubon. Eliot is clearly anxious for us to sympathise with Dorothea's idealistic motives for being open to the idea. Leavis however is, straight away, resistant to this advocacy.

And then, in his view, things go from bad to worse. In particular, for instance, he reacts with allergic ferocity to the great scene in Chapter 76 which brings Dorothea – by now, the widowed Mrs Casaubon – together with the novel's other leading character, Dr Lydgate. Here, Lydgate is a broken man; his reputation ruined because of the scandal engulfing Mr Bulstrode, in which he is supposedly implicated. Dorothea is determined to affirm her, in fact, quite justified confidence in Lydgate; and to see what she might do to help him continue his work as a hospital reformer. Although he despairs of continuing that work, Lydgate is nevertheless deeply grateful for the emotional support she offers him. He smiles:

> The childlike grave-eyed earnestness with which Dorothea [spoke] was irresistible – blent into an adorable whole with her ready understanding of high experience.

But then the narrator-voice adds, in brackets:

> (Of lower experience such as plays a great part in the world, poor Mrs Casaubon had a very blurred short-sighted knowledge, little helped by her imagination.)[5]

Leavis – thinking as he does to see a great deal of authorial projective self-flattery in the portrayal of Dorothea – simply ignores the critical thrust of this latter comment. That is, he treats it as if it were nothing more than a would-be coquettish ploy of false modesty. Meanwhile, however, he squirms at Lydgate's 'adoration'; and squirms all the more when, after the interview, Lydgate, riding away, remarks to himself:

> 'This young creature has a heart large enough for the Virgin Mary.'[6]

For Leavis, the whole element of enthusiastic uplift in the scene represents a quite ghastly 'failure of touch … a radical disorder' on Eliot's part.[7]

And yet, the scene is after all perfectly realistic! Lydgate is a man against whom the whole moralistic herd of his neighbours in Middlemarch is now beginning to turn; it's clear that he's going to be shunned by them. Dorothea doesn't in fact know him all that well. Nevertheless, she's characteristically determined to defy the mean-spiritedness of the herd. We know Lydgate as a man of deep feeling. How could he fail to respond in very much the way that Eliot portrays?

There are in fact only two characters within the novel who really begin to appreciate the latent Saint Teresa in Dorothea. Lydgate is one. The other is the man who ends up becoming her second husband: Will Ladislaw. And, again, Leavis is determined to discredit Eliot's portrayal of Ladislaw's love for Dorothea. Thus: 'Everyone agrees', he remarks, that Will isn't 'substantially ... "there".'[8] Certainly it's true that many critics have been disinclined to consider Dorothea's marriage with Will as an ideal 'happy ending'; supposing that to be what Eliot intends. It may well be agreed that Will isn't substantially 'there', in this specific role; since after all it would surely require a saint, to be a true partner to this saint; and Will isn't a saint. We see him, first, as a drifter. Then as a flirt: in his foolish dalliance with Lydgate's wife Rosamund. Finally, he is redeemed by Dorothea's love – so that, with her loyal support, as his wife, he goes on to find his proper vocation as an energetic political reformer, a radical MP.

Leavis however, for his part, wants to go much further than merely to say that Will is less than saintly. For him, Will 'hardly exists'.[9] That's to say, he hardly exists in such a way as would, so to speak, qualify him as a valid witness in Dorothea's favour, at all. And neither is Dorothea, reciprocally, a valid witness in his favour. Both, Leavis argues, are simple conduits for their author's abstract valuations; to which the narrative adds nothing further of real, concrete moral significance. Thus, he says:

> George Eliot's valuation of Will Ladislaw, in short, is Dorothea's, just as Will's of Dorothea is George Eliot's.[10]

There is in this whole area of the novel, he thinks, a lamentable lack of proper authorial distance, both ways.

Yet, that just isn't true!

Eliot's valuation of Will isn't the same as Dorothea's; nor is Will's valuation of Dorothea the same as Eliot's. For Dorothea, it appears, simply loves Will. But Eliot, on the other hand, from her position of authorial detachment, recognises that *neither* of Dorothea's two marriages was '*ideally* beautiful'.[11] In the Finale to the novel Eliot returns to the viewpoint of the Preface: her underlying critique of a world in which saints are, all too often, unable fully to flourish. And her last word on Will suggests that – notwithstanding all his love and admiration for Dorothea – he is, at least to some extent, still part of the all-encompassing problem here.

I must say, I find Leavis's rage against Eliot's portrayal of Will quite puzzling; oddly over-the-top.

∾

To encounter any sort of virtue in another person, alike whether it be beautiful or sublime, is always, at least to some extent – unless one is a complete psychopath – to feel oneself implicitly challenged: *'Go, you, and do likewise!'* But in the case of sublime virtue the admiration one feels is, straight away, liable to be mixed with alarm, even terror: *'I can't ...'*

Søren Kierkegaard is the great philosophical analyst of this inner resistance. Let's apply his categories to *Middlemarch*. Kierkegaard analyses our resistance to sublime virtue in terms of a distinction between three basic levels.

The first level: *anxiety*, or *dread*.

Sublime virtue is immediately embattled against the herd, the gang, the mob. In *Middlemarch*, Dorothea's whole battle is against the herd-morality of her world: its sheer well-intentioned banality. We're most of us herd-animals, most of the time. And 'anxiety' or 'dread', in the specific Kierkegaardian sense, is definable as what herd-animals feel, when confronted by sublime virtue.[12]

Why does Dorothea opt to marry the Revd Mr Casaubon? It's surely because he alone, amongst the few people she at that stage knows, seems to stand outside the herd. He has no other charms. But, for her, this is enough. Casaubon is engaged on what appears to be a grand scholarly project: *A Key to All Mythologies*. The project is, as a matter of fact, quite futile. It has already been decisively superseded by the latest German-language scholarship; but

Casaubon can't read German, and so he doesn't recognise this.[13] Still less, though, does Dorothea. What attracts her in him is just his hyper-serious eccentricity; his awkward solemnity; everything about him that the Middlemarch herd, so to speak, finds most off-putting.

And why, after Casaubon's death, does Dorothea fall in love with Will Ladislaw? On the one hand, she's responding to Will's love for her. But, on the other hand, he too – at least to some faltering extent – stands out from the herd. Will appreciates her for *her* standing-out from the herd; and she appreciates the qualities in him by which he's equipped for his eventual role as a high-principled political campaigner.

The Middlemarch herd disapproves of both marriages. In later years, Eliot tells us, Dorothea

> was spoken of … as a fine girl who married a sickly clergyman, old enough to be her father, and in little more than a year after his death, gave up her estate to marry his cousin – young enough to have been his son, with no property, and not well-born. Those who had not seen anything of Dorothea usually observed that she could not have been a 'nice woman,' else she would not have married either the one or the other.[14]

The feelings of those immediately around her are more ambivalent. But they also disapprove of both marriages.

In general, she makes them anxious. Here, for example, in an early scene, she is in conversation with Casaubon and her (benign, but generally fatuous) uncle, Mr Brooke, who praises her sister Celia's pretty playing of the piano:

> 'It's a pity you should not have little recreations of that sort, Casaubon' [Mr Brooke said]: 'the bow always strung – that kind of thing, you know – will not do.'
>
> 'I never could look on it in the light of a recreation to have my ear teased with measured noises,' said Mr Casaubon. 'A tune much iterated has the ridiculous effect of making the words

in my mind perform a sort of minuet to keep time – an effect hardly tolerable, I imagine, after boyhood. As to the grander forms of music, worthy to accompany solemn celebrations, and even to serve as an educating influence according to the ancient conception, I say nothing, for with these we are not immediately concerned.'

'No; but music of that sort I should enjoy,' said Dorothea. 'When we were coming home from Lausanne my uncle took us to hear the great organ at Freiburg, and it made me sob.'

'That kind of thing is not healthy, my dear,' said Mr Brooke. 'Casaubon, she will be in your hands now: you must teach my niece to take things more quietly, eh, Dorothea?'[15]

And here, after she is widowed, she is speaking with that good soul, the rector's wife, Mrs Cadwallader:

'You will certainly go mad in that house alone, my dear' [said Mrs Cadwallader]. 'You will see visions. We have all got to exert ourselves a little to keep sane, and call things by the same names as other people call them by ... Think what a bore you might become to yourself and to your fellow-creatures if you were always playing tragedy queen and taking things sublimely ...'

'I never called everything by the same name that all the people about me did,' said Dorothea stoutly.

'But I suppose you have found out your mistake, my dear,' said Mrs Cadwallader, 'and that is a proof of sanity.'

Dorothea was aware of the sting, but it did not hurt her. 'No,' she said, 'I still think that the greater part of the world is mistaken about many things. Surely one may be sane and yet think so, since the greater part of the world has so often had to come round from its opinion.'[16]

The solicitude of both Mr Brooke and Mrs Cadwallader clearly springs from an underlying, dormant state of anxiety, which Dorothea's presence forever threatens to awake.

The second level: *despair*.

Whereas 'anxiety' is the recoil, from sublime virtue, of pure herd-morality – that is, the instinctive reaction of moral individuals lacking any very strong sense of moral individuality – what Kierkegaard discusses under the rubric of 'despair' is, by contrast, the recoil of others more thoughtful, with at any rate the potential therefore to develop a truly individualised, fresh take on reality.

Casaubon is a soul in despair. He indeed has a highly individualised sense of personal vocation. And yet, it's nothing but torment to him.

Kierkegaard distinguishes between 'despair of weakness' ('in despair not wanting to be oneself') and 'despair of defiance' ('in despair wanting to be oneself').[17] When Casaubon first appears on the scene, he's very much an example of the first sort. He's a man of deep feeling, with, one senses, at least some real potential for authentic moral seriousness. Dorothea hasn't entirely misjudged him. Only, having early on mis-identified his vocation in life with an all-consuming scholarly project which – he now secretly realises – lacks any real moral value, he finds himself too weak to change course. He opts to marry Dorothea in the vain hope of being inwardly changed, cured of his misery. But that hope is short-lived. There's no way he can live up to the naïve hopes which she, in turn, has invested in him. And the more he sees that, the more, in his bitterness, he shifts away from 'despair of weakness', towards 'despair of defiance'. Observing the immediate warmth of her response to young Ladislaw, he grows defiantly jealous. He knows himself to be gravely unwell. Out of demonic spite, therefore, he changes his will: specifying that if, after his death, she marries Ladislaw, she must forfeit her inheritance as his widow.

Dorothea's poignant disillusionment with regard to Casaubon begins whilst they're on their honeymoon in Rome. Yet, the moral purpose of the narrator-voice, on the other hand, is to distribute compassion, so far as possible, impartially. And no sooner are the newly-weds back from that honeymoon than Eliot, as it were, breaks cover to address the reader directly, thus:

> One morning, some weeks after her arrival at Lowick [their
> marital home], Dorothea – but why always Dorothea? Was her
> point of view the only possible one with regard to this marriage?
> I protest against all our interest, all our effort at understanding
> being given to the young skins that look blooming in spite of
> trouble, for these too will get faded, and will know the older
> and more eating griefs which we are helping to neglect ...[18]

Having, at some length, awoken the reader's compassion for
Dorothea, next therefore the narrator-voice sets out to do the
same for her husband. Mrs Cadwallader's comment at the time
of Dorothea's first becoming engaged to him has a certain poetic
brilliance:

> 'She says, he is a great soul. A great bladder for dried peas to
> rattle in!'[19]

But the genial contempt of this verdict is just the tone of complacent
herd morality. The narrator-voice pleads with us to look deeper; to
see Edward Casaubon the way Dorothea herself increasingly does.
That's to say: as a proud but vulnerable man; secretly anxious
lest, as seems all too likely, his life's work might peter out in non-
productive failure; and troubled by the emotional demands of
marriage, which truth to tell he hadn't really anticipated.

One of the most remarkable features of *Middlemarch* is its
sacramental enactment of the compassion which Dorothea,
above all, represents. And nowhere is Dorothea's compassionate
nature more admirably apparent than in her relationship to her
despairing husband. The trouble is, though, that she loves the true
self Casaubon does not want to be. Her compassionate presence
in the house therefore becomes, for him, a constant chafing of his
wounded spirit.

The third level: *offence*.

Alas: Casaubon resents what he perceives as the sheer *intrusiveness*
of Dorothea's compassion. And here, finally, we arrive at the

threshold of Kierkegaard's third category of recoil from sublime virtue.

Thus, in Kierkegaard's analysis, 'despair' is the intensification of 'anxiety'; two, in themselves, purely emotional conditions. By contrast however, the third category, of 'offence', is a *theoretic* recoil.[20] One who takes 'offence' at sublime virtue may, or may not, do so out of personal 'anxiety' or 'despair'. But, at all events, they develop theoretic arguments against what they perceive, precisely, as the excessive intrusivenessness of sublime virtue. They plead – on moral grounds – for an altogether more detached attitude of indulgence towards the victims of 'anxiety' or 'despair'.

Yes. And what better illustration, after all, could there be of this than the eminent critic himself, F. R. Leavis; with his *ad feminam* attack on George Eliot as Dorothea's all too intransigent author? All too intransigently idealistic …

∾

Virginia Woolf famously described *Middlemarch* as a 'magnificent book, which with all its imperfections, is one of the few English books written for grown-up people'.[21]

It's a novel that, at the same time, both illustrates the moral necessity of growing up, as vividly illustrated for example by the abiding destructive childishness of Rosamund Vincy, who becomes Rosamund Lydgate; and yet, also, in the figure of Dorothea – with her abiding, adult child-*likeness* – suggests the limitations of grown-up-ness, maturity, *alone*, as an all-determining moral ideal. This is perhaps the most striking sense in which Eliot's atheism remains deeply Christian: the echo here of Jesus's words,

> Amen, I tell you, whoever does not receive the kingdom as a little child shall most certainly not enter into it (*Luke* 18:17; and cf. *Matthew* 18:3, *Mark* 10:15).

Indeed, the theme is announced right at the beginning of the Preface, where Eliot gives her own (somewhat mis-remembered) version of a self-deprecating story which Saint Teresa tells. That is, the tale of how Teresa, as a small child, shared with her brother Rodrigo a wild fantasy of, the two of them, together one day travelling to the 'land of the Moors', there to find glorious martyrdom.[22]

Alas, though, this little story isn't to Leavis's taste at all! At the end of the day, Laurence Lerner is no doubt right:

> The disagreement between Leavis and George Eliot is in fact an ethical one. The heart of Leavis's criticism does not concern falsity [that is, lack of observational realism] in the author's vision, but the value of the Theresa-complex.[23]

In his critique of *Middlemarch*, Leavis is essentially championing a certain ethical notion of 'maturity', against 'the Theresa-complex'; or, more generally, the whole Christian ideal of sainthood.

But what, exactly, *is* this countervailing 'maturity'? I for my part well remember, as an idealistic adolescent, rather hating the condition of adolescence, and impatiently aspiring to get beyond it. Lerner (it appears) diagnoses Leavisian 'maturity' as, in essence, an adult persistence of just such impatience. And he rejects it, on the grounds that

> the presence of a noble nature [such as Dorothea's] generous in its wishes, ardent in its charity, *does* [quite properly] change the lights for us; loving heart-beats and sobs after an unattained goodness ought to have a more complex fate, as the adolescent matures, than simply to be outgrown; and [mere] maturity is a virtue within the range of some very dreary people, and beyond the range of some very fine ones.[24]

I can only say that I agree.

---

1. Leavis, *The Great Tradition* (London: Chatto & Windus, 1948; second edition 1960); p. 9. He later added D. H. Lawrence to the list.

2. Ibid. p. 72.

3. Ibid. p. 75.

4. Ibid. pp. 72—3.

5. *Middlemarch* (London: Penguin Classics, 1994), Chap. 76, p. 765.

6. Ibid. p. 768.

7. Leavis, 1960; p. 78.

8. Ibid. p. 75.

9. Ibid. p. 76.

10. Ibid. p. 75.

11. *Middlemarch,* Finale, p. 838; emphasis added.

12. Kierkegaard, *The Concept of Anxiety* (1844), ed. and trans. Reidar Thomte (Princeton University Press, 1980).

13. He appears, in fact, to be a follower of the late 18th century scholar Jacob Bryant: *Middlemarch,* 1994; Chap. 22, p. 222. That's to say: he posits a common origin to all traditions of mythology, which have supposedly diverged from the days of Ham, son of Noah, onwards. Unfortunately, however, his inability to read German means that he couldn't respond, in particular, to Karl Otfried Muller's 1825 work, *Prolegomena zu einer wissenschaftlichen Mythologie,* which had already, very recently at the time of the novel's action, developed an altogether more sophisticated, and contrary, theory.

    (Although not mentioning Muller's work by name, Ladislaw appears to be aware of this.)

14. *Middlemarch,* Finale, p. 838.

15. Ibid. Chap. 7, pp. 65—6.

16. Ibid. Chap. 54, p. 537.

17. Kierkegaard, *The Sickness unto Death* (1849), trans. Alastair Hannay (London: Penguin, 1989).

18. *Middlemarch*. Chap. 29, p. 278.

19. Ibid. Chap. 6, p. 58.

20. Kierkegaard, *Training in Christianity* (1850), trans. Howard. V. Hong and Edna H. Hong (Princeton University Press, 1991).

21. Woolf, 1925. Essay originally published in the *Times Literary Supplement*, 20th November 1919.

22. C.f. Chapter 1 of *The Life of Saint Teresa of Ávila: by herself*. Eliot represents Teresa 'hand-in-hand with her still smaller brother' as they actually set off:

    > Out they toddled from rugged Avila, wide-eyed and helpless-looking as two fauns ... until domestic reality met them in the form of uncles, and turned them back from their great resolve.

    In reality, Rodrigo was four years older than Teresa. And, as Teresa tells the tale, they never got past the stage of planning the expedition. 'Our having parents', she says, 'seemed to us a very great hindrance.' She makes no mention of uncles.

23. Lerner, 'Dorothea and the Theresa-Complex' (1967), in Patrick Swinden, ed., *George Eliot*, Middlemarch: *A Casebook* (London: Macmillan 1972), p. 246.

24. Ibid. pp. 246—7.

B.

The Recipe
for Sainthood

CHAPTER THREE

The *Amos* Impulse/ the Isaianic Archetype

I

To be a Christian theologian is to take one's place in a still-ongoing story which began just under two thousand, eight hundred years ago. And the same goes for Jewish religious thinkers; Muslim religious thinkers.

It's a story which begins with an earthquake. Namely: the one recorded in the opening verse of the book of *Amos*. For, Amos is the first of the Hebrew prophets whose actual words are preserved for us, in book-form. And here the prophet's work is specifically dated to 'the days of King Uzziah of Judah and the days of King Jeroboam son of Joash of Israel, two years before the earthquake'. We don't know the exact length of the prophet's career within that time frame; the phrasing suggests it may have been quite short, perhaps in the 760s BCE.[1] At that time nothing else in the Hebrew Bible had yet been written, apart from the Song of Deborah, later incorporated into *Judges* 5, and perhaps a few other fragments. There's nothing older to mark out Hebrew religion as having yet become significantly different *in kind* from the sacred traditions of the surrounding world.

In the book of *Amos*, for the first time, we encounter, still in quite inchoate, moral-earthquake form, the vast, multi-faceted *problem* with which the whole 'Abrahamic' tradition thereafter is going to struggle, down to the present day, and no doubt beyond.

Granted, it remains unclear just how much of the book of *Amos* as a whole actually dates back to the mid-eighth century. The scholarly consensus is that, as with more or less all the rest of Hebrew scripture, it evolved over centuries of being copied: with the text re-ordered, and added to, by the scribes. However, there are two good reasons to suppose that much of it does indeed consist of original material.

One reason is its tonal consistency; its distinctiveness; its extraordinarily powerful poetic quality. All of it, up until the very last five verses, is excoriating satire – directed against the wealthy, for their indifference to the plight of the poor – punctuated with eerie little snapshots of the coming disaster they deserve. Other prophets, of course, regularly threaten punishment for corporate sin; but none do so with quite the same sparkle, the same devastating mockery.

The other reason is that the polemic here, very interestingly I think, differs from that in the subsequent prophets, from *Hosea* onwards, inasmuch as it places so little emphasis on the very theme which they make central. According to Hosea, and to all the prophets who follow him, the absolutely primary demand which the god YHWH makes upon his people is that they should worship him *alone*. The norm, of course, at that period in Israel and Judah as in all the nations round about was for people to worship a variety of different gods, for different purposes. Hosea, a generation later, pioneeringly declares this to be spiritual adultery. Amos no doubt *was* hostile to the cults of other gods, besides YHWH.[2] But the fact remains that this isn't what he *focuses on*. If later editors had played a truly major role in reworking the text, one would surely have expected them to add a good deal more by way of post-Hoseanic 'YHWH-alone-ism'.[3]

∾

When one reads the story of Moses, in *Exodus, Leviticus, Numbers* and *Deuteronomy*; or the stories of the earlier patriarchs in *Genesis*; or the later 'history books' of the Bible: one should always bear in mind that these texts, in origin, constitute the campaign literature of a revolutionary movement essentially responding to the challenge that originated with *Amos*. The YHWH whom they portray is a fictional back-projection of the God who first, *in actual fact*, burst into history through that challenge, and then through the response initiated by *Hosea*.

Indeed, the incandescent fury of *Amos* surely is the registering of a moral earthquake. There's actually no reason to suppose that prior to the mid-eighth century BCE the religion of Ancient Israel was all that different in intellectual character from the religion of the neighbouring peoples. But here *is* something quite radically new. Here's a whole new sense of *what a god might want*. Before this, it had been clear to everyone alike. Self-evidently, it had been supposed, what gods want is to be ritually worshipped. They also, insofar as they're associated with rulers, want obedience to those rulers and general conformity to the norms of social cohesion. Everyone, everywhere, knew that, in dealing with the gods, you could never be too obsequious. Flattery was always vital. Yet, here, speaking through the prophet Amos, is a god who, on the contrary, in the most emphatic fashion says, '*Don't flatter me!*'

Addressing his own ordinary devotees – some of them no doubt perfectly sincere, even enthusiastic in their devotion – YHWH declares that he's sick and tired of their liturgies in his honour; their sacrificial offerings; their harp music, their songs in his praise. Far rather, he says,

> let justice roll down like waters,
> and righteousness like an everflowing stream.
>
> (5:21—24)

In Christian corporate memory, *Amos* has largely been reduced to this sound-bite; abstracted from context and so rendered trite. Rabbinic liturgy makes almost no use of the book. For Islamic tradition, Amos is lost in the general crowd of the prophets. But what god had ever previously spoken like this, framing a call for justice with such a rumbustious refusal of merely flattering worship, in general? There's no reason to suppose that the members of the ruling class in Israel were more corrupt than those of other nations. Nevertheless YHWH, speaking through Amos, lays into them as no god, in any culture, had ever done before. Suddenly, YHWH appears to be a completely different sort of god from the others. The very fact that the prophecy of Amos was written down and preserved, as no Hebrew prophecy had been previously, is testimony to the shocking sheer originality of his vision.

How is it to be accounted for? In the first place, if we're to believe the little story in *Amos* 7:10—17, this prophet was, by temperament, a subversive from the outset. Here we see him, an unlicensed prophet from the southern Hebrew kingdom of Judah, who has arrived in the northern kingdom of Israel, and has there been spreading word that, by YHWH's decree, King Jeroboam is going to 'die by the sword', and 'Israel must go into exile away from his land'. He's confronted by the senior cleric Amaziah, priest of the royal shrine at Bethel, who tells him to go home. Whereupon, he further prophesies that Amaziah's wife is fated to become a prostitute, his sons and his daughters will fall by the sword, his land will be confiscated, and he himself, along with all the other notables of Israel, will die 'in an unclean land'. It seems in fact very likely that this story is based on a real historical event, since so far as we know none of these disasters actually came to pass. We surely would have been told if they had! And it's hard to see why any subsequent writer, contributing to the *Amos* tradition, would want to *invent* such a lamentable demonstration of his fallibility, in predicting the future.[4]

But then, in the period immediately following King Jeroboam II's eventual death (by natural causes) matters were further complicated by startling developments abroad. In 745 the emperor Tiglath-Pileser III came to power in Assyria, and set to work organising the world's first ever professional standing army. With this army Tiglath-Pileser proceeded with great efficiency and ruthlessness to subdue the whole region, overthrowing previously more or less independent little states one by one. *Amos* 6:2 clearly refers to the victims of Tiglath-Pileser's campaign of 738; threatening Israel with the same treatment.[5] *Amos* 1:3 – 2:16 consists of YHWH condemning the peoples of Damascus, Philistia, Tyre, Edom, Ammon, Moab, Judah as well as finally also Israel, for their sins, and sentencing them all alike to dire punishment. Assyria isn't named. But the actual threat with which every one of these states was now confronted was Tiglath-Pileser's army. *In response to this step-change escalation in organised mass-cruelty, the prophecy is calling on Israel to become an equivalently pioneering role model, for a quite opposite ethos.*

∾

As I've said, however, *Amos* presents us with a primordial, and enduring, set of problems.

After all, the prophecy doesn't exactly make clear what's meant, in actual policy detail, by 'justice and righteousness' (*mishpat wa tsedaqah*). It simply appears to be an infinite demand: for the rich to stop exploiting the poor. The prophecy renders this infinite demand vividly troubling, in poetic terms. But it doesn't even begin to translate it into an actual reform-programme, with more specific, finite goals; to serve as a basis for organised solidarity, amongst those inspired by it.

The whole tradition of authentic theology may be said, essentially, to stem from *Amos*, inasmuch as it's the devising of strategy to supply just what *Amos*, in this regard, lacks. That is, it serves as back-up to liturgy, attempting to incorporate what one might well call the 'Amos impulse', so far as possible, into effective forms of solidarity-building.

∾

In the first place, then, authentic theology has to remain faithful to the *Amos* impulse.

Abrahamic religious tradition is, as it were, built along a great spiritual fault-line in humanity's crust. Tremors of the *Amos* impulse keep recurring. Some of them are deeply troubling, in more or less the same fashion as the prophet's own original testimony.

Such tremors may, or may not, be politically revolutionary, in the conventional sense. Thus, one might cite Walter Benjamin and Ernst Bloch, say, as two prime twentieth century examples of the politically revolutionary kind: both of them intent on re-grounding Marxist political hope in older, messianic religious traditions, enshrining the *Amos* impulse. Whereas: Kierkegaard is a prime nineteenth century example of the politically conservative – yet nonetheless, in wider cultural terms, absolutely subversive – kind. Indeed, Kierkegaard like Amos was an altogether solitary prophetic figure: embarking as he did, right at the end of his life, on a great pamphlet campaign, demanding that the bishops of the Danish Lutheran Church publicly confess the radical inauthenticity of their church's theology; their complete sell-out to the mere herd-morality of 'Christendom'; the absolute gulf between all that they stood for and the original, true spirit of the gospel. Very much like Amos, before him, Kierkegaard urged his compatriots, for God's sake, to boycott the liturgy of their state church, until its leaders repented. His whole demand was for radical 'honesty', so defined.

But what else is authentic theology, if not a high-stress attempt to marry such sublime honesty with maximum (small 'c') catholic, that's to say, non-manipulative, outreach to all?

I've already referred to Hosea, as the great original pioneer of '*YHWH-alone-ism*'. And 'YHWH-alone-ism' was the earliest proposed solution to the problem here; a solution which eventually inspired the greater part of the Hebrew Bible. So, Hosea represents YHWH raging at his people's 'adultery', their worship of other gods, besides Him. Of course, the people of YHWH are prohibited from the 'idolatrous' worship of other gods in the very first of the Ten Commandments (*Exodus* 20:2—3); and the story of the Golden Calf in *Exodus* 32 notably illustrates the associated demand not to allow the worship of YHWH be corrupted into the likeness of other cults. But the narrative of *Exodus* is legend, back-projecting the world-view of its much later authors; who belonged to the movement which, it seems, Hosea effectively founded. And the same applies to the historian author or authors of 1 *Kings*, which, in legendary fashion, tells of the struggle waged by the prophet Elijah, rather more than a century earlier than Hosea, against Hebrew worship of the Canaanite god Baal. Moreover, even as the YHWH-alone-ist historian presents it, this was only a struggle over the cultic practice of the royal court. Hosea, by contrast, was demanding that no Hebrew *anywhere* should worship any other god but YHWH; an altogether more revolutionary call.

So, what justified such radicalism; entirely unparalleled in any of the other peoples of the age? It was surely, above all, the sheer qualitative uniqueness of YHWH, *as now reconceived by Amos and his followers.* The true rationale of Hosea's polemic remains latent, inasmuch as the actual novelty of that conception couldn't easily be admitted; it lacked the accumulated gravitas usually associated with immemorial antiquity. That was why the legend of Moses was overlaid upon the *actual* origins of YHWH-alone-ism. Yet, the underlying argument was compelling: *because of the uniqueness of YHWH's (freshly revealed) moral character, and the absolute difference of YHWH from all other gods, YHWH alone deserved worship.* At the same time, however, Hosea's argument also provided just what Amos hadn't: a clearly defined, finite and therefore realisable political goal, around which to rally. Non-worship of other gods was something which, if the advocates of YHWH-alone-ism could only gain the necessary power, might very well be policed, and enforced.

Granted: this strategy *was* highly ambivalent. It involved a cathexis of the *Amos* impulse with a good deal of crude xenophobia and tribal aggression; reflected most distressingly in the violent fiction of *Deuteronomy* 13:12—18, 20:16—18, *Joshua* 6—7, 1:10—15. Yes, but xenophobia and tribal aggression, in one form or another, tend to be features of human life everywhere. Only in this instance were they, at least potentially, sometimes mixed with, and transcended by, that very much rarer phenomenon, the *Amos* impulse.

Eventually, in 622 BCE, the eighteenth regnal year of the then twenty-six-year-old king Josiah, a YHWH-alone-ist regime did in actual fact come to power in Jerusalem (2 *Kings* 22:3 – 23:25; 2 *Chronicles* 34:1 – 35:19). Hardliners like the prophet Jeremiah may still have been impatient. But in the long run the victory of the Josianic Reform proved decisive. During the subsequent period of rule by foreign powers, successively the Babylonians, the Persians, and the Greeks, the dominance of YHWH-alone-ist principle in Hebrew culture appears finally to have consolidated. And, in consequence, the cathexis of the *Amos* impulse with campaigning YHWH-alone-ism gave way to another, second species of cathectic strategy: a grand project of evangelism among the Gentiles.

Because Judaic evangelism was subsequently surpassed by Christian evangelism and by Islamic evangelism, and because these two projects then suppressed it, we tend to forget just how energetic it appears to have been in the six centuries between Alexander and Constantine. After that, as well, outside the Roman Empire Judaism still continued to evangelise. It spread into Yemen, under Jewish Himyarite rule up until the early sixth century CE, and on into Abyssinia. It spread into the Berber regions of North Africa. It spread among the Khazars, whose kings had their capital not far from where the Volga flows into the Caspian Sea. Those kings, and no doubt many of their people, are said to have converted to Judaism in the mid-eighth century; their kingdom survived until some point in the eleventh century.[6]

And subsequently – where Judaic evangelism was blocked, and morphed into Jewish cultural survivalism – Christian and Islamic evangelism took over the model that it had pioneered. All three enterprises alike, I'd argue, have their most fundamental justification in the way that they potentially channel the *Amos* impulse; incorporate it into viable forms of cosmopolitan community life.

Again, the sheer pursuit of institutional growth, which with such urgency is innate to both Christianity and Islam from the outset, constantly threatens to become a merely self-sufficient goal. Evangelistic impatience, down the centuries, has generated so many spurious intellectual short-cuts, manipulative dishonesties, crimes of coercion.

Still, the pearl of great price remains.

II

I'm intent here on tracing the *genealogy*, so to speak, of the concept of sainthood; sublime virtue at its fullest pitch. How did that concept originally become thinkable? The book of *Amos*, in the mid-eighth century BCE, is the beginning of the story. But the *Amos* impulse, considered on its own, only gets us half-way to where we need to go. There's still another key development to observe: occurring, in fact, some two hundred years later.

Thus: the basic trouble with the *Amos* impulse, considered on its own, is quite simply its corruptibility by the element, within it, of sheer rage.

The *Amos* impulse is a furious vindication of ideal truth-as-openness, embattled against the closed-mindedness of the herd, the gang, the mob. The trouble is, though, that then it tends to become embittered, by the struggle; to be infected by resentment; to grow fanatical. And this is liable to generate another, new form of closure. Namely: the impatient closed-off-ness, from all outsiders, of the angry moralistic *sect*, as such.

∿

The core narratives of the Hebrew Bible are the work of YHWH-alone-ist writers, intent on giving the richest possible imaginative substance to their theological world-view. At the heart of the resultant project is the narrative most directly related to their core political ambitions, the legend of Moses. Thus, the question here is: why *should* the people of Israel heed those who tell them that their national god, YHWH demands exclusive worship? What actually gives this god the *moral right* to issue such a most unusual decree?

Yahweh-alone-ism answers this question with epic narrative.

It systematically translates the *Amos* impulse into a solidarity-building project, based on stories. YHWH, it teaches, is properly to be worshipped alone, above all, because he's the great Liberator, the God of Exodus. But also: because he's the one and only Creator. Moreover, he alone has been Exodus-people's one true national god from time immemorial. He was the God of the patriarchs, from whom they're ultimately descended. And he's been involved with their national history, ever since: he alone, the acknowledged God of all their people's heroes.

So far, so straightforward! What happens, though, when this national god with such singular ambition *fails* in one of the supposedly most basic tasks of any national god, as such, in the ancient world: the protection of his people from military and political catastrophe?

King Josiah, the monarch during whose reign a radically YHWH-alone-ist regime for the first time came to power, had the good fortune to rule over a small but autonomous state. Given the power politics of the day, however, this autonomy was unsustainable. First, in 609, the Egyptians invaded. Josiah himself (aged just thirty-nine or forty) was killed in battle. Then, it was the turn of the Babylonians. In 605 they won decisive victories over the Egyptians at Carchemish and Hamath; and in 598—7 followed up by conquering the kingdom of Judah, which consequently ceased to be a client state of Egypt and became a client state of Babylonia instead. According to *Jeremiah* 52:28—30, some three thousand Jews were, at that point, deported to places elsewhere in the empire. After a subsequent futile rebellion, the Jerusalem temple, the royal palace, all the great houses of the city were burnt to the ground. The city's defensive walls were demolished. More of the people were deported; according to Jeremiah, in two waves. Others, meanwhile, fled to Egypt, and presumably to other safe havens abroad.

How were the YHWH-alone-ists to respond? By this time, they had roughly a century and a half of impassioned, and not altogether unsuccessful, campaigning behind them. But in terms of customary magic thinking, such a catastrophe was of course a disgrace for any god; and all the more humiliating, surely, for one who claimed monopolistic status, as theirs did, over the ritual life of the defeated people. In *Jeremiah* 44:15—19 we hear the voice of the sceptics. The prophet, in this scene, has been compelled to join the exiles in Upper Egypt; and there, we're told, many of the women have gone back to worshipping a goddess, the queen of heaven, with cake offerings and libations. Moreover, their husbands approve of their doing so. (Fifth century papyri found at Elephantiné, by Aswan, show the Jewish community there *still*, in fact, combining the worship of YHWH with that of the goddess Anath.) The reasoning of these women is simple. Before the YHWH-alone-ist reforms, they say, 'We used to have plenty of food, and prospered, and saw no misfortune. But from the time we stopped making offerings to the queen of heaven and pouring out libations to her, we have lacked everything and have perished by the sword and by famine ...' One may well imagine that this was quite a widespread reaction, also among the exiles in Babylonia, and among the remnant in Palestine.

'By the rivers of Babylon – there we sat down and there we wept' (*Psalm* 137:1). Time passed. And then there emerged fresh hope: with the conquest of Babylon by the Persian king Cyrus, in 539. The distinctive second section of *Isaiah*, Chapters 40 to 55, dates from this time; or at any rate situates itself in this context. We know nothing of its anonymous author, or (perhaps more likely) authors, simply known to scholarship as 'Deutero-Isaiah'. Was it, for instance, actually written in Babylonia, or in Palestine? There's no clear evidence. But the inner coherence of these chapters, as a whole, consists in their developing what effectively amounts to a threefold YHWH-alone-ist argument, against the doubters. Indeed, I think that it's, above all, the cumulative compacted energy of that argument, as such, which justifies our continuing to treat '*Deutero-Isaiah*' as a single unit.

Thus, first, the traumatic destruction of Jerusalem, just thirty-five years after the YHWH-alone-ist reform under Josiah, is set here in a larger historical context. With whatever degree of inside information or wisdom of hindsight, the prophet is assured that

Cyrus will enable the rebuilding of what the Babylonians had destroyed; just as eventually proved to be the case.[7]

> Comfort, comfort my people,
> says your God;
> speak tenderly to Jerusalem,
> and cry to her
> that her time of service is ended,
> that her iniquity is pardoned,
> that she has received from YHWH's hand
> double for all her sins.

(*Isaiah* 40:1—2)

Deutero-Isaiah's case for YHWH-alone-ism begins with that promise of imminent relief, at any rate as some mitigation of the all too obvious immediate factual counter-evidence.

Second: he goes on to attack the elementary presuppositions of the doubters' argument. They for their part simply assume that YHWH is just one among a whole multitude of national gods; each to be accorded authority according to the manifestation of their magic power, to confer military success and economic prosperity on their mortal clients. However, the prophet represents YHWH declaring that this isn't so. And here the uniqueness of YHWH – first truly articulated in the surviving literature of Israel by Amos – is decisively reinterpreted. With pioneering boldness, Deutero-Isaiah converts the monolatry, or liturgical exclusivity, of older YHWH-alone-ism into, if not quite full-blown philosophic monotheism, at any rate, something very like it. The true reason for worshipping YHWH alone, according to this prophet, is quite simply that YHWH is the only *real* god there is. The others are all counterfeits. As truth is one, so there's only one God. And the truth in question is the deep truth of history. The proper criterion for recognising what's authentically divine isn't, as the doubters suppose, the mere apparent display of magic power. No, it's the capacity of the one and only true God's prophets truthfully to interpret the course of historical events: in accurately predicting the future, to render events spiritually educational, morally productive. Five times the prophet represents YHWH summoning all the other gods, as a corporate body, to a civil trial, with a view to adjudicating his claims: *Isaiah* 41:1—5; 41:21—29; 43:8—15; 44:6—8; 45:20—25. He claims, in particular, to be wholly responsible for the rise of the Persian emperor Cyrus. In elevating Cyrus, certainly, he has the welfare of his people first and foremost in mind; and yet it's an historic intervention quite outside his allotted sphere of influence as a national god. Cyrus himself, after all, has no inkling of how he's being used. What, YHWH taunts the other gods, have *they* ever done, to rival this?

And then, third, this section of *Isaiah* contains yet another, still more momentous fresh thought-development – which really is *the* key thing that I have been manoeuvring towards, all along. The doubters based their doubts on the simple fact of their people's suffering. *Deutero-Isaiah* paradoxically takes *that very fact* and converts it, from being a source of doubt, into the exact opposite: itself, a fundamental *justification* of YHWH-alone-ist faith!

This is admittedly not the argument of the trial scenes. There YHWH boasts, merely, of his prophets' predictive accuracy. But, of course, other gods also delivered oracles, which were no doubt sometimes accurate. And, as we've seen, you could predict the future quite wrongly, as Amos had done, and yet still be widely acknowledged as a genuine prophet. Again, the true uniqueness of YHWH-alone-ist faith was grounded, far rather, in that furious yearning for 'justice and righteousness' which opens like a chasm in Amos's earthquake-prophecy. Amos's oracular warnings, and the oracular warnings of Hosea, (First) Isaiah, Micah, Jeremiah, Zephaniah, the YHWH-alone-ists in general – that whole tradition of warnings so appallingly, it appeared, fulfilled in the eventual destruction of Jerusalem – were intended to inspire a wholesale moral transformation of YHWH's people. The urgency of the warnings reflected YHWH's unique repudiation of ritual business-as-usual.

Deutero-Isaiah highlights that uniqueness of YHWH, as perceived by the tradition stemming from *Amos*, for instance in

41:6—7; 44:9—20. Here, the worship of other gods is mocked on the grounds that they're mere idols, manufactured by a craftsman. The manufacturing process is described, with scathing sarcasm: implicitly suggesting that these idols are nothing more than the product of wish-fulfilling fantasy. But YHWH isn't. There can, after all, be no element of wish-fulfilment in the worship of a god who demands of his own people that they submit, patiently and prayerfully, to such acute misery; as coming from his hands.

What's most original of all, however, in *Deutero-Isaiah* is, surely, the thinking behind the four so-called 'Servant songs':

- 42:1—4
- 49:1—6
- 50:4—9
- 52:13 – 53:12

Although not strictly speaking songs, these four passages were given that name in the late nineteenth century by the pioneer exegete Bernhard Duhm. He in fact suggested that they were written by another author, not 'Deutero-Isaiah' himself. Duhm's theory has been immensely influential. Hans Barstad, on the other hand, trenchantly describes it as 'one of the biggest scholarly myths in the history of biblical exegesis' and one that 'is long, long overdue for demolition'.[8] This seems a bit harsh. One may well be sceptical of Duhm's separate-authorship hypothesis; but these texts surely do have a certain, intriguing inter-relationship.

Thus: all four of the 'songs' in question portray a figure, simply called 'the Servant of the Lord'. In the first 'song', YHWH speaks, praising him; in the second and third 'songs' the Servant speaks, in the second 'song' he also quotes YHWH; in the fourth 'song', first YHWH speaks, then a crowd of onlookers, and finally YHWH again. Much of the extensive scholarly literature following Duhm has focused on the question of the Servant's identity. Is he a personification of Israel as a whole? In the second 'song', the Servant does actually describe YHWH as saying to him

'You are my servant,
Israel, in whom I will be glorified.'

(49:3)

And in a number of other places in *Deutero-Isaiah* as well, outside the 'songs', Israel is named as YHWH's 'servant'. But then, again in the second 'song', the Servant is described as having a mission *to* Israel:

Now, thus says YHWH,
who formed me from the womb to be his servant,
to bring Jacob back to him,
and that Israel might be gathered to him ...
[he says]
'It is too light a thing that you should be my servant
to raise up the tribes of Jacob and to restore the preserved of
    Israel:
therefore I make you a light to the nations,
that my salvation may reach to the ends of the earth.'

(49:5—6)

Is he then a specific individual figure, a promised leader, representatively embodying the best of Israel? Is he Deutero-Isaiah himself? Is he some other prophet, a second Moses (c.f. *Deuteronomy* 18:15—22)? Is he a king, as the first 'song' especially would suggest? Is he the whole group of YHWH-alone-ist campaigners, represented as a single corporate person?

Or might he, as I'm inclined to think, be any of these – any individual, any group – representing *the truth-claims properly associated with unjust suffering, fully recognised as unjust, and yet nevertheless endured, in exemplary fashion, without bitterness*? In this sense, it seems to me that these texts are re-interpreting the suffering of the people of Israel, as illustrative of a universal moral ideal.

The Servant here is, in short, precisely an archetype of true *sainthood*, in general.

Above all, in the fourth 'song', as it describes the persecution, the suffering, the sacrificial death of the Servant, we have a profoundly original *argument-through-archetype*; an attempt to define the very highest form of sacred authority. Namely: the authority of the saint, as something altogether higher than that of the priest, or even that of the righteous prophet.

The third 'song' is related to the fourth, inasmuch as in it the Servant speaks subjectively of the experience of being tortured, which, in the fourth, is objectively observed by the onlookers. We have already seen how the second 'song' affirms the universality of the truth represented by the Servant. And the first does the same. But it's the fourth, the longest of the 'songs', that really spells out what's new in the universal gospel of *Deutero-Isaiah*; the truth simply described as 'justice' (*mishpat*) in 42:1, 4, and as 'salvation' (*yeshua*) in 49:6.

~

When Amos contemplated the imminent future affliction of Israel, this was punitive suffering; to be endured, in penitence, because it was only what Israel deserved. And so were the coming catastrophes envisaged, after Amos, by Hosea and the various other prophets of YHWH-alone-ism, prior to Deutero-Isaiah. But the fourth 'Servant song' is, very differently, concerned with an unmerited superfluity of suffering. The book of *Amos*, as I have said, constitutes the breakthrough-moment in which the worship of YHWH first became radically different in nature from all the other sacred cults of that era: with YHWH's great refusal, there, to be bought off by mere ritual flattery; his furious assault on the sheer *greed and complacency* of Israel's ruling class. But this species of vice is, after all, only one potential source of injustice. Another – quite distinct, yet almost equi-primordial – is *bitterness arising from self-pity*: resultant in the festering of jealousy and grievance; the channelling of resentment into a lust for revenge; the moralising of that lust; all that Nietzsche for instance considered most quintessentially Judaeo-Christian! But the fourth 'Servant song', *Isaiah 52:13 – 53:12*, tackles this whole

48

other type of temptation, inasmuch as it celebrates a saint, one who, although acutely exposed to the temptation of moralised resentment, does *not* succumb. The Servant here, the archetypal saint, suffers the very uttermost affliction; yet does so entirely without self-pity; to the point of inspiring an astonished admiration amongst those who observe it, whose own consciences are moreover painfully pricked by the spectacle.

The 'song' thus begins with YHWH affirming the true moral glory of this figure; who, *in secular terms*, seems to rank among those most devoid of glory.

> Behold, my servant shall prosper;
> he shall be exalted, lifted up, and very high.
> As many were aghast at you
> [viz. the people of Israel, when Jerusalem was destroyed?]
> so many nations shall be astonished at him
> kings shall shut their mouths;
> for that which was never told them they see,
> and that which they had never heard they perceive.
>
> (52:13—14a, 15)

The universality of the Servant's mission to the nations has already been declared in the first and second 'Servant songs'. Now we are to be shown just what is so astonishing about this mission, to those hitherto seduced by the conventional boastfulness of 'kings'; that's to say, the rich and powerful in general.

Next, the chorus-members report what they have observed.

> Who could have believed what we have heard
> and to whom has the arm of YHWH been revealed?
> He grew up before him like a young plant,
> and like a root out of dry ground.
> He had no form or comeliness
> that should have made us give heed to him;
> there was no beauty that should have made us desire him;
> his appearance was so marred, beyond human semblance,

and his form beyond that of the sons of men.
He was despised and rejected by men;
a man of sorrows, and humiliated by sickness.
He was like one before whom men hide their faces,
despised – we esteemed him not.

(53:1—2; 52:14b; 53:3)

Even as the Servant's sufferings escalate, on the other hand, still he doesn't complain. And the chorus places great emphasis on his evident lack of self-pity:

> Tortured, he endured it submissively,
> and opened not his mouth;
> like a sheep that is led to the slaughter,
> like a lamb before its shearers is silent,
> he was dumb and opened not his mouth.

(53:7)

Eventually, it appears that he is killed. At any rate, he dies:

> And they made his grave with transgressors,
> and his place of burial with miscreants,
> although he had committed no crime
> and there was no deceit in his mouth.

(53:9)

However much one may sympathise with those who are sorry for themselves, self-pity leaves less of a job to be done, in this regard, by others. The chorus members, however, seeing the fate of the not at all self-pitying Servant, find themselves, in retrospect, compelled by aching compassion to acknowledge their own complicity, somehow, in the injustice suffered by the Servant. They've confessed their previous indifference to him –

> Yet *ours* [they now confess] was the sickness that *he* carried,
> and *ours* the pains *he* bore.

50

> Yet we supposed him stricken,
> smitten of God and humiliated.
> Yet he was pierced on account of our sins,
> crushed on account of our iniquities.
> Chastisement that led to our welfare lay upon him,
> and by means of his stripes there was healing for us.
>
> All we like sheep have gone astray;
> we have turned everyone to his own way,
> but YHWH laid on him the iniquity of us all.
>
> He was carried off from prison and judgment,
> and who gave a thought to his stock?
> For he was cut off from the land of the living,
> put to death because of our sins.
>
> (53:4—6, 8)

And the 'song' concludes with more words of YHWH:

> Therefore I will give him a portion with the great,
> and he shall divide the spoil with the strong;
> because he poured out his soul to death
> and let himself be numbered among the transgressors.
> Yet he bore the sins of many
> and made intercession for the transgressors.
>
> (53:12)

∼

How though, exactly, is the Servant a bearer of sins? I think it's in three ways.

In the first place: he bears a burden of boundless compassion; a deep concern for the moral welfare of others, around him. There's no angry reproach here – compare *Amos*, *Hosea*, first *Isaiah* – but simple grief. He makes intercession for the transgressors. Isn't it just this basic, exemplary attitude of his that so moves the chorus?

Secondly: even where the members of the chorus are themselves, directly, his persecutors, he isn't vindictive. Being free of self-pity, he is, so to speak, a non-transmitter of wrong. He breaks the cycle – of resentment leading to revenge, and so generating further resentment, leading to further revenge – by which evil is perpetuated. Every non-transmitter of wrong may well be said to 'bear' the burden of what they don't transmit. And the Servant here becomes a symbolic representative of all such non-transmitters.

But then, thirdly: it seems that he's being persecuted precisely *in order to* serve as a scapegoat. In other words, the fact that he's suffered 'on behalf of' the chorus is not only a matter of his own chosen response to persecution; his representativeness was also their malicious choosing. The chorus members may not have been the Servant's actual torturers; but their confession, at the very least, suggests that they didn't themselves resist the torturers' general scapegoating policy. Insofar as such policy is a discharge of social tensions, an all too easy way of generating a sense of community in shared aggression against the scapegoat, they've surely more or less colluded with the policy, as its beneficiaries. 'YHWH laid on him the iniquity of us all'. This is said here with deep penitential grief: it absolutely shouldn't have happened. But in other contexts, of course, what *René Girard* has called the 'scapegoat mechanism' involves crowds filled with persecutory glee; or at least an urgent sense of therapeutic necessity at work.

Compare for example that other primordial archetype, the figure of Oedipus in Greek myth. Girard compares the story of Oedipus especially to the story of Joseph, in *Genesis*.[9] Thus, both stories alike are concerned with the fate of an outsider. Both begin with an expulsion: the infant Oedipus is exposed on a hillside, to die, so as to thwart the prophecy that he'd grow up to kill his father; the young man Joseph is sold into slavery by his jealous brothers. Both heroes nevertheless eventually prosper, and rise to become great rulers: Oedipus by solving the riddle of the Sphinx, and thereby magically liberating the city of Thebes from a major curse, for which he's rewarded by being made king, and married to the newly widowed queen Jocasta; Joseph, by interpreting

Pharaoh's prophetic dreams, and then, on Pharoah's behalf, organising an appropriate famine-prevention policy. At length, however, in both stories, there comes a second crisis. In the Greek story, Thebes suffers a terrible plague, which is then revealed to be a consequence of the fact that Oedipus, all unawares, has indeed killed his father, in a quarrel with a stranger on the road; and that Queen Jocasta is actually his own mother. So, he's punitively marked by being blinded, and expelled a second time. But the Hebrew story, very differently, ends in reconciliation. Joseph's brothers are driven, by famine, to seek grain in Egypt. He meets them. They don't recognise him. He plays at revenge: planting the money they had paid, plus a silver cup, in the grain sacks with which they return; then having them arrested as thieves. But it's only a game, a device to highlight his, in actual fact, making the opposite choice, to forgive them. One story, in short, ends with healing for the city of Thebes brought about by the outsider being quite rightly expelled; the other, on the contrary, with healing for the family of Jacob brought about by the outsider's forgiveness of those who had, as they now acknowledge, quite wrongly expelled him.

But Oedipus also stands opposed, in still more radical fashion, to the Suffering Servant.

Girard's general theory is that early notions of the sacred typically begin from deep-seated memories of scapegoating events: the resolution of social conflicts by a consensual projection of blame onto scapegoat-figures; the violent persecution of scapegoats, as a means of restoring harmony in the wider community. These memories, he suggests, have then been processed somewhat in the way that dreams work; they've been disguised, sanitised, in myths like that of Oedipus; and then, further, worked into sacred rituals for remembrance, in which the scapegoat may even, sometimes, be honoured for the social benefits that their scapegoating has brought about, by being transformed into a god. Such, he suggests, is really the norm. And maybe he's right. The prehistoric evidence, by its very nature, can only ever be circumstantial. But ancient Hebrew religion –

he further argues – insofar as it begins to diverge from the other sacred cults of the age, breaks with this antique norm.

Certainly, the fourth 'Servant song' does appear to be a direct *unmasking* of the 'scapegoat mechanism'; which is on the contrary just reaffirmed by the Oedipus myth. For, in order to work well, the 'mechanism' needs to have its actual cruelty, and irrationality, well disguised. But in the fourth 'Servant song' there it is, with no disguise at all. The 'mechanism' works by transferring the persecutors' guilt, for their part in the general malaise of their world, onto the scapegoat. In this 'song' however, the Servant, the scapegoat, is retrospectively acknowledged to have been entirely innocent; indeed, not only innocent, but positively saintly. And the chorus, evidently made up of erstwhile persecutors, confesses to having been altogether wrong in their moral judgment of him. The very act of scapegoating itself, it would seem, is recognised here to be intrinsically sinful. And, as a result, this 'song' enacts a truly momentous step-change in religious thinking.

~

In the context of *Deutero-Isaiah* as a whole, the 'Servant songs' look both backwards and forwards. They look back towards the destruction of Jerusalem by the Babylonians, and the whole displacement of populations associated with that disaster. Here we have the basic question again, how is the continuing worship of YHWH to be justified, at all, in the light of such horrors afflicting his people; let alone the worship of YHWH alone? The fourth 'song' in particular suggests the radical answer: '*YHWH is true God, like no other, just because of the way that he, in principle, inspires his people to suffer as this Servant does; and because he thereby evokes the sort of response we see in the chastened chorus here.*' (Never mind to what extent this was actually how the Israelites responded to their misfortune: what matters is just the originality of the ideal!)

And, at the same time, especially the first and second 'songs' also look forwards, now that the grand project of YHWH-alone-ism, within Hebrew culture, has largely prevailed, to the grand project that was to succeed it: the spreading of YHWH's truth to 'the nations'.

But, immediately, along with evangelistic ambition come the temptations of evangelistic impatience. Already, the book of *Job* represents a great cry of protest against this. Thus, it's after all only natural that evangelists impatient to make fresh converts are tempted to dwell upon the supposed power of God, to confer material benefits on the properly devout. And, again, if such benefits fail to accrue, it's only natural that they're therefore inclined to attribute this failure to some, perhaps concealed, fault of the unlucky one. Job is a 'servant' of YHWH who, like the Servant of the fourth 'Servant song' in *Deutero-Isaiah*, suffers both appallingly and unjustly. The one great difference is that, whereas the latter 'was dumb and opened not his mouth', Job – being oppressed by the advice of 'friends' whose thinking is effectively formed by the most stubborn evangelistic impatience – responds volubly, in protest against that impatience.

Girard has dedicated a substantial book to the interpretation of *Job*: interpreting it as the dialogue of a scapegoat with a scapegoat-persecuting crowd.[10] Such a reading admittedly goes a good way beyond the actual text. But yes, the impatient evangelist always wants to please the crowd; this sort of impatience may very well therefore contribute to complicity with the scapegoat-persecuting tendencies of a crowd, in all sorts of contexts. How then shall we interpret YHWH's great culminating speech in *Job* 38 – 41? For his part, Girard deplores it. He sees this portrayal of YHWH as nothing more than celestial back-up for those bullies, Job's 'friends'. I disagree. It's unquestionably a very different version of YHWH from that which appears for instance in *Amos*. The prophecy of *Amos* is deadly serious; YHWH's speech in *Job* is comedic, mock-sublime bombast; it's largely buffoonery. YHWH boasts here of his creative exploits in general, and not least of the wild creatures he has created, each of which reflects something of his own untamed magnificence: the lion, the raven, the mountain goat, the deer, the wild ass, the wild ox, the rearing horse, the hawk, the vulture or eagle (38:39 – 39:30) All except one is invoked with rhetorical questions; as, again and again, YHWH asks Job, do you really dare challenge the Creator of these? But there, right in the midst of all this splendid oratory, we *also* meet the ostrich, ludicrously flapping its wings in vain: the ostrich which, according to ancient folklore,

> leaves its eggs to the earth,
> and lets them be warmed on the ground,
> forgetting that a foot may crush them,
> and that a wild animal may trample them.

The ostrich, we're told,

> deals cruelly with its young, as if they were not its own;
> though its labour should be in vain, yet it has no fear;
> because God has made it forget wisdom,
> and given it no share in understanding.

> (*Job* 39:14—17)

If, though, one accepts the undiscriminating view of divine omnipotence suggested by evangelistic impatience, one actually ends up with a view of God – in relation to sufferers such as Job or the Servant in *Deutero-Isaiah* – effectively resembling this (erroneous) image of the careless ostrich's relationship to its offspring! Isn't there at least a hint, in this passage, of YHWH laughing at his devotees' misconception of himself; as being ostrich-like?

At all events, there's no actual condemnation of Job here. On the contrary, in the appended epilogue, it's the 'friends' who are condemned by YHWH; whilst Job is adjudged to have spoken the truth (42:7). YHWH's speech is a humorous rebuke to self-indulgent self-pity; but *not* to a victim's bearing of truthful testimony, simply in itself. If YHWH is demanding anything of Job, it's just that he resemble more the Servant of the fourth 'song', at any rate now that he has quite rightly had his say. Thus, Job is finally silenced; he transcends his bitterness; even as the Servant – a model of saintliness, transcending all bitterness – is, earlier, silent (40:3—5; 42:1—6).

❧

And then, of course, the fourth 'Servant song' in *Deutero-Isaiah* clearly also played a key role in helping the first Christians recognise a crucified dissident as their messiah. The pioneering archetypal notion of sainthood which appears, compacted, in the original form of the 'song', so to speak, provides the seed. Christianity, in the most ambitious fashion, plants it afresh into history, as the gospel narrative. So, the primordial insight of the 'song' expands; it's made absolutely central to a whole system of liturgy.

But, alas, the essential truth-potential involved here is as fragile as it's profound! Caught up into the grand project of the Church, the ideal is exposed to a truly massive pressure of distorting evangelistic impatience.

Both *Amos* and *Deutero-Isaiah* bear witness, in pioneering fashion, to the proper offence of sacred truth. That is: its offence to inert thoughtlessness. *Amos* envisions a violent future in which the thoughtless rich and powerful will be brutally compelled to sympathise with the plight of the poor, by being, themselves, dispossessed, and so made to share that plight. The fourth 'Servant song' pictures the scapegoating crowd being shocked into penitence by sheer admiration for the saintliness of the victim. But the impatient evangelist – by contrast – is naturally inclined to flatter the crowd of potential converts; the more easily to win them over. To the extent that such impatience has prevailed in Christian history, the *Amos* impulse has, in effect, been altogether suppressed. And the critical message of the fourth 'Servant song' has been positively reversed.

Thus, how did it happen that – far from recognising the authentic truth-potential of the gospel to be a fundamental subversion of the 'scapegoat mechanism' – the Church, from the Constantinian Revolution onwards, has so often sought to apply that very 'mechanism' to pagans, to 'heretics', to Jews, to 'witches', and to gay people, all in Christ's name? In large measure, this depended on a theology of 'atonement' which, notwithstanding any remaining echoes, set Christ decisively apart from the archetype of the Servant in the fourth 'song'. The Christ of such theology is imagined as a mythic superman, with magic powers; quite different from the not at all magically endowed figure of the Servant, representing all scapegoats.

Accordingly: in earlier 'atonement' theory Christ's death is understood as a necessary 'ransom' paid to the devil. God, it's supposed, has here tricked the devil; Christ is like the bait on a fish-hook (Gregory of Nyssa), or the bait in a mouse-trap (Augustine). By suffering in superhuman-divine fashion, he buys the devil off. This notion beautifully recurs for instance in Milton's *Paradise Lost*, Books Three and Twelve; and underlies *Paradise Regained*. Or else, in later mediaeval thought, the devil drops out of the picture, and instead we have the sort of doctrine classically developed by Anselm in *Cur Deus Homo* (1094—98). Anselm's argument possesses a more sophisticated internal logic. It presumes that the gravity of any wrong is determined by the social status of the one sinned against. Even the slightest sin is a wrong done to God, who is infinite. Cosmic justice requires a commensurate punishment, but no mortal can ever pay the infinite price required; only God can suffer infinitely, so as to restore proper order. Therefore, God must become incarnate as a superhuman representative being, in order to suffer on our behalf. An infinitude of debt, accrued in relation to God, balanced and cancelled by an infinitude of penal repayment, by God incarnate ... This surely is quite different from the representative suffering of the Servant in the fourth 'Servant song'! That 'song', considered purely and simply in itself, contains nothing equivalent to the essentially magic element in these theories. Indeed, both the 'ransom' theory and the Anselmian 'two infinities' theory arise out of a thinking that has altogether lost touch with the original, trans-mythic rationale of the fourth 'song'; intrinsic to the chorus's horrified recognition that the Servant's scapegoat-suffering is unjust. They're attempts *nevertheless* to vindicate the basic affirmation of Christian faith, that God is revealed in the figure of the crucified Christ. There's simply no need for such theories, once one recognises the true essence of divine revelation, here, to lie in that older trans-mythic rationale, taken up into the gospel story, and thereby dramatically counter-posed to the whole imperial-Roman propagandist symbolism of crucifixion.

Cur Deus Homo: 'why a God-man'? Anselm's mythic answer is altogether superfluous! It's enough to say, quite simply, that God becomes man in order to register the absolutely basic theological importance of debunking the 'scapegoat mechanism'.

And why, more exactly, a *crucified-yet-resurrected* Saviour? This isn't a question Anselm asks, at all. His theory has no bearing on the institution of crucifixion, as such; or, therefore, on the significance of Christ's resurrection as the divine verdict on that institution, and hence on everything it was intended by the Roman authorities symbolically to mean. Yet, this is of vital importance. Indeed, I'd argue that the full potential of faith in Christ to effect 'salvation' *depends upon* his having been, precisely, crucified. If he'd died any other sort of death, Christian faith would never have acquired its true power to 'save'. The story of the Resurrection, abstracted from this specific context, would then be reduced to just another miracle-legend, like many another.

Thus: that God is definitively revealed in the figure of a *crucified* victim is nothing other than divine strategy for debunking the 'scapegoat mechanism' in the most *dramatic* fashion possible. It's God exploiting the intrinsic drama of the Roman-imperial practice of crucifixion – the sheer imaginative energy, the deterrent horror, the ostentatious cruelty of that practice! – so as to subvert all that the crucifiers themselves intended to achieve by it. Crucifixion is the 'scapegoat mechanism' raised to the level of state terrorism at its most flamboyant. And the resurrection of the Crucified Dissident, in principle, then renders it the primary symbol of everything from which we need salvation. For it surely has to be understood as an icon encapsulating the all-pervasive collaboration, in human affairs, of the gang, the mob, the herd: the gang of rulers condemning the Dissident to this death; the mob loudly assenting to the verdict; the herd of passive onlookers. God's raising to life of one who's been crucified is, accordingly, the ultimate symbolic vindication of sublime virtue, as the sheer antithesis to all that, in general, brings gang, mob and herd together.

And, as a Christian theologian, my argument in what follows is not only that we need once and for all to drop all attempted merely mythic justifications of Christ's death on the cross, as a pernicious distraction. But also, that, in so doing, *we should explore all possible means of imaginatively opening up the* trans-*mythic Isaianic archetype of the Suffering Servant, now recognised as the one true, alternative model for salvation, instead.*

III

Nowadays, novels surely are amongst the most significant such potential resources. How can they help? Quite simply: by portraying sublime virtue, in all of its problematic relation to the reality of a world in which such goodness is by no means at home.

Theology prescribes for beautiful ritual designed to help create the most homely of spiritual homes, for all sorts of folk; ritual, however, which *also* honours sublime virtue. There's a palpable tension in this, between two opposing imperatives. The more homely the spiritual home – the more effective in integrating its various inhabitants together – the more liable they are simply to forget the undomesticated nature, the sublimity, of the rare goodness that its ritual is meant to honour as the highest of all. And, by the same token, the more rigorously theology holds fast to sublime virtue, the less easily it will tend to relate to its home community.

For the theologian, there's something particularly fascinating about the capacity of novels (at least a few of them) to develop a beautiful re-imagining of sublime virtue. That is, their potential energising contribution to the *dis*-integrative moment here. This has two elementary aspects. Sublime virtue is lifted clear from every sort of conventional herd-ethos, or gang-code, or mob-excitement, as such, in the first place by its *exemplary agency*. And then, secondly: by its *exemplary suffering*.

Exemplary agency: namely, that which springs from the *Amos* impulse.

Exemplary suffering: namely, that which corresponds to the Isaianic archetype; the suffering of the Suffering Servant.

By the '*Amos* impulse' I don't mean any particular form of moral rigour. I mean *all* forms of high standard, held fast without fear of offending the adherents of ordinary herd / gang / mob (a)morality. Novels may well portray such rigour as informing a wide variety of perhaps quite contradictory ethical projects; in a wide variety of different contexts. But the common factor, in each case, is just a principled, resolute determination not to be merely ingratiating. It's the pure moral antithesis to every species of merely propagandist impulse; the integrity that consists in preferring, where necessary, to *confront* moral banality as such, rather than *manipulate* it with charm.

The book of *Amos*, for the first time in history proper, serves up this impulse neat. By contrast, novelists who want to make the characters in question here sympathetic tend to serve it up in small quantities. One can scarcely say that the prophet himself, raging against the high priest (7:10—17), is a sympathetic character! His oracles range from the wonderfully sardonic to the thunderously exasperated; he's a remarkable poet. But, as a spectacle, such unrelieved rage is just exhausting. The *Amos* impulse on its own isn't yet the fullness of sublime goodness. Ranters aren't saints; and Amos is a ranter. True saintliness precisely, I think, consists in the coming-together of the *Amos* impulse with the Isaianic archetype, as a fundamental corrective. *It derives, first, from the incorporation of the individualistic* Amos *impulse into effective solidarity-strategy; and then, secondly, as a precaution against fanaticism, from a strong admixture of the spirit evoked in the Isaianic 'Servant songs'.*

In the case of the *Amos* impulse the primary initiative is with the social critic. But in the case of the Isaianic archetype, it's with others: it's with the human herd, as such; it's with the authorities, the ruling gang, doing what's needed to preserve their control over the herd; or, when the worst comes to the worst, it's with the lynch mob. The Suffering Servant is defined, in the first instance, by the manner of his or her suffering, how it affects his or her relationship to these others. In the mildest cases, the herd just doesn't know how to help; the passers-by pass by in embarrassment. Maybe they positively don't want to help. Or, again, maybe it's worse than that, and they're delighted for the gangster-authorities, or for the mob, to persecute the sufferer. In *Isaiah* 52:13 – 53:12 we're shown that highest level of affliction, at its most extreme. But, always, what's crucial is that, come what may, the Suffering Servant remains un-embittered. In retrospect, the chastened chorus is inspired by the exemplary way in which this outcast has come to terms with being outcast. The persecuted suffering of the Suffering Servant is transfigured; merging with the very purest suffering-with, that is, com-passion, even for the persecutors. And, astonished by being so radically forgiven, the chorus-members are inspired, after all, to look beyond the confines of their previous herd-worldview.

What then is the recipe for a proper representation of true sainthood, in the primordial sense; that's to say, sublime virtue, fundamentally uncorrupted by the corporate egoism of the religious institutions whose calling is to celebrate it?

I'd answer:

Take a modicum of that extravagant passion for justice which informs the book of Amos. *Add a generous helping of the un-embittered readiness for innocent, vicarious suffering exemplified by the Servant in* Isaiah 52:13 – 53:12. *Stir together; and then bake in the oven of a modern novelist's imagination …*

---

1. Bible quotations, unless otherwise specified, from the New Revised Standard Version (Cambridge: Cambridge University Press, 1989).

    King Uzziah of Judah reigned 786—736, King Jeroboam II of Israel reigned 786—746. Geologists studying the layers of sediment on the floor of the Dead Sea have found evidence of a major earthquake in the region, of approximately magnitude 8, occurring around the middle of the eighth century BCE.

For the tentative suggestion of the 760s, see for instance Jörg Jeremias, *The Book of Amos: A Commentary* (Louisville, Kentucky: Westminster John Knox Press, 1995), p. 2. This is largely based on the lack of any mention, by name, of the Assyrians.

2. *Amos* 5:25—27 and 8:14, would be evidence of this – supposing that they do belong, as is possible, to the original stratum of the text.

3. *Amos* 2:4—5 looks very much like just such an addition, by a later Judaean editor, interrupting as it does the flow between the sequence in 1:3 to 2:3, denouncing the *political*, as opposed to liturgical, crimes of Israel's neighbours, and 2:6—16 denouncing the equivalent crimes of Israel. Everywhere else Amos is a prophet engaging with the northern kingdom of Israel; not, as here, with the southern kingdom of Judah. The odd thing is, precisely, that there's so little else in the book, as we have it, that resembles 2:4—5.

4. In some circles at least, it appears that Amos's fallibility in this regard was in fact critically remembered. He had prophesied that, in Jeroboam's reign, an enemy nation would 'oppress' Israel 'from Lebo-hamath to the Wadi Arabah' (6:14). Yet, as the historian-author of 2 *Kings*, with striking use of the very same phrase, reports, Jeroboam, far from being on the defensive, was very much an aggressor: indeed, he 'restored the border of Israel from Lebo-hamath as far as the Sea of the Arabah' (2 *Kings* 14:25). He did so, the historian further informs us, 'according to the word of the Lord, the God of Israel, which he spoke by his servant Jonah son of Amittai, the prophet, who was from Gath-hepher'. Amos isn't named here; but the implicit contrast with Jonah is clear. Thus, the historian goes on: 'the Lord had not said that he would blot out the name of Israel from under heaven', as Amos had mistakenly declared, with reference to the near future; but, on the contrary, 'he saved them by the hand of Jeroboam son of Joash'. Jonah got it right, although his prophecies haven't been preserved. (The little book of *Jonah*, with its surreal narrative, appears to be a very much later work.) Amos got it wrong.

5. 'Cross over to Calneh, and see;
from there go to Hamath the great;
then go down to Gath of the Philistines.
Are you better than these kingdoms?'

Calneh and Hamath were two principalities in Syria, both conquered according to Assyrian texts by Tiglath-Pileser in that year. Gath, meanwhile, was conquered (presumably around the same time) by King Uzziah of Judah; in 2 *Chronicles* 26:6 we are told that Uzziah 'broke down its wall'.

If Amos himself flourished in the 760s, perhaps these later verses come from a 'school of Amos', rather than the prophet himself? And perhaps the same goes for Chapters 1—2: a survey of peoples threatened by the expansion of Tiglath-Pileser's Assyrian Empire? C.f. Petrus D. F. Strijdom, 'Reappraising the Historical Context of Amos', in *Old Testament Essays*, 24 / 1, 2011.

6. See Shlomo Sand, *The Invention of the Jewish People* (London: Verso, 2009); Chapter 4.

7. In what follows I use the translation in Claus Westermann, *Isaiah 40—66* (London: SCM Press, 1969.)

8. Barstad, 'The Future of the "Servant Songs": Some Reflections on the Relationship of Biblical Scholarship to its own Tradition', in Balentine and Barton, eds., *Language, Theology and the Bible: Essays in Honour of James Barr* (Oxford University Press, 1994.)

9. The myth of Oedipus is a recurrent topic in Girard's writing. For the comparison with the story of Joseph, see especially Girard, *I See Satan Fall Like Lightning*, trans. James G. Williams (New York: Orbis, 2001), pp. 106—15.

10. Girard, *Job the Victim of His People*, trans. Yvonne Freccero (Stanford University Press, 1987).

CHAPTER FOUR

Dostoevsky:
The Idiot and
The Brothers Karamazov

Some novels help show the turmoil that may result where both basic elements of what I've called the 'recipe' for sainthood are present, in full. That's to say: not the Isaianic archetype alone, but the Isaianic archetype clearly infused with the *Amos* impulse; and, conversely, not the *Amos* impulse alone, but the *Amos* impulse as mediated, in the truest sense, by the Isaianic archetype.

Other novels, by contrast, illustrate what it means for just one of these two sides to predominate; out of kilter.

Thus, consider for example Dostoevsky's work: his portrait of Prince Myshkin in *The Idiot* (1868) and of Alyosha in *The Brothers Karamazov* (1880). It seems to me that, in both cases, Dostoevsky has in fact essentially abstracted the Isaianic archetype from the *Amos* impulse.

Observe how that distorts it!

∿

Ford Madox Ford – whose own very striking novelistic portrayal of true sainthood I'll also be discussing below – published a brief review of both *The Idiot* and *The Brothers Karamazov*, dated February 1914. This begins with a sort of retraction:

The other day [Ford writes] I chanced to utter some rather careless words about Dostoevsky. I wish I hadn't. For the poor chap was a miserable man, and I hate hitting even at the ghosts of the unhappy. For heaven's sake let him have all the glory that the world can offer him, so that his shade may be mightily rejoiced. And the poor chap had to drag his weary pen over miles and miles of paper to find himself an insufficient sustenance. May then, all the peaches and all the caviar of the world be piled upon his altar, and all the Vouvray of France be poured over them as a libation ...[1]

(Ford, after all, was *himself* forever 'dragging his weary pen over miles and miles of paper'; being, like Dostoevsky, a full-time writer without any great resources of inherited wealth, constantly struggling to make ends meet.) Nevertheless, he goes on, he still wants to 'stick to his guns'. In response to those who have challenged his previous remarks, he now seeks to refine them. The basic point is as follows:

The Brothers Karamazov is not a finished book. It is a mere preparation for writing the life of a saint. In that sense I was simply careless when I wrote that the monastery scene (and by that I was thinking only of the scene of the dead monk whose body gave out an evil odour) was an excrescence in *The Brothers Karamazov* as it stands. It is no doubt only an excrescence to that extent. As part of the preparation of Dostoevsky's hero for a saintly life, to be described in subsequent volumes, it is easy enough to see that what is for the moment an excrescence would have been no doubt a necessity for the finished work and so perfectly in accordance with the form.

The Brothers Karamazov as it stands is in fact merely the pedestal to an immense statue. What I stupidly said is that the pedestal bulges out too much upon one side.

The critics have denied that it bulges. But what they should have said is, far rather:

66

'Yes, the pedestal appears to bulge; but how beautifully that will be accounted for when the great statue stands upon it leaning over to the other side!'[2]

If only – that's to say – Dostoevsky hadn't died too soon to complete his work!

Dostoevsky did, indeed, make an explicit promise, in his preface 'To the Reader', that he would follow up *The Brothers Karamazov* with a second volume; and that 'the principal novel is the second'.[3] The two novels, he says, will be linked inasmuch as they'll both have the same hero, the saintly Alyosha Karamazov. But, whereas the first is set some thirteen years ago, and deals with events of the hero's adolescence, the second will deal with his activity in 'the present day', namely the period around 1880.

Alas, though, just a few months after making that promise the author was dead. And therefore, we can only speculate about what he left unwritten.

Ford, next, proceeds to discuss *The Idiot*. Here, he professes grim foreboding:

The essence of my self-appointed task is to record my own time, my own world, as I see it. It is an ambition like another, and I trust it will pardoned to me. In that sense, and in that sense alone, I can say something about this great writer. I almost wish he had never written; I regard his works with envy, with fear, with admiration. I seem to see him on the horizon as a dark cloud, and the thought of his heavy books is as of so many weights upon my soul; as of so many labours for my poor brain.[4]

Dostoevsky is a Romantic. Ford's fastidious taste is for French Realism; or for Turgenev.

[Dostoevsky's] characters are extraordinarily vivid, but they are too vivid for the Realist School. They are too, always, in one note; they develop little; they are static. His strong scenes are strong to the point of frenzy, but they are too full-dress; everybody has to be in them at once. And they are entirely unprepared – or any rate the author very frequently doesn't. trouble himself to prepare them. There does not seem to me to be any particular reason why Nastasya should come to the house of Ganya, why she should find so many of the characters there; and there does not seem to me to be any particular reason why Rogozhin should at precisely that moment rush in with another crowd. It is mere coincidence.

(The reference is to *The Idiot*, Part I, Chapters 8—10.) Turgenev, for instance, would never permit himself such licence. And neither would Tolstoy. But Dostoevsky simply doesn't care. He wants to prepare you for one episode of the Christ legend, and he wants to have a lot of spectators. So he just pulls them in, and the Christ-Myshkin is struck on one side of the cheek and, in the proper romantic tradition, he goes one better than our Lord. He turns away to the wall and weeps for the shame that his persecutor will feel. And the persecutor duly feels the shame.[5]

To Ford, however, this all seems somehow too '*ready-made*':

Frankly speaking, I am tired of variations of the Christ legend. Or, no, I am not tired of them; I simply never liked them at all.

Is this an oblique reference to works like Ernest Renan's famous *Life of Christ*? Or to any sort of writing, whatsoever, intended to be edifying to the Christian public, as such, at large? At all events, he goes on:

I seem to want something fresher, something brighter, something sharper than the Myshkin Christ. For Myshkin is the same thing all over again. But if you ask me what I want ... ah, there! that again is not my job. And indeed I don't know. If I did I should try to do it myself.[6]

Ford is writing here some ten years before he embarked on *Parade's End*; in which he actually did make just such an attempt.

It seems to me that three questions arise out of this article as a whole:

1. Why, exactly, the 'bulge' in *The Brothers Karamazov*, as 'statue-pedestal'?

2. How might the finished 'statue' have looked, had Dostoevsky lived, and had he persevered in his commitment to it?

3. To what extent is Ford's verdict on 'the Myshkin Christ' more than just an expression of purely subjective literary taste? How justifiable is it, also, in theological terms?

∾

The 'bulge' in *The Brothers Karamazov* is not only, as Ford puts it, 'the scene of the dead monk whose body gave out an evil odour'; but it surely also includes the whole of Book VI, as background to that scene. It's a bulge, in that it interrupts the narrative revolving around the Karamazov family, with a set of documents in which the Karamazovs don't appear at all: (a) the autobiography of Alyosha Karamazov's spiritual guide, Father Zosima, covering his early life, many years prior to the events described in the rest of the novel; and (b) sundry 'Discourses and Sermons' of Father Zosima. Who then dies, and exits the novel entirely.

What's the function of this large chunk of material, so poorly integrated into its immediate context? I think Ford is right. Fully to appreciate *The Brothers Karamazov* one has to read it very much as a book that points beyond itself to the larger project announced in the preface, but never fulfilled. The ultimate rationale of the 'bulge' only begins to become, speculatively, apparent when one considers it in this light.

Dostoevsky sets out to write a two-novel depiction of true Orthodox saintliness. This is both a vindication of traditional

Russian folk religion, and also an invitation to rethink the traditional folk-religious notion of sainthood, in the fresh medium of a modern novel. Alyosha isn't yet, in the full sense, a saint in *The Brothers Karamazov*; only a potential saint. The fully realised saint in this novel is Father Zosima. In the grand scheme of Dostoevsky's implicit argument, Alyosha and Zosima surely represent two stages in the transition from the initial folk-religious notion of sainthood to a fully developed novelistic notion. Thus, by comparison to the probable future, promised Alyosha, Zosima is a much more conventional type of Orthodox saint: a priest and elder in a monastery. His autobiography is novelistic in tone, and already points beyond the standard forms of traditional hagiography; but he's otherwise just the sort of figure whose life would be celebrated in such literature. When we first encounter Alyosha, he's a novice at the monastery in question. Come the end of Book VII, however, at Zosima's bidding he leaves.[7] The second, projected novel was presumably intended to show him leading a saintly life out in the secular world; as far removed as possible, in social context, from the older norms of hagiography. And so, the purpose of the 'bulge', portraying Father Zosima, is to juxtapose and compare two altogether different notions of sanctity.

The obvious weakness of the more primitive notion is its liability to be hijacked by an essentially manipulative clericalist ideology; and so, to be corrupted into mere kitsch. Again: novels, in principle, offer a potential therapy for such corruption. In a novel, sainthood can be shown, with real intimacy, truly put to the test; truly refined. When Zosima dies, at the end of Book VI, such is his popular reputation that at first there's a clear possibility of his becoming the object of an officially sanctioned cult. But folk-religious thinking, in this environment, requires that the bodies of saints, after their death, remain miraculously more or less incorrupt. In Zosima's case this doesn't happen. His corpse soon starts to stink. Symbolically, what does this signify? We, the novel-readers, know that he *is* a genuine saint. *To us*, the corruption of his dead body doesn't signify any argument to the contrary; as it does to the practitioners of folk-religion. So, the scandal here marks a first clear point of division. The people's scandalized reaction to the corpse's stink represents the failure of old-time folk-religion fully to appreciate sublime virtue simply in itself.

Moreover, the resultant furore also brings about a decisive transition in Alyosha's own understanding of sainthood, and hence of his own vocation. For, at first, he'd simply shared in the widespread popular expectation of an incorrupt body, and attendant miracles. Then, however, once this hope has been dashed, he finds himself confronted with a basic choice: either to hold fast to the ethos of traditional Russian Orthodox folk-religion and therefore to moderate his veneration of the supposedly 'discredited' Father Zosima; or else, persisting in that veneration, to step decisively out of the intrinsic limitations of traditional folk-religious thinking. He chooses the second option. For, after all, what he thirsted for was justice:

> justice, and not simply miracles! ... He could not without a sense of personal outrage, of embittered deep-seated animosity, even, face the fact that the most righteous of righteous ones had been delivered up to the mocking and malicious jeers of such a frivolous multitude, so clearly his inferiors.[8]

This is the moment which, for him, decisively dispels the intrinsic ambiguity of traditional folk-religion as such, between testimony to genuine saintliness, and mere trivialisation of the same.

At first, indeed, the clarification of Alyosha's thought is emotionally tinged with rebellion. Traditional folk-religion, of course, values strict adherence to clear rules. It's Lent. But when the mischievous seminarist and future theologian Rakitin finds him – prostrate in grief under a tree – to Rakitin's amazement he agrees, in principle, to share in an illicit breakfast of sausage and vodka. No vodka is actually to hand, but Rakitin leads him away to visit Grushenka; the woman with whom both his brother Dmitri and his father are infatuated. There Alyosha takes a sip of champagne. And when Grushenka flirtatiously sits herself on his knee he doesn't object.

Almost at once, however, rebellion gives way to a fervent sense of spiritual rebirth. Praying by night in the elder's cell, where Father Zosima's body lies in the coffin, he becomes drowsy during the reading of *John* 2:1—1, the story of Jesus at the wedding in Cana; and starts to dream. Father Zosima appears to him, as one of the wedding guests. 'Let us be merry', says Zosima in the dream.[9] Alyosha goes out. Again, he throws himself flat upon the earth.

> Why he embraced it he did not know, he did not try to explain to himself why he so desperately wanted to kiss it, kiss it, all of it, but weeping he kissed it, sobbing and drenching it with his tears, and frenziedly he swore to love it, love it until the end of the ages. 'Drench the earth with the tears of your joy and love those tears of yours ...' resounded in his soul. What did he weep about? Oh, he wept in his ecstasy even about those stars that shone to him out of the abyss, and 'was not ashamed of this frenzy'. As though threads from all these countless of God's worlds had all coincided within his soul at once, and it trembled all over, in 'the contiguity with other worlds'. He wanted to forgive all creatures for all things and to ask forgiveness, oh, not for himself, but for all persons, all creatures and all things, while 'others asked the same for me' – resounded again in his soul. But with each moment that passed he felt plainly and almost palpably that something as firm and unshakeable as this celestial vault was descending into his soul. Something that was almost an idea took mastery of his intellect – and now for the rest of his life and until the end of the ages. A feeble youth had he fallen to the earth, yet now he arose a resolute warrior for the rest of his life and knew and felt this suddenly, at the same moment of his ecstasy. And never, never for all the rest of his life would Alyosha be able to forget that moment. 'Someone visited my soul in that hour,' he would later say with resolute faith in his words ...[10]

Why the 'bulge' in Book VI? It's surely to prepare us for this crucial moment of transition in Alyosha's spiritual career.

The significance of the moment is somewhat obscured by the fact that it comes a little less than half-way through the novel, and that thereafter Alyosha, although a recurrent presence, rather fades into the background of a narrative now for the most part dominated by his brother Dmitri's trial for the murder of their father, and his brother Ivan's lapse into madness. But the promised sequel would have restored Alyosha to centre stage. And then no doubt, in retrospect, the necessity of the 'bulge' would as Ford suggests have become much clearer.

~

What then of that unwritten sequel, Dostoevsky's definitive portrayal of saintliness, in the person of an older Alyosha Karamazov: that is, Alyosha once he has reached the age of Christ crucified?

We have the pedestal in *The Brothers Karamazov*. To what extent does this already indicate what Dostoevsky would have erected, on the foundation it provides?

Rowan Williams draws attention to a suggestive remark of Paul Evdokimov's: that the Dostoevskian saint typically tends to resemble an icon in the room, a "face on the wall".[11] That's to say, their saintliness is first and foremost a mode of simply *being present*. Beyond the act of making themselves present, and so available for others to approach, they mostly *do not take the initiative* in their relationship to others. But, rather, they respond to the initiative of others, with unconditional generosity; leaving those others as far as possible free, either to approach or not. Their listening, often counselling, presence is not, in this sense, as Williams puts it, a form of 'active engagement' so much as 'a site of manifestation and illumination'.

The purest example of this mode of sainthood is Christ himself, as he appears in Ivan Karamazov's fable of the Grand Inquisitor. Thus, Ivan's Christ walks the streets of sixteenth century Seville 'saying nothing ... with a quiet smile of infinite compassion'.[12] He doesn't have to do anything else in order to be recognised; he works miracles where it's demanded of him. When he's arrested, he listens in perfect silence to the Inquisitor's rant. And at the end he merely kisses the perfidious old man on the lips.

As for Father Zosima: he isn't silent. But, as an elder, his role in the monastery is, again, just to be an available presence, waiting for pilgrims to come; giving guidance to those who take the initiative of asking for it. Also, in *The Devils* there's a chapter – which the censor excised – featuring another holy man, Bishop Tikhon. Like Zosima, Tikhon has retired to a monastery; and there receives those who come in order to confess, and seek spiritual guidance. In the censored chapter, the demon-possessed Stavrogin visits him.[13] It won't be so easy for Alyosha, outside the monastic context, to play such a role. But will he, nonetheless, try?

The Dostoevskian saint, as a type, is qualified for the role purely and simply by virtue of being a great ego-transcendent sufferer, one who has learnt an ever-deeper compassion for all those around them, through his or her own suffering. In short: their saintliness consists in an approximation to the Isaianic archetype. For the Isaianic-archetype aspect of sainthood, after all, is surely just what, in the first instance, icons represent.

But where – given that the *Amos* impulse is, by contrast, absolutely a mode of taking-the-initiative – is *that* in the Dostoevskian picture?

Again: to be shaken by the *Amos* impulse is to take the initiative in challenging the mere inertia of herd-morality, for the sake of justice in the world at large. In Book VI, Chapter 3 of *The Brothers Karamazov* we're given a glimpse of Father Zosima's preaching. Dostoevsky evidently does recognise that without at least something of this sort there will be a significant gap in the portrayal of his saintliness. But these sermon-fragments are edifying in character, rather than campaign-initiatives. And they aren't at all well integrated into the novel as a whole. They're a bulge in the bulge!

In *The Brothers Karamazov* we already see Alyosha's potential with regard to the Isaianic-archetype aspect of sanctity; albeit in somewhat troubling fashion. He's very much a Karamazov in his capacity for great suffering. Only, in his case, it's a capacity sublated into selflessness: his response to being bereaved, after Father Zosima's death, clearly illustrates this. He's consistently compassionate. In his relationship to Liza Khokhlakova, above all, he takes compassion to quite disturbing lengths. Liza is confined to a wheelchair; a wildly impulsive and self-destructive, one might well say typically Dostoevskian personality. She and Alyosha become engaged. Of course, it's she who takes the initiative, proposing to him. And one immediately wonders: is his self-abnegating pity for her, in the end, going to be an adequate sustaining basis for marriage? The bond between them seems to be so entirely founded upon it. Nor does he seem capable of ever taking the necessary initiative to confront and challenge her where she needs to be confronted and challenged. This is most appallingly illustrated in Book XI, Chapter 3. Here she tests him, confessing to masochistic desires, fantasies of arson and suicide. She tells him that she loves him; then goes on to say, with great emphasis, that she loves no one. In other words: she's in hell. She tells him that she no longer wants to be his wife. Alyosha responds very gently. But then, in the midst of it all, she abruptly asks: "Alyosha, is it true that the Jews steal little children at Passover and kill them with knives?" To which he replies: "I do not know". And she goes on to share a fantasy with him, in which she herself has crucified a four-year-old child, and afterwards sits eating pineapple *compôte*, watching as the child dies.[14]

The novel was written just before the outbreak of sustained antisemitic violence in the Russian Empire. Dostoevsky's personal antisemitism was essentially aesthetic in character: an intensifying ingredient in his Russian Orthodox nationalism, giving added flavour to his rhetoric.[15] And in this context it's clearly just the Gothic-horror quality of the fantasy that counts, as a symptom of Liza's insanity. Alyosha, one may presume, surely *does* know that it's madness. But he doesn't want to affront Liza by suggesting that she's stupid.

Yes, but still, how can we continue to believe in the *potential saintliness* of someone whose response to the demonic is, after all, so spineless? In general, the basic objection to Dostoevsky's proposed canonisation of Alyosha is a pervasive sheer fuzziness with regard to his participation in the *Amos* impulse, inasmuch as this involves confrontation and challenge. Embracing his vocation, just before he leaves the monastery, he rapturously declares himself to be 'a resolute warrior for the rest of his life'.[16] A warrior *for what cause* though, exactly? It remains unclear. In Book X, and then in Chapter 3 of the Epilogue, Alyosha converts the gang of schoolboys around Kolya Krasotkin from their original scapegoating persecution of 'little Ilyusha', to being a crowd of caring friends, gathered first around Ilyusha's sickbed, then around his grave. There's an element of Dickensian sentimental pathos in this; alongside a good deal of malicious comedy in the depiction of Kolya, who's so very anxious not to be laughed at. In general, it's the weakest strand in the novel as a whole. But it does at any rate serve the purpose of showing Alyosha's capacity for leadership. What it doesn't yet show, on the other hand, is how that capacity is actually going to be exercised in the adult world; that is, to what cause it will be harnessed.

Elsewhere in the novel something like the *Amos* impulse appears, transmuted into rebellion against God and therefore completely cut off from the Isaianic archetype, in the anguish of Alyosha's brother Ivan. And again, at the opposite extreme, there's a parody of the *Amos* impulse, channelled by a crude ascetic fanaticism, in the thinking of Father Ferapont, Zosima's chief opponent within the monastery. Ferapont's gleeful rejoicing when Zosima's dead body starts to decay reveals his long-festering jealousy. Whereas Zosima preaches universal love, Ferapont stands for strict fasting as the highest form of holiness, which is reserved for monks alone; an altogether more overt contestation of herd-morality. Ferapont however is, plainly, psychotic. Dostoevsky is by no means inviting us to consider his standpoint as a serious option.

One of the first critics of *The Brothers Karamazov* was Konstantin Leontiev. His worldview was, so to speak, a sophisticated, intellectualised version of the same species as Father Ferapont's; he sought to outflank Dostoevsky in representing a yet more militant form of Russian Orthodox nationalism. Leontiev thus accused Dostoevsky of using the figure of Father Zosima to promote an alien-to-Russia, 'Franciscan' model of sanctity. And (notwithstanding the counter-evidence, especially, of *The Demons*) he also expressed the suspicion that, under cover of his professed Russian Orthodoxy, Dostoevsky secretly sympathised with the Western European, secular ethos of utopian socialism. This is, to say the least, a highly fanciful reading! If Leontiev's xenophobic misgivings were justified, then yes, utopian socialism certainly would have provided a framework for the *Amos* impulse, in the unwritten sequel to *The Brothers Karamazov*. But the only real evidence for that hypothesis in what Dostoevsky actually *did* write is the all too apparent absence there of any *other* such framework, truly adequate to the task in question.

∾

And how does the depiction of sanctity in *The Brothers Karamazov* relate to that in Dostoevsky's earlier work *The Idiot*? Unfortunately, Prince Myshkin, the 'idiot' of the title, is precisely the most extreme example possible of the self-same imbalance, between vivid embodiment of the Isaianic archetype and all too fuzzy intimation of the *Amos* impulse.

No one, in short, could be less capable of taking a serious Amos-like initiative than Myshkin. He arrives on the train from Switzerland, where he has been undergoing long-term treatment for epilepsy, into St. Petersburg, where he knows no one. And then he makes straight for the house of the Epanchins, for the simple reason that General Epanchin's wife appears to be a distant relation. He hasn't warned them that he is coming. And, though the general finds it hard to understand, Myshkin really has no particular purpose in mind, other than to say hello. Indeed, throughout the novel this remains his typical mode of action. A sort of secular, untethered, wandering equivalent to Father Zosima or Bishop Tikhon – although quite without their accumulated wisdom – again he simply goes about, making himself benevolently present to the other characters in the novel. He pursues no further strategy; neither an egoistic nor an ego-transcendent one.

The Idiot was published in serial form, beginning in January 1868. A week after he had sent off the first five chapters to *The Russian Herald*, we find Dostoevsky declaring in a letter to Apollon Maikov that his aim here was to *'depict a perfectly beautiful human being'*; three months later, in his notebook, this has been contracted to the emphatic formula, 'PRINCE CHRIST'.[17] Myshkin, when he's introduced to us, is described in terms very similar to the conventional depiction of Christ in Russian icons.[18] Nastasya Filippovna, when she first meets him, feels somehow that she has seen him before; she hasn't, but it's no doubt the Christ-likeness of his appearance that she's registering.[19] Note, however, his actual *non*-Christ-likeness in practice. The Christ of the Gospels is absolutely driven by the *Amos* impulse: he proclaims the imminence of 'the kingdom of heaven'; insurgently declares God's blessing upon the poor; recruits and organises a band of followers; and affronts the established political and religious authorities of his homeland, to the point that they feel obliged to eliminate him. There really isn't the slightest approximation to any of this in the story of Prince Myshkin!

Insofar as sainthood, in a Christian context, means Christlikeness, Myshkin isn't, therefore, a saint at all. He's a pure innocent. But innocence is scarcely the same as sainthood. Myshkin isn't a saint; he's an innocent *instead*. In effect: *it isn't so much the historic model of Christ that he follows, as the purely fictional one sketched out by Rousseau, in the figure of Émile.*

Thus, in the book *Émile*, Rousseau imagines a grand educational experiment.[20] The eponymous subject of this experiment is an orphan brought up purely and simply as a child of nature; in absolute isolation from other children, so as not to be corrupted, as all others more or less are, by a foolish concern for status, rivalries leading to jealousy, the lust for domination. His tutor's over-riding interest is just to produce a truly *free* individual, in the sense of one who is emotionally self-sufficient; whose contentment is dependent neither on the submission of others, nor on their approval; and who is, thereby, systematically kept from being socialised into the mutual manipulation of human herd-existence as such. In his infancy, Rousseau argues, it's crucial that the adults around Émile show they can't be manipulated by his tears. As he grows older, on the other hand, he isn't to be rewarded for successfully following a set curriculum. Rather, the tutor lets himself be guided by Émile's natural curiosity; gently prompting it at times, but never engaging in even the slightest battle of wills with him. For the one thing that he's determined Émile shall, so far as possible, *never* learn is an inflamed *'amour propre'*, or conceit. By which is more specifically meant: the conceit of an all-too-needy self-consciousness; preoccupied not with a pursuit of what's intrinsically good, but rather with mere concern for what other people will think and say about one, alike whether for good or ill; inasmuch as this is the root-source of all competitiveness.

What Émile's education is deliberately meant to do, it seems, Myshkin's epilepsy has somehow also done, for him. He has no *amour propre*, beyond the minimal *amour de soi*, or elementary self-regard, necessary for the preservation of life and the enjoyment of purely natural goods; perhaps not even that, in view of the way he almost seems to invite Rogozhin's potentially deadly attack in Part II, Chapter 5. No matter what people do, however hostile, he takes no offence.

Some of those whom Myshkin encounters respond with immediate warmth, sensing that his is an innocent benevolence one can confidently trust. But others call him an 'idiot'. And, in a sense, these latter aren't mistaken. Again, compare Rousseau's great treatise. Émile ends up, as a young man, going on a two-year tour around Europe, essentially *as a disengaged observer*: comparing different political and moral cultures. Rousseau supplies him with plenty of money, which Myshkin also has; but, still more importantly, with a bride already faithfully waiting for him at the end of the journey. This makes it easy for him to preserve his necessary aloofness – in a sense, one might say, Rousseau has rather cheated in this regard! But Myshkin, by contrast, has no sooner arrived in Saint Petersburg than he's caught up into two simultaneous love affairs, plus a whole swirl of other emotionally charged relationships around them. Free as he is of inflamed *amour propre* himself, he encounters a range of people driven more or less crazy by the disease. And the trouble is that, in his innocence, he has developed no effective strategies for coping with the difficulties of life in such a fallen world.[21]

There's thus a sense in which, as Williams puts it, Myshkin 'makes no adult choices'.[22] He has no strategy for coping with the plight into which he has drifted; never takes charge of the situation; lacks any apparent skill either in solidarity-building with potential allies, or in discernment of when to compromise, when to hold firm. Dorothea Brooke in *Middlemarch* may, as F. R. Leavis argued, represent an 'immature' ideal. However, she does at any rate make 'adult choices'; Myshkin is a much more extreme case. And, therefore, there's no way he could become a channel for the *Amos* impulse. The *Amos* impulse is surely a sublimation of *amour propre*, in the broader sense of pride, not just its absence. It draws its energy from the proper spiritedness of a campaigning dissident; but Myshkin has none of the skills of a campaigner.

And how is this sublimation, where it does occur, made possible? Not by an education like Émile's – but far rather, I'd argue, by active, loyally critical membership within a vigorous moral community. Although Amos stormed against the religious authorities of Israel, he did so in the name of Israel's God; appealing to all that, as he saw it, was most particular to Israel's calling as a nation. Myshkin, for his part, is a member of the Russian Orthodox Church, but he has been abroad for a long time, and the only time we see him in church, at the funeral of General Ivolgin, he confesses to never having previously attended such a service.[23] 'Adult choices', with regard to religious practice, are ideally founded on adult belonging, within a shared historic tradition. But Myshkin's most vivid confession of faith is based on his altogether *private* experience of epileptic fits, the moment before collapse:

> 'In that moment' [he says to Rogozhin] 'I somehow begin to understand the extraordinary phrase *"there should be time no*

longer" [*Revelation* 10:6]. Probably ... that is the very second that was not long enough for water to be spilled from the epileptic Mahomet's overturned water-jug, though in that very second he was able to survey all the habitations of Allah.'[24]

Subsequently, just before succumbing to another epileptic attack in Part IV, Chapter 7, during a soirée at the Epanchins, Myshkin does, for once, engage in fighting talk: a ferociously anti-ecumenical rant, in fact, upholding Russian Orthodoxy, but denouncing Roman Catholicism as 'worse than atheism itself ... the teaching of the Antichrist'.[25] Once again, though, this is quite alien to the *Amos* impulse, which is fundamentally grounded in corporate *self*-critique.

Hegel has a name for those who – although they're sincerely conscientious individuals, with real individuality – nevertheless fall short of what he considers full ethical wisdom, just because they fail to take seriously the necessity for proper solidarity-building activism; energetic actual engagement in the struggle for justice. He calls them *'beautiful souls'*. And in the *Phenomenology of Spirit*, he analyses two basic variants of this general mentality.[26] First, there's what one might perhaps term the 'sweet-tempered beautiful soul': whom Hegel pictures as a solitary, vainly yearning figure; in terms of social impact, little more than 'a shapeless vapour dissolving into thin air'. And then: a rigidified version, perhaps integrated into a whole other-worldly sect, the 'hard-hearted beautiful soul'; a bitter figure, moralistically condemning any form of tactical compromise with potential allies as a sell-out. If Hegel had had Dostoevsky's work to hand, he might well have cited Myshkin as a prime case in point. Myshkin is a generally sweet-tempered beautiful soul, who however in his rant at the Epanchins' soirée mutates into hard-heartedness: fantastically projecting his own apolitical innocence onto the Russian Orthodox Church, and all the wickedness associated with political realism onto Roman Catholicism.

Beset as he is by the wild interplay of other people's blazing *amour propre*, and quite incapable of effective strategy in coping with this phenomenon – which, as it's so alien to him, he can't truly comprehend – there's no realistic prospect of Myshkin's story having a happy ending. For there to be any true closure at all, it has to be tragic. And so it proves: at the end, he has collapsed into insanity, and is finally returned to the clinic in Switzerland from which at the beginning of the novel he'd just been discharged. Earlier, this bleak conclusion is enigmatically prefigured by the symbolism of Holbein the Younger's painting of the dead Christ, a copy of which hangs in Rogozhin's house. Myshkin, visiting, is startled by it:

> 'That painting!' [he] exclaimed suddenly, under the impact of a sudden thought. 'That painting! Some people might lose their faith by looking at that painting!'[27]

(And the nihilistic youth Ippolit, later on, also discusses it at some length in his extended suicide note, or 'Necessary Explanation.')[28] As Williams remarks, Holbein's painting

> is a kind of anti-icon, a religious image which is a nonpresence or a presence of the negative. This is true in a purely formal sense: in classical Orthodox iconography, the only figures ever shown in profile are demons and – sometimes – Judas Iscariot. The icon seeks to confront the viewer / worshipper with a direct gaze informed by the divine light. Holbein's painting shows (though this is not explicitly described in the novel) a corpse seen from alongside – not only a dead man fixed at a moment in the past (there are Orthodox depictions of the dead Christ and his entombment), but a dead man in profile, a double negation of the iconographic convention. In a fairly literal sense, this is a "diabolical" image.[29]

What Holbein's painting shows is Christ not yet risen, in other words, not yet re-entered into the struggles of history, but simply *emptied of fight*. Pure Suffering Servant, therefore, nothing else: *like Myshkin*, who's never a real fighter, and ends up reduced to complete passivity.

Why do both his two love-affairs founder? What Nastasya Filippovna, herself a great fighter, surely wants is not only a man who won't exploit her – as Totsky, her original patron, has – but one who also has the strength effectively to battle her demons, resist her own self-punitive impulse to self-destruction. Clearly, Myshkin won't exploit her. She sees that straight away. Just a few hours after initially meeting him, she's able to declare:

'He is the first man I have ever met in my whole life in whom I can believe as one who is truly devoted. He believed in me at first sight, and I trust him.'[30]

However, she fears that he lacks the necessary fight to withstand her own self-destructiveness; and that, in any close relationship with her he too will be ruined by it. So, for a spell, she seeks to promote his affair with Aglaya Ivanovna; whilst half-submitting, for her own part, to the lethal passion of Rogozhin. And she wavers between the two men right to the bitter end.

Whilst, as for Aglaya Ivanovna: what she ideally wants, besides love, is a fighter who'll have the strength, and the daring, to rescue her once and for all from a domestic environment that she finds all too confining; and give her a role within some much larger struggle. So, in the Conclusion, we see her eloping with, she thinks, a wealthy Polish count – who, shame to say, turns out neither to be wealthy nor a count – but who recruits her to the cause of Polish nationalism. Again, it's Myshkin's lack of fight which, after much toing and froing, prevents his relationship with Aglaya coming to fruition.

This prevailing lack of fight is essential to his innocence. However, I come back to the nub of the matter: innocence alone isn't yet sainthood. Williams relates the issue here to the fundamental question of Christology, 'whether the humanity taken on by the eternal Word in the Incarnation is fallen or unfallen'.[31] In the West, by way of answer to that question, the dogma of the Immaculate Conception of the Blessed Virgin Mary says: unfallen. But the novelistic imagination, by its very nature, pulls the other way.

Fallen human beings are much more interesting. Novels about saints have to do with fallen human beings who have confronted their fallenness with exceptionally honest self-awareness; and who thus are – surely just by virtue of their honesty – Christ-like.

Myshkin is indeed absolutely honest, within the limits of his self-awareness. Yet, his innocence restricts that self-awareness, to such an extent that, in the final analysis, his honesty lacks the *hard-won* character of a true saint's. He's good more by nature than by grace. Compare, as an example of a true saint, Father Zosima: in his case, it's very much the other way round.

---

1. Ford, *Critical Essays*, ed. Max Saunders and Richard Stang (Manchester: Carcanet, 2002), p. 126.

2. Ibid. p. 127.

3. Dostoevsky, *The Brothers Karamazov*, trans. David McDuff (London: Penguin Classics, revised edition, 2003) p. 10.

4. Ford, *Critical Essays*; p. 127.

5. Ibid. p. 128.

6. Ibid. pp. 128—9.

7. See *The Brothers Karamazov*, Book II, Chapter 7, p. 104, where Zosima, near to death, says to Alyosha:

    > As soon as God sees fit to let me pass away, you must leave the monastery. You must go away entirely … I give you my blessing for your great task of obedience in the world at large. You have much travelling yet to do. And you will have to get married. You will have to endure everything before you return again. And there will be much work to do. But I have faith in you, and that is why I am sending you. With you is Christ. Cherish him and he will cherish you. You will behold great woe and in that woe you will be happy. Here is my behest to you: in woe seek happiness.

8. Ibid., Book VII, Chapter 2, pp. 439—40.

9.   Ibid. Chapter 4, p. 468.

10. Ibid. p. 469.

11. Paul Evdokimov, *Gogol et Dostoievski, La descente aux enfers* (Paris: Desclée de Brouwer, 1961), pp. 88—9. Rowan Williams, *Dostoevsky: Language, Faith and Fiction* (London and New York: Continuum, 2008), pp. 28—9. (Williams describes Evdokimov's work on Dostoevsky, in general, as being 'unfairly neglected'.)

12. *The Brothers Karamazov*, Book V, Chapter 5, p. 325.

13. The chapter in question, 'Stavrogin's Confession', omitted in earlier translations, is printed in David Magarshack's 1971 Penguin edition, as an appendix. Bishop Tikhon is modelled on the real-life eighteenth-century Saint Tikhon of Zadonsk. Dostoevsky had a special devotion for Tikhon Zadonsky, a saint who suffered bouts of acute depression, with various psycho-somatic symptoms.

14. *The Brothers Karamazov*, pp. 746—47.

15. See his article, dated March 1877, Chapter 2, 'On the Jewish Question', in Dostoevsky, *The Writer's Diary*, trans. and annotated by Kenneth Lantz (Evanston Ill.: Northwestern University Press, 1993.) Here he denies being antisemitic; but then launches into a sustained attack on Russian Jews in general for their supposed hostility towards their Gentile neighbours, especially those poorer than themselves; building up to some really very ugly speculation as to what would happen if roles were reversed, with Jews the majority and Russian Christians the minority; before however finally advocating equal civil rights, so as to remove any appearance of justification for the hostility he deplores.

16. *The Brothers Karamazov*, Book VII, Chapter 4, p. 469.

17. See Dostoevsky, *The Idiot*, trans. David McDuff (London: Penguin, 2004), Introduction by William Mills Todd III, p. xxiii. The letter to Maikov is dated 12 January; the notebook formula appears three times in the margin of a page, dated 9—10 April, at which point Dostoevsky was at work on the opening chapters of Part II.

18. Ibid. Part I, §1, p. 6.

19. Ibid. Part I, Chapter 9, p. 123; Chapter 10, p. 138. See Williams, *Dostoevsky*, 2008; p. 48.

20. Jean-Jacques Rousseau, Émile, trans. Allan Bloom (New York: Basic Books, 1979).

21. Things do in fact, also, go wrong for Émile: in an unfinished supplement, we find him writing to his tutor of his anguish, when he finds that his beloved wife Sophie has (it seems) been raped by another man. Rather shockingly, he blames her. His solitary education hasn't included learning how to forgive.

22. Williams, *Dostoevsky*, p. 48.

23. *The Idiot*, Part IV, Chapter 10, p. 682.

24. Ibid. Part II, Chapter 5, p. 265. C.f. Williams, *Dostoevsky*, p. 49.

25. *The Idiot*, Part IV, Chapter 7, pages 633—7.

26. Hegel, *Phenomenology of Spirit*, VI. C. c. (*Die schöne Seele*: usage of this phrase was widespread in German literature of the period; although it's Hegel who gives it the most sharply thought-through philosophic meaning.)

27. *The Idiot*, Part II, Chapter 4, p. 255.

28. Ibid., Part III, Chapter 6, pp. 475—7.

29. Williams, *Dostoevsky*, p. 53.

30. *The Idiot*, Part I, Chapter 14, p. 181.

31. Williams, *Dostoevsky*, p. 56.

CHAPTER FIVE

Saints and Holy Warriors

Now, though, let's distinguish between three basic different types of ethical sublimity:

- the sublimity of angels

- the sublimity of the hero

- the sublimity of the saint, in the strict sense.

Angels are sublimely untroubled by fear of death, because they're immortal. And in their sublime, unfallen state they're untroubled by any requirement to overcome egoism, because they quite simply lack egos. By human standards, they possess no real individuality. (The fallen angels fall by acquiring egos. But, judging by the myths, these are still only somewhat hazy ones! Angels, alike whether they're unfallen or fallen, lack individual life-stories, of the human kind.)

Sublime heroes, by contrast, are sublime by virtue of their having overcome mortal fear, perhaps even of death. But they differ from *saints, in the strict sense*, inasmuch as their egos are well-bolstered by all the praise they receive from the communities to which they belong.

Saints, in the strict sense, have not only overcome great mortal fear, perhaps even of death, but have also had to undergo a substantial degree of ego-loss. To some considerable extent, they've passed through the process which the Sufis call *fanā' wa baqá'*, 'annihilation and abiding': the 'annihilation' of their surface egos, the 'abiding', only, of the 'that of God', so to speak, deep down within their selves.

∽

Why turn, as a theologian, to novels? Not least, because of novels' rich potential as a medium for ironic critique of *propaganda-myth*, in general; very much including the propaganda-myths generated by evangelistic impatience.

By definition, a 'propaganda-myth' falls short of authentic revelation for the simple reason that, in the end, it remains all too subservient to the corporate egoism of the movement it seeks to serve. Thus, propaganda-myth is a form of aesthetic production which right from the outset excludes the true sublimity of the saint, inasmuch as the sublimity of the saint, on the contrary, precisely represents the *dissolution* of self-assertive egoism, both individual and corporate.

Consider, for instance, the dialectic of propaganda-myth and anti-propaganda played out in the mainstream Christian theological tradition. By the 'ego', to which propaganda-myth appeals, I mean that self which is constituted by imitating other people, competing with other people; failing, in the process, either fully to respect the real individuality of other people, or to become a truly free individual oneself; and thereby being rendered opaque to the 'that of God' within. Christ, potentially, comes to signify the supreme opposite. In him, perfect transparency to God is also an absolute openness to all others: solidarity with the victim; 'bearing' the sin of those who victimise. His being crucified, in this case, viscerally represents that 'bearing' of sin, according to the Isaianic archetype. The deterrent propagandist purposes of those who crucify already, dramatically, render anyone who is crucified a representative figure: representing all those who are to be intimidated, by witnessing their own potential fate, anticipated here. But behold a crucified dissident, a victim of that extreme propaganda, raised from the dead! That he's also hailed as the

Son of God gives this event the most all-encompassing symbolic significance. It isn't just a one-off judgment on a particular case, but a universal divine verdict on the underlying purposes of crucifixion in general; and, by extension, a verdict on any regime, of whatever kind, that to any degree resembles the one which crucified Christ, in its dependence on propaganda. Ultimately, it's a judgement on the essential *libido dominandi*, the 'lust for domination', of the ego, in all its forms, synecdochally symbolised by the cross. Ascended into heaven, Christ incarnates the pure sublimity of the saint, accorded in principle an absolute maximum of anti-propagandist authority.

Confronted with the resultant challenge however, the propagandist impulse – *also at work within the Church* – fights back. It seeks to reframe the gospel in other terms; render it less threatening to the ego. One strategy serving this purpose we've already noted, in Chapter 3: the hollowing-out of Christ's humanity by magical salvation-myth, culminating in Anselm of Canterbury's 'two infinities' theory. Here, what matters is no longer so much the paradigmatic *ethical* value of Christ's iconic 'Suffering Servant' ego-transcendence; but rather the *magic* efficacy of his salvific pain. The human phenomenon of sublime virtue morphs into mere super-human power. And then, another, complementary strategy is for the sublimity of the saint to be, in effect, swallowed up into the flashier, yes, but altogether more amenable sublimity of angels. In the New Testament, this ploy appears most obviously in the *Revelation of John*.

So, the opening vision of *Revelation* is a fantastical appearance of Christ. First, the prophet hears a loud voice hail him from behind, causing him to turn round. And then, he reports,

> I saw ... amid the lampstands one like a son of man ... And his head and hair were as white as wool – a white like snow – and his eyes like flames of fire, And his feet like fine brass, as if fired in a furnace, and his voice was like a sound of many waters, And he held seven stars in his right hand, and a sharp, two-edged sword coming out of his mouth, and his face was

like the sun shining at full strength. And when I saw him I fell down at his feet like a dead man ...

(1:12—17)[1]

Never mind that this figure bears no resemblance whatsoever to the Jesus of the Gospels: clearly, the author is aiming at all-out sublimity, of a certain kind, for propaganda purposes. The fiery eyes recur, as does the rather grotesque, lip wielded sword, when Christ reappears, at the culminating crisis of the narrative. Here the prophet reports:

I saw heaven opened, and look: a white horse, and the one sitting on it called Faithful and True, and he judges and wages war in justice. And his eyes are [like] a flame of fire, and on his head are many diadems, he who has a written name that no one except him knows, And who has been clad in a robe deep-dyed in blood, and his name is called the Logos of God. And the armies [who were] in heaven followed him on white horses, clothed in bright, clean, fine linen. And from his mouth comes forth a sharp sword, so that with it he might strike the gentiles; and he will shepherd them with a rod of iron; and he treads the winepress of the wine of the vehemence of God the Almighty's ire. And on the robe and on his thigh he has a name written: KING OF KINGS AND LORD OF LORDS.

(19:11—16)

Nothing indeed could be more remote than this 'shepherding with a rod of iron' *bully* sublimity from the saintly sublimity of the Suffering Servant in *Isaiah*!

Revelation records two great outbreaks of war in heaven. The other, earlier one is at 12:7—9. Here the commander of God's forces isn't Christ, but the Archangel Michael. But how do the two wars differ? And how, after all, do the two commanders differ? On both occasions a great victory is won: Michael's army throws down Satan and all his angels out of heaven; Christ's army defeats the various 'beasts' representing pagan Rome, kills them, and imprisons Satan. The second victory is more complete. Of course, Christ, who wins it, outranks Michael. Nevertheless, his authority appears to be absolutely *of the same kind.* To all intents and purposes, he is pictured here in the guise of a supreme warrior angel. And this notion of Christ as a quasi-angelic celestial warrior naturally recurs, throughout Church history, wherever there are crusades; or wherever the *Amos* impulse is warped into mere hate preaching. The crusading fervour that issued in the English Civil War, for instance, also afterwards gave birth to Milton's *Paradise Lost*. So, Milton gives us the propaganda-mythic sublimity of angels, magnificently rendered, in various guises: Satan and his hosts in Books One and Five; the dissident seraph Abdiel in Book Five; the vast armies of heaven and hell confronting one another in the climactic battles of Book Six.[2]

These battles end with Christ simply outbidding Satan in the same angelic sublimity. But compare the *Letter to the Hebrews* 1:1—4:

> God, having of old spoken to the fathers by the prophets, in many places and in many ways, At the end of these last days spoke to us in a Son, whom he appointed heir to all things, and through whom he made the ages. Who – being a radiance of his glory and an impress of his substance, and upholding all things by the utterance of his power – took his seat at the right hand of the Majesty in the places on high once he had accomplished a purification of sins. Becoming as far superior to the angels as the name he has inherited surpasses theirs.[3]

Why is the anonymous author so anxious to affirm Christ's absolute superiority to angels? There's no evidence of any group *explicitly* regarding Christ as an angel. But is this intended as a polemical thrust against the sort of apocalyptic Christology to be seen in *Revelation*: its whole tone? 'For surely', he also remarks,

> [Christ] does not reach out to angels, but rather reaches out to the seed of Abraham. Hence it was necessary to become like his brothers in all things, so that he might become a merciful and

faithful high priest of God's affairs, in order to make expiation for the people's sins. For inasmuch as he himself has suffered in being tried, he is able to help those enduring trials.

(2:16—18)

The Christ-like sublimity of the saint, in other words, is really quite different in kind from the sublimity of angels; and of a much higher order.

༄

'Onward, Christian soldiers, marching as to war,/With the cross of Jesus going on before!' In general, the protagonists of Christian propaganda-myth are intent on stirring up that militant spirit. Sometimes, they invoke the sublimity of warrior-angels to do so. And sometimes, again, they invoke the sublimity of mortal heroes: heroic holy warriors.

Inasmuch as the true sublimity of the saint essentially involves ego-loss, it tends to be hampered by ego-bolstering *fame*. This indeed is another major advantage of novels, in exploring it: their ability to evoke lives lived in historic obscurity. By contrast, the elaborate bureaucratic canonisation-process run by the Vatican – like the less formal equivalent processes at work in Eastern Orthodoxy and in Anglicanism – inevitably tends to fix upon the famous.

So many 'official' saints have been famous holy warriors for the Church; either metaphorically, or else quite literally. Think of all those heroic warrior-kings who have been canonised: St. Oswald, king of Northumbria in the early-seventh century; St Alfred the Great, king of Wessex in the late-ninth century; St Alexander Nevsky, ruling in mid-thirteenth century Russia; his contemporary, the piously Jew-hating, book-burning St Louis IX of France; and so forth. There have indeed been many others ...

Or consider for example that great one-off, *Joan of Arc*.

Here we have, as it were, the holy-warrior ideal supremely incarnate, in a heroine.

∼

My mother came from Penzance. I know the local churches well. Amongst them, one stands out for the exceptional quality of its interior artwork: St Hilary, just inland from Marazion. In the 1920s the parish of St Hilary had a very enterprising Anglo-Catholic vicar, Father Bernard Walke; whose wife Annie was an accomplished painter. The Walkes recruited numerous others from the nearby Newlyn artists' colony, to help decorate the place.[4] But one of the most impressive paintings there is actually by Annie Walke herself: a full-length portrait of Joan of Arc, in full armour.

What does it mean for this great icon of *French* patriotism, this strange warrior, so fiercely embattled in her lifetime against the forces of the King of England – this martyr-saint, burnt at the stake by clerics loyal to that King – to be honoured here, in a Church of England parish church? Walke's painting of Joan dates from just after Joan's eventual canonisation, in 1920. If it's her gender as a warrior, rather than her nationality, that counts in this instance, the image is perhaps primarily a monument to the victory, still only half-achieved at that point, of British suffragette militancy. It looks very much like a baptising of the suffragette cause.[5]

But Joan's career very strikingly, I think, illustrates the relationship between the sublimity of the hero-as-holy-warrior and the sublimity of the saint, at its most problematic. For, whilst there can surely be no questioning the sublime nature of Joan's courage as a warrior, I must confess, I am rather less sure how compatible this is with authentic sainthood, in the specific sense determined by the Isaianic archetype. The sublimity of the hero-as-holy-warrior is by no means incompatible with the raw *Amos* impulse; but it quite clearly does preclude the pacific saintliness of the Suffering Servant in *Deutero-Isaiah*.

Little rural settlement though St Hilary is, the Walkes were well connected with the literary world. George Bernard Shaw once came to visit. This wasn't long after his play *Saint Joan* had been premiered, in 1923. Seeing Annie Walke's portrayal of Joan, in the church, Shaw was moved to exclaim, 'Ha, this is *my* Saint Joan!' To which the artist replied, 'Oh no, Mr Shaw, this is the *real* Saint Joan'. But that's just the problem with Joan of Arc! She was, right from the outset – namely, from the age of thirteen, when she first started seeing her visions of the Archangel Michael, and the heroic martyrs, Saint Margaret and Saint Catherine – such a great weaver of propaganda-myth, around herself. Joan's genius lay in her instinctive ability to render herself into a more or less mythic figure. But her *reality* is more or less lost behind the myth of her own weaving. That she has meant so many different things to different people is surely due to the very nature of such propaganda-myth-making: the manipulative way in which it seeks to play upon, and so is shaped by, wishful fantasy. In this regard, Joan, as a sublime heroine of such myth, actually represents the exact opposite to the Suffering Servant in *Isaiah*. For, effective propaganda-myth meets the urgently felt need of its addressees, for encouragement. But, by contrast, the memory of the Suffering Servant reveals *what has hitherto been unfelt.* Namely: the, in principle, still more urgent need of the chorus, for repentance and forgiveness. Remembering the Suffering Servant, the chorus members grow ashamed of their past aggression. Joan's propaganda-myth, however, is designed for the rallying of an army, the troops of one feudal sovereign fighting against those of another. No matter how legitimate any sovereign's claim might be, to represent his people, I would query whether such a blood-soaked warrior-enterprise could *ever* be the truly primary task for a saint, in the fullest sense.

~

There are, it seems to me, five basic species of myth-making impulse. 1. There's myth simply intended as a form of *entertainment.* Think, for example, of the comic-book mythic superheroes of today: Superman, Batman, Spiderman and the rest. 2. At other times, myth serves as the theoretical framework for a rather more serious belief in *magic*. Here, it consists of narratives informed by superstitious anxiety, or hope. 3. In pre-literate societies, on another level, myth-making is not least a lyrical project of finding, expressing and celebrating a sense of straightforward *at-home-ness* in the natural world; such as we can no longer share, but can only honour with respectful remembrance. 4. Then, on the other hand, there's myth issuing out of profound *alienation* from the world. Gnostic myth is the prime example: essentially, a sacralised attack – framed in terms of grandiose theogony, and cosmogony – on the malign effects of evangelistic impatience, seen as pervading other, more mainstream Abrahamic traditions. 5. But by '*propaganda-myth*' I mean any sort of wondrous narrative intended to help energise the corporate ego of a campaigning movement. When it comes to specifically *propaganda*-myth, I absolutely believe in 'demythologisation'!

Thus, consider how the sublimity of the hero-as-holy-warrior gets caught up into that fifth species of myth in Joan's case. Joan's mystique has been, and still is, invoked by a range of different political movements. Often, it's the political right that has sought to appropriate her. In the early twentieth century *Charles Maurras*, of the proto-fascist Action Française, was one such admirer; another, no less notable, was *Maurice Barrès*, the great original 'anti-intellectual' intellectual. Maurras was a monarchist, Barrès a republican; but they were friends, both alike energetic protagonists of the antisemitic cause in the Dreyfus Affair; both belligerent advocates of revenge for the humiliation of the 1870 Franco-Prussian War. And both saw Joan as a sublime symbol of the ideal political conjuncture between devout Roman Catholicism and loyalty to 'France'. Both, therefore, greeted her canonisation in 1920 as a great national triumph. More recently, again, the Front National/Rassemblement National has followed in the path pioneered by Maurras and Barrès. And yet it isn't only the right who have claimed her. As the martyr-victim of a church court, she has also served as an icon of left-wing anticlericalism; and as a peasant girl, rising up as a leader, she has obvious potential as a socialist icon. *Anatole France* – an atheist, and socialist, Dreyfusard – was another prominent devotee, for instance. And her most thought-provoking celebrant of all, *Charles Péguy*, was likewise very much a man of the left.

Péguy was an ardent patriot, whose life was cut short, at the age of forty-one, when he was killed in action in 1914, the day before the beginning of the Battle of the Marne. As a young man, in 1897, he had published a substantial drama portraying the career of Joan of Arc.[6] This drama, however, pre-dated his personal conversion to Christian faith. And his major work on Joan is actually a later, lyrical reworking, and major theological expansion, of the first two scenes of that earlier work: *La Mystère de la charité de Jeanne d'Arc* (1910).[7] Joan, here, is a thirteen-year-old girl; not yet embarked on her public career, just about to begin it; spinning as she tends her father's sheep, on a hillside by the River Meuse. She encounters, and engages in dialogue with, two other figures: first, briefly, with her ten-year-old friend, Hauviette; then at much greater length with a young Poor Clare nun, Madame Gervaise. Much of the text consists of a grand set-piece poetic meditation, by Madame Gervaise, on the life and death of Christ.[8] But the three characters are also in sharp conflict. Joan represents the wild form of sublimity that will eventually inform her career; Hauviette, a common-sense, moderating scepticism; Madame Gervaise, a scepticism informed by devout loyalty to established ecclesiastical authority. All three points of view are sympathetically represented. We, the audience, are left to judge for ourselves between them.

But, again, which species of sublimity does Joan, in fact represent, in Péguy's play? Superficially, it might appear that it's the sublimity of the saint: a devoutly Christian, anguished 'bearing' of the sins and suffering of humanity at large. However, I don't think so. Far rather, it's just the sublimity of the hero-as-warrior, sacralised with splendid theatricality. Soon after Madame Gervaise's arrival – it's true – Joan abruptly confronts her with a bitter recitation of the cruelties and, above all, the blasphemies of war.

Do you know, Madame Gervaise, that the soldiers are everywhere storming the market towns and breaking into churches? ...[9]

She taunts her, almost. Repetitively! In effect, she's asking: 'Do you *really* care?' Only, what would it mean, in Joan's view, really to care? In her earlier conversation with Hauviette, it emerges: she wants to see war "killed". "And war does not kill itself through peace". To which Hauviette replies:

> You are right, big sister, you are right. The best thing, if one could, would be to kill war, as you say. But in order to kill war, you have to make war; in order to kill war, you need a war lord, *[laughing as she would at the most enormous joke, at the most unthinkable flight of fancy]* and it isn't us, is it, who are going to make war?[10]

Well, Joan of course *is*. At this point in the story, though, that laughable prospect hasn't yet emerged.

Joan, further, goes on to scandalise Madame Gervaise with a weirdly challenging prayer:

> Oh, if in order to save from the eternal flame
> The bodies of the dead who are damned and maddened by
> pain,
> I must abandon my body to the eternal flame,
> Lord, give my body to the eternal flame;
> My body, my poor body, to that flame which will never be
> quenched.
> My body, take my body for that flame.
> My wretched body.
> My body worth so little, counting for so little.
> Of little weight.
> My poor body of so little a price.
> [A pause.]
> And if to save from eternal Absence
> The souls of the damned maddened by Absence,
> I must abandon my soul to eternal Absence,
> May my soul go to eternal Absence.[11]

In short, she volunteers for hell.

What good could such a sacrifice actually do for the damned? None whatsoever! But that isn't the point. She doesn't exactly make this absurd gesture out of compassion. Rather, she's just boasting. The point is to affirm, in extreme metaphysical terms, her boundless courage.

Thus: Joan here is working with the most crudely manipulative notion of hell, as an extremity of punitive physical and psychological torment, stretching out into an endless expanse of extra time. She takes this deplorable picture for granted; she doesn't in any way question its compatibility with divine love. There's no protest here. Her prayer is a boast. It's meant to express, with the most extravagant flourish, the heroic 'sublimity of the hero-as-holy-warrior': her being undaunted even by the infinite terror of hell. Yet, note: this is, in actual fact, the *exact opposite* to what I'm calling the true sublimity of the saint! For that other sublimity consists, on the contrary, precisely in being undaunted by the (not at all manipulative) *terror of heaven*. It confronts the terror of ego-loss; the terror intrinsic to the revelation of God's presence, insofar as the barrier of ego has gone; the terror of Moses, ascending Mount Sinai.

Joan prayerfully expresses her willingness, if need be, to be damned. Mother Gervaise immediately rebukes her: such a prayer is nothing but blasphemy! The sheer flamboyance of it is sublime, yes; but it's also quite monstrously egoist, in its hubris. For how after all can one *pray* (however hypothetically) to be damned? This is a self-contradiction. As Madame Gervaise argues, authentic Christian prayer involves an aspiration, at least, to be of the Church. Yet, there can by definition be no Church in hell. Christ is poetically imagined as descending into hell on Holy Saturday: this expresses God's unbounded love for all. But how could Christ share the *lostness*, as such, of the damned? To be damned is wilfully to have separated oneself from God. As the Son of God, Christ, again by definition, represents the most perfect integration of humanity into God. Christ, we read in the Gospel of Matthew (27:46) cried out on the cross, in the words of Psalm 22, verse 1,

'My God, my God, why have you forsaken me?' Here he takes upon himself all the grief of earth, including grief *for* the damned; but, still, scarcely the grief *of* the damned, as Joan prays to do. (The grief *of* the damned is, in any case, surely anaesthetised by sin ...) 'Why, sister', asks Madame Gervaise, 'should you want to save better than Jesus the Saviour?'[12]

Why indeed? For my part, I must say, I am fully with Madame Gervaise in her protest.

Then, the conversation turns to the story of Christ's arrest in the Garden of Gethsemane. Madame Gervaise recalls that 'the master Saviour did not want Peter to draw his sword against the soldiers in arms: we mustn't go to war'.[13] 'So they had swords ...', Joan interjects. Well, yes, they did have swords, but when one of the disciples struck out at the slave of the high priest, cutting off his ear, Jesus stopped him; immediately, according to Luke 22:51, healing the wound. And then all of the disciples fled.

Joan	I believe ... I believe.
Madame Gervaise	Daughter, child, what dare you say?
Joan	I believe that, had I been there, I would not have forsaken him ...[14]

That's to say: notwithstanding the hopelessness of the situation, *she*, embodying the sublimity of the hero-as-holy-warrior, would still have fought back, with her sword. Those disciples, she goes on to insist, in effect represent the timorous mentality of the herd, at its absolutely most contemptible. 'They were happy once.' For, they had enjoyed the actual earthly presence of Christ. And yet, by not violently resisting, they had all betrayed him.

> French knights, French peasants, people from our country
> would never have forsaken him.
> People from the country of France. People from the country of
> Lorraine ...
> Never would the people of these parts have forsaken him.[15]

She nags and nags away at the theme; driving poor Madame Gervaise to distraction.

Certainly, Péguy's Joan is sublime. In her frenzied obsession, magnificently so! But I'm less sure that what we see in her is sublime *virtue*. On the contrary: there's something demonic about such sublimity.

---

1. Again, the New Testament passages cited here are as translated by David Bentley Hart, *The New Testament: A Translation* (New Haven and London: Yale University Press, 2017).

2. Milton actually rejected the traditional Homeric / chivalric focus on warfare as providing the subject matter for epic poetry: *Paradise Lost*, Book Nine, lines 14—47. Book Six, however, depicts epic *spiritual* war. There is of course something ludicrous in the fact that, although swords flash and slice, and the demonic artillery blazes away, none of those engaged, either righteous angels or fallen angels, can actually be killed; or even be subjected to anything more than the most fleeting pain! But, in ghostly pantomime fashion, it's still glorious.

3. C.f. also *Ephesians* 1:20—21, *Philippians* 2:9—10, *Colossians* 1:15—18, *1 Peter* 3:21—22.

4. The story is told in his 1935 autobiography: Walke, *Twenty Years at St. Hilary* (St. Agnes: Truran Books, 2002). He was also famous for the religious plays he wrote and produced in St. Hilary, for broadcast on the BBC. His Anglo-Catholicism however provoked conflict: in 1932 a bus-load of militant Protestants arrived, broke into the church and vandalised it.

5. There's also a statue of Joan in Winchester Cathedral; installed in 1923.

6. Péguy, *Jeanne d'Arc: drame en trois pièces* (Paris: Gallimard, 1952). This originally appeared in the *Revue Socialiste*.

7. English translation by Julian Green: *The Mystery of the Charity of Joan of Arc* (London: Hollis & Carter, 1950).

8. This soliloquy runs from pp. 100—167. It covers the whole life and death of Jesus; especially as viewed by his mother. A curious detail is the emphasis on his supposed role as a carpenter. With reference to the throwing out of the moneychangers from the Temple, Madame Gervaise oddly remarks that, as a workman from a family of workmen, 'He instinctively disliked tradespeople' (p. 157). I must say, this was theological news to me!

9. Ibid. p. 69.

10. Ibid. p. 40.

11. Ibid. pp. 83—4. Repeated, more briefly, on p. 92, this prayer already in fact features in the earlier *Jeanne d'Arc*, pp. 21—2.

12. *The Mystery of the Charity of Joan of Arc*, p. 167.

13. Ibid. p. 170.

14. Ibid. p. 171.

15. Ibid. pp. 172—3.

CHAPTER SIX

Nikos Kazantzakis:
Christ Recrucified

Nikos Kazantzakis's work *Christ Recrucified*, first published in Greek in 1948, seems to me a prime example of confusion between the sublimity of the saint and the sublimity of the hero-as-holy-warrior, developed in the form of a novel.[1] Thus, whereas Dostoevsky's depiction of sainthood, in the figures of Prince Myshkin and Alyosha Karamazov, is one-sided, in that it represents the Isaianic archetype pretty well altogether abstracted from the *Amos* impulse, Kazantzakis's depiction of sainthood is instructively one-sided in just the opposite fashion. For here, on the contrary, we have a celebration of the *Amos* impulse quite unbalanced by any adequate appreciation for the Isaianic archetype. Although Kazantzakis does indeed pay a sort of lip-service to the Isaianic archetype – and even does so with a certain melodramatic flourish – in a crucial sense, I want to argue, his thinking at this point lacks real conviction.

Two novelists both from the world of Eastern Orthodoxy, Dostoevsky and Kazantzakis essentially represent opposing poles of the true ideal.

∾

Kazantzakis, be it noted, wasn't only a novelist. He also very much believed in being, and sporadically was, a political activist.

102

The narrative of *Christ Recrucified* is set in Anatolia, just before the final mass exodus of the Greek population, following the catastrophic defeat of the invading Greek army in the 1919 – 1922 war against the Turks, and the associated wave of terror. And the plight of refugees is central to the plot. Several political experiences in Kazantzakis's own life clearly help inform *Christ Recrucified*. One is his work, at the age of thirty-six, as Director General of the Greek Ministry of Welfare in 1919—20; a post to which he'd been appointed by the great republican prime minister Eleftherios Venizélos, with particular responsibility for the resettlement, in Macedonia and Thrace, of Greek refugees fleeing conflict in the Caucasus. Another is his significant contribution as an agitator, during the years 1924 – 1925 in his native land of Crete, to the insurgent movement centred on the newspaper 'The Voice of the Reservist'. Here he was collaborating with a Communist cell in Iraklion. The readership of the newspaper was primarily made up of men discharged from the army; many had been under arms right from the beginning of the 1912 – 1913 Balkan Wars, through the First World War, and then the debacle in Anatolia. Returning home, alongside a great number of refugees from Anatolia, they found a drastic lack of jobs, of housing and, in particular, of available farmland – a central demand was that they should be granted land owned by monasteries. Matters actually came to a head when, on February 1st 1925, Communists, shouting 'Peace!' and 'Down with War!' clashed with a crowd enraged by the expulsion of the Ecumenical Patriarch from Istanbul, and calling for a renewed attack on Turkey. Then, a few days later, some of Kazantzakis's comrades broke into the belfry of Iraklion Cathedral, and started to ring the bells. After that, however, the authorities cracked down, quite effectively. Kazantzakis himself, after twenty-four hours in prison, wasn't exactly silenced – but, always restless as he was, nevertheless found himself starting to wonder about his previous Communist loyalties. In order to work through the questions that he increasingly had, he set off for the Soviet Union, as a journalist, to record his impressions of the great experiment being undertaken there. Subsequently, he dated the decisive onset of his eventual disillusionment with Marxism as an ideology to that moment.[2]

After another twenty years of wandering and writing, at the end of the Second World War he at length returned to politics, as the founder of his own political party; aiming to draw together all the various splinter groups of the non-Communist Greek left. For a brief while in 1945 – 1946 he was actually Minister without Portfolio in a coalition government. The political context in which, shortly thereafter, he wrote *Christ Recrucified* was the Greek Civil War, between Communists and anti-Communists. The novel has, fundamentally, to be understood as part of Kazantzakis's general attempt to develop an alternative 'myth'-framework for socialist politics aesthetically far richer than anything compatible with standard Communist Party propaganda. That's to say: just the sort of 'myth', in general, advocated by Péguy's friend Georges Sorel; just the sort which Péguy had also been intent on developing, in his depiction of Joan of Arc.[3]

To this end, he sets out to re-appropriate the prophetic core of the Christian gospel. *Christ Recrucified* is, not least, an attempt to liberate the gospel from the dominant mind-set of the Greek Orthodox Church, as a reactionary institution. It's a project of 'Liberation Theology', long pre-dating that actual term. Kazantzakis had already infuriated elements in the leadership of the Church before he wrote *Christ Recrucified*. In 1930 he had faced a serious threat of prosecution, on a charge of atheism, for his extended lyric-philosophical essay *Askitikí*, subsequently translated under the title *Saviours of God: Spiritual Exercises*.[4] And later on, in 1953 – 1954, he was to face another storm of similarly motivated criticism, focused on passages in his novel *Freedom and Death* and his novelistic adaptation of the gospel story, *The Last Temptation of Christ*.[5] The latter was placed on the Roman Catholic Index of Forbidden Books. Back home in Greece, hard-liners campaigned to have him excommunicated, although in vain.

∾

Christ Recrucified is a tale of two small Greek communities. One is the village of Lycovrissi, 'Wolf's Fountain'. The other: a band of fugitives, refugees from another village, St George's. When the invading Greek army arrived, these latter had risen up in support. And when the invaders were driven off, the Turks had come and burnt their village; raped and killed. For three months, when the novel begins, these refugees have been on the road, carrying their icons, the Gospel and the banner of St George.

Lycovrissi, for its part, has so far been spared from the turmoil. Its people still live in peace, under the governance of an alcoholic Turkish Agha. The only other two Turks in the village are the Agha's boy concubine, and his bodyguard. Every seven years, at Easter, the village stages its own passion play. The novel opens at the beginning of the seventh year, shortly before the arrival of the refugees, with the selection of actors for this: two wealthy men, the archon Patriarcheas and 'Father' Ladas to be Pontius Pilate and Caiaphas; the warm-hearted village prostitute Katerina to be Mary Magalene; the saddler Panayotaros to be Judas; three other young villagers, Yannakos, Kostandis and Michelis, to be the apostles Peter, James and John; and finally, the shepherd Manolios to play Christ. The selections are all predictive of the actual roles these characters will go on to play in the narrative.

When the refugees arrive, they're represented by their pope, that is, village priest, Fotis, who pleads with the pope of Lycovrissi, Grigoris, for land on which they might settle and re-establish their village. But Pope Grigoris represents the Church at its most corrupt. Although land is available, he immediately rejects the appeal, on the grounds that the refugees are a cholera-risk. And the other notables of the village agree. Manolios (Christ in the passion play) protests against their cold-heartedness; he's supported, in the first instance, by Yannakos, Kostandis and Michelis (Peter, James and John in the passion play). The refugees retreat into makeshift accommodation up the nearby Mount Sarakina. This leads to steadily escalating conflict which, in the end, erupts in lethal violence.

There are in fact two main saints in *Christ Recrucified*: old Pope Fotis and young Manolios. The pope is a gaunt ascetic, with a haunting past, who is associated with the prophet Elijah (*1 Kings*

17—19, 21; 2 *Kings* 1—2); there being a little chapel dedicated to the prophet high up on Mount Sarakina. He has all the fieriness of the Hebrew prophetic tradition; and he transmits this to Manolios. But the basic problem, I'd argue, with Kazantzakis's depiction of sainthood is that, for him, a saint is simply a warrior of exceptional high chivalric morale, expressed in terms of Christian rhetoric.

Kazantzakis enjoyed mixing together ideas: Christianity and Buddhism at one level; Schopenhauer, Nietzsche, and Shestov at another. He certainly warmed to Sorel's high-minded apology for violence. But above all he professed himself a follower of Henri Bergson, whose lectures he had attended in 1908. No doubt part of the attraction, for him, of Bergson's thought was its principled imprecision; the polyvalent suggestiveness of Bergson's 'vitalism'; that is, Bergson's celebration of '*élan vital*', the life force, in whatever form it might take. The influence of Bergson may well be traced right through Kazantzakis's work. But Peter Bien, his most prominent English-language interpreter, argues that

> Bergsonism's most subtle presence [actually] occurs in *Christ Recrucified*, where it governs the very structure of the plot since the refugees – forever moving, forever producing effects by means of which their own reality expands and transcends its being – are the developed organisms through whom the continuity of genetic energy passes like a current, upwards, toward composition, whereas the established citizens who resist them in the village represent matter's inverted evolution toward decomposition. The meeting of these two streams is the luminous interval called life, the interval between the one dark abyss from which the refugees enter the book at the start (as energy longing to express itself via materiality) and the other dark abyss into which they pass out of the book at the end, defeated in materiality but with their creative potential intact. If we allow the images to guide us to an intuition of duration ['*durée réelle*', Bergson's term for pre-theoretic ultimate reality, apprehended in direct proportion to the sheer intensity of one's vital energy] we will appreciate the degree to

which this remarkable novel is governed in its deep structure by a vitalistic theory of the world and of human destiny.[6]

To what extent, though, does this Bergsonian scheme, in itself, really provide a sufficiently nuanced framework for moral judgement?

Pope Fotis and Manolios are two prime embodiments of ethically inspired high-intensity *élan vital*. But is this as saints, in a strict sense, or is it simply as righteous warriors? There's a slippery slope here. If after all it's the latter, then what *other* forms of high-intensity *élan vital*, shaped by the 'sublime of the warrior', may we be invited to admire, as being kin to theirs? Kazantzakis in the diary entry I have already cited, which records the onset of his disillusionment with Marxist ideology, starts to formulate an alternative form of political hope. He writes:

> The positive, creative role has always been taken by the *"barbarians"*. Only they possess the seed.[7]

'Barbarian', here, has a range of connotations. At one level, it has the mischievously provocative meaning of 'non-Greek'. Then, more broadly, it means 'uncivilized'. But, above all, to be 'barbarian' is to be untamed by the sheer inertia of the *status quo*, or opened up, so far as possible, to *élan vital*. Kazantzakis is still at this point, in the mid-1920s, thinking about the Russians, as bearers of revolutionary hope for humanity as a whole. 'But Russia's present leaders', he remarks 'are disregarding their true mission and looking to Europe for seed: materialism, Marx, etc.'[8] And, later, he comes to think of other peoples as bearers of 'barbarian' promise. In his epic reworking of the *Odyssey*, Odysseus joins a band of Cretan rebels in league with blond Dorian 'barbarians' from the north; and then travels south, to the source of the Nile, in search of African others.

There is of course an element of 'barbarian' promise, in Kazantzakis's very broad sense, also at the source of biblical and qur'anic monotheism: it's there in the story of the Exodus, the slave revolt; in the Christian perception of God revealed incarnate as the crucified dissident; in the apocalyptic hope common to

Judaism, Christianity and Islam. Kazantzakis's saints represent this particular form of 'barbarian' promise at its most urgent.

But then the trouble is that his taste for *all things* 'barbarian', simply as such, is all too indiscriminate. Thus (like Sorel) he was in turn an admirer of both Lenin and Mussolini. For, were not Lenin and Mussolini – each in their different ways, alike – two great stirrers-up of *élan vital*? Likewise, also, he was for a while seduced by the charisma of Generalissimo Franco; whom he interviewed in 1936. And again, at the end of his life, for the same reason, he became a quite uncritical admirer of Chairman Mao, visiting China as an honoured guest of the state in 1957. In short: he had a truly lamentable weakness for revolutionary despots, and their personality cults! Moreover, his vitalistic way of thinking had the unfortunate effect of altogether obscuring the radical opposition between any such cult and a proper honouring of saints. It's as if for him both phenomena are, in essence, just variants of the same.

Kazantzakis's lousy judgement when it came to revolutionary despots is I think very much of a piece with the basic one-sidedness of his thinking about saints: its being all *Amos* impulse, unbalanced by any authentic approximation to the Isaianic archetype. The vision of Christ in *Christ Recrucified* is, in his own terms, essentially 'barbarian'. So much so that, as the novel approaches its climax and the refugees on the mountain are preparing to descend for a final confrontation with the people of Lycovrissi, the impulsive Yannakos/'St. Peter', determined to support them against his fellow-villagers, bursts out:

> "If Christ came down on earth today, on an earth like this one, what do you think He'd have on his shoulders? A cross? No, a can of petrol."[9]

Yannakos intends holy war, in the form of arson. Michelis/'St. John' protests. But Manolios / 'Christ' is with Yannakos. He has seen just such a vision of the Saviour in a dream. 'You're right,' he says to Yannakos, 'not a cross; petrol.'[10] He carves a wooden image of what he has seen. At first Michelis is startled:

"What is it?" he cried; "it's War!"

"No, it's Christ," replied Manolios, wiping the sweat from his forehead.

"But in that case, what's the difference between Him and War?"

"None," replied Manolios.[11]

Nor does it take long for Michelis, too, to be convinced ...

∽

As I've said, Kazantzakis does, it's true, pay a certain 'lip-service' to the Isaianic archetype. The identification of Christ with the Suffering Servant is, after all, deeply rooted in Christian tradition; and he's keen to reproduce the tradition as far as he can, at any rate superficially, as a source of ingredients for his own plot.

So, for example, in Chapter 5 Manolios is heading down the mountain, from his shepherd's hut, intending to visit Katerina the prostitute/'Mary Magdalene' who, he knows, loves him. He's both intending to 'save' her and, at the same time, also seething with sensual temptation – when, all of a sudden, he finds his face grotesquely swollen over and 'flowing with muck'. This is certainly a very graphic illustration of Deutero-Isaiah's verses:

> He had no form or comeliness
> that should have made us pay heed to him;
> there was no beauty that should have made us desire him;
> his appearance was so marred, beyond human semblance,
> and his form beyond that of the sons of men.
> He was despised and rejected by men,
> a man of sorrows and humiliated by sickness.
> He was like one before whom men hide their faces,
> despised – we esteemed him not.
>
> (*Isaiah* 53:1—2 / 52:14 / 53:3)[12]

Manolios's first thought is: can this be leprosy? Or is it some other disease? At all events, it preserves him from giving way to the immediate temptation.

(It so happens that Kazantzakis himself suffered from recurrent extreme bouts of facial eczema.)

And then, with regard to the chorus's crucial chastened recognition in *Isaiah 53:4—5* that the Servant has gone to his death *on their behalf*: note, first, Manolios's heroic response to the crisis that hits the village when the Agha's boy concubine is found murdered (Chapters 8—10). In actual fact, the murderer is the Agha's bodyguard, Hussein. But, unaware of this, and incandescent with rage, the Agha threatens to hang the 'notables' of Lycovrissi one by one, in the middle of the village, until the guilty party confesses. Hearing the news Manolios, without hesitation, goes down and confesses to the crime himself. His face is miraculously healed on the way! The Agha doesn't at first believe him, but locks him up all the same, along with the village 'notables'; to be hanged at sunset. In order to save Manolios, Katerina then confesses to the crime. The Agha, in his fury, stabs her to death. He nevertheless orders the hanging of Manolios, also, to proceed. Manolios is only saved when Hussein's guilt is discovered. In the most literal sense we thus see him, like Christ, volunteering to die on behalf of others; specifically, moreover, on behalf of those who are now his greatest enemies, the 'notables'.

So too, when later on – in the course of the climactic battle between the refugees and the main body of the villagers – Pope Grigoris's brother, the schoolmaster, is killed, struck on the head by a stone, Grigoris quite falsely informs the Agha that it was the 'bolshevik' Manolios who had thrown the fatal stone. To this Panayotaros/'Judas Iscariot' adds his own invention: that Manolios had been calling on the refugees to burn down the Agha's house. Manolios hands himself in to the Agha, who – even though Manolios does indeed call himself a 'bolshevik' – re-enacts the New Testament role of Pontius Pilate with Jesus, inasmuch as he recognises Manolios's actual innocence of the crimes with which he is charged. Nevertheless, in order to appease the mob, the Agha decides to deliver Manolios into their hands. They drag Manolios off into the church (which is dedicated to 'the Crucifixion'). Manolios cries out, 'Kill me! Kill me!' And, just as Pope Fotis, Manolios's friends and all the refugees arrive at the church doors the village mob does as he demands. Pope Fotis – with a bitterness of despair, mind you, which is quite alien to the gospel, and to *Isaiah* – mourns him:

> 'Dear Manolios, you'll have given your life in vain,' he murmured; 'they've killed you for having taken our sins upon you; you cried: "It was I who robbed, it was I who killed and set things on fire; I, nobody else!" so that they might let the rest of us take root peacefully in these lands … In vain, Manolios, in vain will you have sacrificed yourself …'[13]

It's in vain because the Agha has, in the meantime, sent for a Turkish regiment, complete with artillery, to suppress the disorder in the village. Manolios has died as a martyr in a much more restricted sense than the Isaianic Suffering Servant, whose scapegoat death surely serves to show the intrinsic folly and injustice of all scapegoating, in the most general terms. Manolios's scapegoat death was, in a much more limited way, intended, by him, to make peace between two particular communities. Heroic – but to no avail! The refugees will still be obliged to move on.[14]

∾

What, though, does it mean truly to evoke the truth of the Isaianic archetype in a novel? To recapitulate, one might say that, ideally, it involves three things:

1. The novel needs to show the clear innocence of an innocent sufferer who is – or innocent sufferers who are – more or less set over against a morally critical or accusatory human herd.

2. Then, it needs to show them responding to the hostility of the herd, the gang, the mob without resentment, or desire for

revenge; as it were, soaking up the sin of others, the sinfulness which comes to expression in that hostility; hence, 'bearing' it; cutting short its self-replicating process.

3. Above all it needs to prompt, in us its readers, the same general attitude as is expressed by the chorus in *Isaiah* 52:13 – 53:12. That's to say, not only a sense of unsparing distaste for the folly or destructiveness of such sin as is highlighted by the narrative; but also, a sense of shocked fellow-feeling with the sinners. So that we in turn are compelled to confess: "these sins, that the saint is shown 'bearing', *are ours*".

Although the case of Manolios does indeed fit the first two criteria, *Christ Recrucified* clearly fails with regard to the third.

So: consider the village 'notables' who are in the first instance responsible for rejecting the refugees; and eventually for the murder of Manolios. The retired sea captain Fortounas, who goes boozing with the Agha, is a jovial figure, and actually quite open to the refugees. However, he dies already in Chapter 6. The schoolmaster seeks to mediate between the two warring groups. He, though, is weak and ineffective. Whilst, as for the trio most committed to the conflict – Pope Grigoris, the archon Patriarcheas, and old Father Ladas – they have scarcely any redeeming features at all! There is, in the end, nothing here that could inspire any sort of real, chastened fellow-feeling in the reader. Grigoris is a bully; Patriarcheas is a snob; Ladas is a miser. They're comic caricatures. And to this extent, the novel isn't so much a true, *searching* confrontation of saintly virtue with the norms of herd- or gang-morality as such; but rather a brash work of quasi-Manichean kitsch, essentially just upholding one still-emergent form of herd- and gang-morality, labelled 'revolutionary', against another older one, labelled 'reactionary', represented by these odious types. It rises above propaganda, by virtue of its not being hitched to any particular partisan cause (Manolios's confessed 'bolshevism' notwithstanding); which also saves it from being triumphalist. Yet, it nonetheless still remains quite disturbingly close kin, in spirit, to standard propaganda-triumphalism.

Again, compare Dostoevsky's work. The great sinners among Dostoevsky's leading characters are strange, tormented individuals, who demand our respect; albeit respect more or less mixed with horror. Kazantzakis's chief sinners, on the contrary, elicit mere contempt – which inevitably, then, does rather compromise our appreciation for his saints, matched in conflict against such unworthy adversaries!

---

1   Here I'm using the second edition of the English translation by Jonathan Griffin, (London: Faber & Faber, 1962). The first edition of this translation had originally been published in Oxford by Bruno Cassirer, 1954; and separately in the USA under the title *The Greek Passion* in New York, by Simon and Schuster, 1953.

    For a previous theological discussion of Kazantzakis's work: see F. W. Dillistone, *The Novelist and the Passion Story* (London: Collins,1960.) I generally concur with Dillistone's verdict. (The other authors he discusses in this survey of novels addressing the passion story are Melville, Faulkner, and Mauriac.)

2   See the diary entry quoted in Peter Bien, *Kazantzakis: Politics of the Spirit*, vol 1 (Princeton University Press, 1990), pp. 96—7.

3   C.f. Sorel, *Reflections on Violence*, trans. T. E Hulme and J. Roth (Mineola, NY: Dover Publications, 2004). These 'reflections' first appeared, as a series of newspaper articles, in 1906. Sorel was a socialist, arguing against his comrades' inhibitions with regard to revolutionary violence. He invokes the concept of 'the sublime': 'Socialists must be convinced that the work to which they are devoting themselves is a *serious, formidable, and sublime work*; it is only on this condition that they will be able to bear the innumerable sacrifices imposed on them by a propaganda, which can procure them neither honour, profits, nor even immediate intellectual satisfaction' (Ibid. p. 139; and c.f. pp. 210—11). To inspire this 'sublime work', he thinks, there's a need for 'myth', ideally of comparable power to the apocalyptic Christian 'myth' in the book of *Revelation*. This 'myth', in his view will naturally focus on the idea of an all-transformative general strike (pp.125—39).

4   This was actually first published in 1927; then reissued in a revised edition in 1945.

5   *Freedom and Death* was first published in 1953 as *O Kapetán Mihális*. *The Last Temptation*, written in 1950—51, wasn't actually published in the Greek original until 1955; but that it was on the way was known earlier, and it was this foreknowledge which provoked the scandal.

6   Bien, *Kazantzakis*. vol. 1, p. 50.

7   Ibid. p. 96. My emphasis.

8   Ibid. pp. 36—7.

9   *Christ Recrucified*, p. 417.

10 Ibid. p. 418.

11 Ibid. p. 427.

12 As reconstructed in Claus Westermann, *Isaiah 40—66* (London: SCM Press, 1969), pp. 253—4.

13 *Christ Recrucified*, pp. 466—7.

14 C.f. *The Last Temptation*, trans. Peter Bien (London: Faber & Faber, 1975), pp. 394—8. Here Jesus, in conversation with Judas, cites *Isaiah* 53:4—5, 7. The letters of the text appear, 'filling the air'. He commits himself, as the Messiah, to follow the way of the Suffering Servant, and die a scapegoat's death. Judas protests: *he* is looking for quite a different sort of Messiah, one 'with a sword'. Jesus insists otherwise. And yet, he gives no *reason* why it can't be that way.
    In *Christ Recrucified* Manolios's death has a salvific rationale – but appears to be a defeat. *The Last Temptation* represents the Passion of Christ as a triumph – without, however, any clearly indicated salvific rationale, even where the question 'why' is explicitly asked. It's just not a question that really seems to interest Kazantzakis.

C.
Negative Revelation

CHAPTER SEVEN

The Solidarity of the Shaken

The darker the background, the brighter sublime virtue shines. One might speak, here, of *negative revelation*. The worse it gets, the clearer it gets.

This already applies to the book of *Amos*. For, how after all was it possible for that revolutionary re-envisioning of the divine, in *Amos*, essentially as infinite intensifier of ethical concern for the oppressed poor – the demands of *mishpat wa tsedaqah*, 'justice and righteousness' – to take hold? It surely required the dark shadow cast by the Assyrian emperor Tiglath-Pileser III; his creation of the world's first ever standing army; the clear threat which this posed to all the surrounding peoples; and the prophet's resultant sense of crisis, calling everything urgently into question. So, in *Amos*, the prophet's fresh understanding of God is juxtaposed to terrible, fleeting images of impending catastrophe. It's predicated upon the sheer impossibility – as the prophet and his followers saw the situation – of business as usual.

And the same principle applies to *Deutero-Isaiah*. Yes, there's a promise of coming relief here. But this is relief consequent upon pretty much the very worst having already happened; nothing less. Thus, the message of *Deutero-Isaiah* is addressed to a still-traumatised people. The image, here, of the Suffering Servant is rooted in the collective trauma of people who've been driven from their homeland; whose Temple has been destroyed, and the city around it devastated; whose whole sacred culture has been systematically assaulted.

Sublime virtue is, by definition, always embattled. But where it's embattled only against the moral banality of the herd, the chiaroscuro effect is much less intense than in a social context where government has fallen into the hands of truly ruthless hostile gangs; gangs orchestrating mobs, military or otherwise.

George Eliot, in the Preface and Finale of *Middlemarch*, laments the historic near-invisibility of people like the saintly Dorothea Brooke. As a study of sublime virtue, *Middlemarch* is indeed a struggle waged against that near-invisibility; especially as it derives from the nineteenth century social disadvantages of women. However, it isn't only their gender which renders saints of Dorothea's kind almost invisible to the historian. There's also the fact that Dorothea's sainthood is simply counter-posed to the Middlemarch *herd*. Teresa of Avila, for her part, had altogether more formidable opponents!

And other novels, by contrast, grapple with far more spectacular manifestations of sublime virtue, lit up by negative revelation.

∿

Positive divine revelation is what lays the foundation for particular confessional traditions: Jewish, Christian and Muslim forms of scripture and liturgy, the deep truth of which consists in celebration of sublime virtue. *Negative* revelation, serving to highlight that deep truth, is mixed in with this. And yet, it also transcends the confessional particularity of positive revelation.

Gradually, through God's history, something new is working its way to the fore. Within and beyond the solidarity of Jew with Jew, or of Christian with Christian, or of Muslim with Muslim – in fact, beyond every species of particularistic confessional solidarity – a universal *solidarity of the shaken* is emergent. Not just bland, abstract 'humanism'! But very much a product of negative revelation: solidarity on the basis of shared *shaken-ness* by such revelation; solidarity on that basis alone. Beyond ethnic solidarity, beyond class-based solidarity, beyond any easier sort of solidarity laced with mere prejudice against outsiders – fully explicit solidarity of the shaken is a late-comer, just because it's the most difficult sort of solidarity to organise, the noblest sort.

Solidarity of the shaken: *solidarita otřesených*. As a philosophical term, the phrase is originally Czech. It was coined by Jan Patočka, who in 1977 co-founded, with Václav Havel, the Charter 77 civil rights campaign in Czechoslovakia.[1] For Patočka it was a name for the ideal ethos of that movement. An upsurge of protest against the Czech Communist Party's reign of terror, Charter 77 emerged from, and went on to inform a whole underground counter-culture. This counter-culture invited the participation of all Czechoslovak citizens, entirely regardless of their other political views; entirely regardless of their attitudes to religion, for or against; entirely regardless of social class; entirely regardless of their aesthetic likes and dislikes, or their various different interests, in general. But what united the signatories, besides their citizenship, was *just* their shared, 'shaken' concern for the defence of free, civilised public debate; their shared, 'shaken' determination, come what may, to speak truth to power. And so, the movement went on to inspire a fundamental reckoning, precisely, with the element of negative revelation bound up in the history of East-Central Europe, as a whole, under Communist totalitarianism, from 1945 onwards.

As I understand it, the 'solidarity of the shaken' is none other than what in the New Testament is called the 'kingdom of God', or the 'kingdom of heaven'. It's a modern, secular name for God breaking into history. That's to say: for God – it may be openly, or it may be anonymously, but, either way, in the most decisive practical fashion – at work in the world.

∾

In this section of the book I discuss three novels grappling with heightened intensities of negative revelation.

One comes from modern China; one, from the African-American experience, in the southern USA; one, from the history of the Jewish diaspora, culminating in Nazi-occupied France. But the first isn't just of Chinese significance. The second isn't just of African-American significance. And the third isn't just of Jewish significance. In the end, all three surely speak to the solidarity of the shaken.

1. Patočka, *Heretical Essays in the Philosophy of History*, translated by Erazim Kohák (Chicago and La Salle, Illinois: Open Court, 1996). The key passage is at the end: pp. 133—6. But the whole text builds towards this. And c.f. Havel, *Living in Truth*, translation edited by Jan Vladislav (London: Faber and Faber, 1987), p. 157.

    Patočka actually died just three months into the campaign: collapsing, at the age of 69, after a gruelling ten-hour interview with the police. He was a professor of philosophy, banned however from university teaching from 1951 – 68, and again from 1972 onwards; and mostly unable to publish in the ordinary way. The *Heretical Essays*, a major work, were completed in 1975. Only after his death, however, were they widely copied and circulated, by informal means.

CHAPTER EIGHT

Yiyun Li: *The Vagrants*

What negative revelation, in the first instance, reveals is quite simply the proper sacredness of sublime virtue. The positive revelation of Abrahamic religion at its best nurtures sublime virtue; develops liturgy celebrating it. But sublime virtue, *in itself*, is by no means dependant on such nurture. Thus, Yiyun Li's novel *The Vagrants* presents us with a spectacle of sublime virtue set in a cultural environment completely untouched by Abrahamic tradition: north eastern China, Jilin province, the city of Muddy River near the Korean border (Hunjiang, population 80,000) in the late 1970s.[1]

Truly, the Muddy River of this novel is a seedy, cruel place. There's nothing much that's homely about this town. As indicated in the novel's title, it's a community of 'vagrant' souls.

After Chairman Mao's death in 1976, there'd appeared to be a real chance of liberalising change. In 1978 a brief 'Democracy Wall' experiment began in Beijing: many hundreds of people writing and displaying 'big character posters' on a long brick wall in the city centre, critical comments on current affairs; great crowds gathering to read them. And tentative calls for reform were being made throughout the country. Li's novel tells the story of one such call – and of its brutal suppression.

✌

Li emigrated from China, to the United States, as a young woman in 1996. The language of her novels is English. But in the spring of

2003, she published an essay, in the *Gettysburg Review*, meditating on a true story from her original homeland.[2]

In 1968, at the height of the Cultural Revolution, in Hunan province, a nineteen-year-old girl, the Communist Youth League secretary in her high school class, wrote a letter to her boyfriend, a young soldier. In the letter she expressed her revulsion from the mob-ethos, the sheer hysteria, of the Red Guard student movement in which she was caught up - she'd seen too many people tortured, and even murdered!

Mistakenly, she thought she could trust her boyfriend. But he handed the letter in to his company commander. One thing led to another, and three days later the girl was arrested.

There followed ten years in jail, during which she bombarded all and sundry with letters, protesting and appealing. Eventually, there was a retrial. Those letters had exasperated the authorities; they were presented as evidence of her incorrigibility. She was sentenced to death. In the spring of 1978, she was taken to a stadium and there, in front of a great crowd of spectators, she was executed by firing squad.

Moments before she was shot, an ambulance had raced onto the pitch. A team of medical workers had jumped out, man-handled her into position, and then proceeded, without anaesthesia, swiftly but carefully to remove her kidneys. These were then air-lifted to the hospital where the father of a high-ranking provincial Communist Party boss was waiting for a transplant.

Her family were required, as was customary, to pay for the bullet that had killed her. (It cost twenty-four cents. Li remarks: this was the price of one thin slice of pork in those days.) But they didn't dare go and collect her corpse. Instead, it was dumped on a rubbish heap outside town, where unfortunately a necrophiliac pervert was the first to find it. This man later confessed to having raped the body; and to having then further mutilated it by excising the sex organs, which he'd pickled in formaldehyde.

These things happened just a few months before the beginning of the 'Democracy Wall' experiment. A number of the girl's fellow-citizens did in fact try to appeal on her behalf. After her death, moreover, they persisted: arguing for her to be posthumously rehabilitated, 'de-purged' (*Ping-Fan*). Hundreds joined in the protest, unnerving the authorities. All the protesters were eventually punished: some lost their jobs, others served prison sentences. And one thirty-two-year-old woman, judged to have been the prime mover of the protest – the mother of a two-year-old boy – was herself executed.

In her essay, Li goes on to recall an incident in her own childhood, dating from the same time; when she was five and a half years-old. She remembers how, one day, all the children of her Beijing primary school were made to line up along a rope, and process to an open field nearby, full of a great crowd, both other children and adults; how a bamboo stage was quickly erected; how a truck drove up and four bound men were pushed out, then led onto the stage. She remembers the policemen there 'in snow white uniforms'; how one of them came onto the stage with a loudspeaker, to announce that these four 'counterrevolutionary hooligans' had been sentenced to death; and how he raised his fist to lead the chant of 'Death to the counterrevolutionary hooligans!' She remembers how the 'aunties', the primary school teachers, signalled, and she raised her fist – along with all the other children, and all the 'uncles and aunts' from the local factories, shops and offices, and all the retirees – shouting out the slogan, together. She remembers in particular her teacher Auntie Wang, the uneasy relationship she had with her. And how immediately after the event

> Auntie Wang walked up to me and put her hand to my head, in the shape of a handgun. 'You see that? If you have too much of your own will, you will become a criminal one day. Bang,' she said, pulling her finger as if to trigger the gun, 'and you are done.'[3]

Li's novel is then a coming to terms with such memories; as foundational moments, in her life, of negative revelation.

It's constructed upon a frame of actual historic fact: the tale of the two martyrdoms. Li shifts the story's location; and moves it forward a year, for dramatic effect, to the height of the Democracy Wall period. She also adds a cast of other fictional characters. But the figure of Gu Shan, in the novel, is closely modelled on the first martyr, who died such a grotesque death; whilst the figure of Wu Kai is, in essence, modelled on the second martyr, executed for her role in organising the protest against that first death.

～

We aren't made privy to Gu Shan's intimate thoughts and feelings; we don't hear her speak. The novel begins on the day of her death. But we see her only in the distance, from a vantage point within the spectator-mob, at one of the six denunciation-ceremonies before the actual execution: a slumped figure in her prison uniform, the hair roughly torn from the crown of her head.

What we learn about her as a person comes, largely, from the bitter memories tormenting her parents: old 'Teacher Gu' and his wife. Extrapolating from the basic historical facts, Li imagines Gu Shan as having been, from the age of fourteen, a fanatical Maoist; at first, a leading student activist during the Cultural Revolution; an extreme zealot, gangster-bully and mob-stirrer, who'd then repented.[4] At one public gathering in 1966, we learn, her parents themselves had been amongst those paraded on stage by Gu Shan and her Red Guard comrades – although Gu Shan had, in their case, left it to some of the others to perform the ritual whipping and kicking. But she'd whipped and kicked others, and not only on that occasion. Once, in pursuance of her Red Guard militancy, she'd kicked an eight-month pregnant woman in the belly. The child, Nini, was then born with a deformed hand and legs. Nini is a central character in the novel. Her parents rejoice on the day of Shan's death: they slaughter one of their only two hens, for a celebratory chicken feast.

We're given just two glimpses of Gu Shan in prison, the two occasions that she was visited there by her father. The first visit was just after she'd been sentenced the first time. On that occasion teacher Gu had vainly attempted to console her, saying that ten years would soon pass. 'Shan', we're told, 'was sneering the entire time that he spoke'.[5] The second visit was after her retrial, when she'd been sentenced to death. Teacher Gu had then been shocked at her squalid condition; utterly transformed from ten years previously. All her old bounce had vanished. She'd gone crazy.

> She started talking when she sat down. She told him that she had written letters to Chairman Mao and he had replied, apologizing for the wrong decision and promising a release. It had been two years since Chairman Mao had passed away, but Teacher Gu, sitting in a cold sweat, did not point that out to Shan. She talked fast, about all the things she planned to do after her release...[6]

Is Gu Shan a 'saint'? It seems odd to apply the epithet, either to the 'sneering' eighteen-year-old, or to the hysterical, broken twenty-eight-year-old!

And yet, the effect of her martyrdom, in Muddy River, certainly is reminiscent of the effect the death of the Suffering Servant in *Deutero-Isaiah* has on the chorus there. The manner of Gu Shan's death is of course meant to be shocking; but in the period of the Democracy Wall, the shock of such propaganda events has ceased to be quite as intimidating as before. Many of her fellow-citizens are evidently moved to penitence by the shock, regretting their complicity in the regime that killed her. Many are filled with admiration: 'She died for her commitment to *our* liberation.'

Of the Suffering Servant, again, it's said:

> He was maltreated, yet he was submissive
> and did not open his mouth;
> like a sheep led to the slaughter,
> like a ewe that is dumb before the shearers,
> he did not open his mouth.
>
> (*Isaiah* 53:7)

Gu Shan goes to her death, likewise, silently. But in her case, this is no voluntary silence. Rather, so as to silence her, since she's such an unruly victim, the authorities have taken the precaution of surgically excising her vocal cords. Her throat is thickly bandaged, after the operation.

Mutilation after mutilation!

∾

Perhaps the real saints here, though, are the dissidents who, throwing off their herd-identities, rise up in the most civilised, non-violent fashion, after Shan's death, to demand that she be officially 'de-purged'. Above all: Wu Kai, their chief spokeswoman; but also, Jialin, the young man through whom Wu Kai is brought into contact with a whole informal network of intellectual malcontents.

These hidden dissidents can't hope to stop the execution. But they *are* able to ride the wave of public disgust prompted by the horror of that event. So Jialin mobilises a team – 'a doctor from a workers' clinic, a clerk in the optical factory, a retired middle school teacher, a department store accountant, a pharmacist, and a few educated youths who had recently returned from the countryside'[7] – to circulate door to door, on the eve of the Ching Ming public holiday, handing out white tissue paper flowers, and inviting people to bring them to a protest gathering the next day, in the town's central square, right next to the statue of Chairman Mao, where there will be an opportunity to sign a petition.[8]

It's Wu Kai who becomes the chief public face, and voice, of the enterprise. Her job equips her perfectly for the role. Muddy River isn't a glamorous place, but she's the nearest approximation to a glamorous local celebrity there. She's the news presenter on local radio. (This is at a time when very few people in the town as yet have televisions). And she represents the Communist Party as master of ceremonies, hosting official events such as May Day, the anniversary of the founding of the Party, National Day, and other occasions which the local authorities decide to register with mass gatherings. Indeed, it's she who hosts the main denunciation ceremony (fifteen thousand people in the East Wind Stadium) preceding Gu Shan's execution. Yet, just a few days later, her voice comes over the loudspeakers in town, saying:

> 'Greatly respected citizens of Muddy River … As you may not know, there is great historical change happening in our nation's capital, where a stretch of wall, called the democratic wall, has been set up for people to express their ideas on where our country is going. It is a critical moment for our nation, yet news about the democratic wall did not reach us. We've been taught for years that in our Communist state we are the masters of our own country, and of our own fates. But is this ever true? Not long ago, Gu Shan, a daughter of Muddy River, was wrongfully sentenced to death. She was not a criminal; she was a woman who felt immense responsibility for our nation's future, who spoke out against a corrupt system with courage and insight, but what became of this heroine who acted ahead of her time?'[9]

And it's Wu Kai who persuades Gu Shan's mother, to attend the demonstration, and receive people's condolences there.

Jialin has initiated their alliance, some time ago, with a speculative letter, to which Wu Kai has immediately responded by going to visit him at home. After which they arrange to meet, and exchange letters, from time to time, in the reading room of the town library.

Wu Kai was a contemporary of Gu Shan's in the first grade, at school in Muddy River. But then she'd gained a place at the theatre school in the provincial capital. And she'd had a brief career as a child star; before eventually marrying Han, an ambitious Party official back in Muddy River, with pushy parents.

Li embroiders the original historic material she's working with, by having Wu Kai's husband Han be the official who has organised the donation of Gu Shan's kidneys, sorting out all the practicalities. In the novel, the recipient of the kidneys is none other than the provincial boss of the particular gang, within the

Communist Party, to which Han and his parents belong. Han has no advance warning of his wife's subversive intentions. On the eve of the Ching Ming holiday, we actually see him in a state of panic: it looks, for the moment, as if a rival gang, within the Party, is about to take his gang down. These others are intent on making a scandal out of Gu Shan's death, and in particular the business with her kidneys. And perhaps the mayor of Muddy River is going to protect himself by making Han the fall-guy. Before rushing off to the provincial capital in a desperate attempt to avert this threat, Han drafts a little document for Wu Kai to sign, in case the worst should come to the worst: an application for divorce. If he should be disgraced, Han is anxious that, as far as possible, she and their infant son Ming-Ming will be sheltered from the fall-out.

Over three hundred people sign the petition, for Gu Shan to be 'de-purged'. For a brief moment, at first, Wu Kai and Jialin are elated. But then the tide abruptly turns. When Han returns home, neither Wu Kai nor Ming-Ming are there. Only the nanny remains. Wu Kai has been arrested. Han's parents have spirited Ming-Ming away. And now it's they who, against his feeble protests, insist upon an instant divorce.

Apart from Wu Kai, all the other signatories to the petition are given jail sentences, ranging from three years to life. But

> upon reviewing the cases, the provincial officials pointed out that a warning to the masses would not be effective without a death sentence. *Kill a chicken to frighten all the mischievous monkeys into obedience*, one top official urged in writing, and several others chimed in with their consent.[10]

Wu Kai is chosen for exemplary punishment.

At the denunciation ceremony in the East Wind Stadium, Han is the final speaker, telling of his shock and humiliation at the discovery of his wife's delinquency.

Sometime later, the other dissidents are in fact 'de-purged' and released. One of them writes his memoirs. He remembers listening to Wu Kai singing in her cell: *The flowers of May bloom on the prairie, and the red petals fall and cover the martyrs' blood,* a song originally commemorating heroic Communist martyrs.[11] 'What is there to fear about death?' she asks, when the sentence is read out to her ...

---

1. Li, *The Vagrants* (London: Fourth Estate, 2009). There's a real place that used to be called Hunjiang, 'Muddy River'. (In the 1990s the authorities renamed it Baishan, 'White Mountain', in the hope of attracting tourists.) It was Li's husband's original hometown. See her memoir *Dear Friend, from My Life I Write to You in Your Life* (London: Penguin, 2017), p. 175.

2. Li, 'What Has That to Do with Me? *Gettysburg Review* Vol. 16, No. 2. Reprinted in the 'P.S.' at the back of her collection of short stories, *A Thousand Years of Good Prayers*, London: Harper Perennial, 2006.

3. *A Thousand Years of Good Prayers*, 'P.S.', p. 13.

4. Gu Shan, at 28, is a year younger than the historic woman on whom she's modelled. This, coupled with Li's moving the action of the novel forward by a year from the actual historic events on which it's based, has the effect of making Gu Shan two years younger at the time of the Cultural Revolution. The way that the Cultural Revolution messed with the heads of such young teenagers was of course a major feature of its horror.

5. *The Vagrants*, p. 100.

6. Ibid. p. 102.

7. Ibid. p. 220.

8. Ching Ming ('Tomb Sweeping Day') is all the more auspicious as an occasion for such an event, in that it's a family festival for the honouring of the deceased.

9. *The Vagrants*, p. 229.

10. Ibid. p. 332.

11. Ibid. p. 333.

CHAPTER NINE

Colson Whitehead:
The Nickel Boys

'God is love' we read in the New Testament, *1 John* 4:8, 16. And Aelred of Rievaulx – writing in the mid-twelfth century – plays upon that theme. Thus, Book One of his dialogue *On Spiritual Friendship* comes to a climax when Aelred's friend, and fellow monk, Ivo is moved to ask the daring question:

> What does this all add up to? Shall I [also] say of friendship what John, the friend of Jesus, says of charity: *"God is friendship?"*[1]

To which the answer is surely yes!

Aelred had been educated as a child at Hexham Abbey in Northumbria; and either there, or perhaps a little later on in life, at the court of the King of Scotland in Roxborough, had become familiar with Cicero's Latin dialogue *On Friendship*. His own book is partly inspired by Cicero's pagan work, but is partly also intended as a corrective to it; a meditation on the proper Christian ethos, as he saw it, of the Cistercian community of which he'd become abbot …

The Greek word for 'love', throughout the New Testament, is *agapé*. When Plato, by contrast, had wanted to celebrate a certain sort of love he used the word *eros*. Anders Nygren in his classic work *Agape and Eros* (first published, in Swedish, 1930 – 1936) argues that the New Testament notion of *agapé* has to be understood very much as an implicit polemical antithesis to Platonist philosophic *eros*.[2]

Divine *agapé*, in which the Christian saint ideally participates, is, as Nygren understands it, a majestic spirit of generosity, differing from *eros* by virtue of its complete freedom from any admixture of *need*. It transcends all sorts of *eros*, from the most vulgar to the most exalted; very much including the pagan philosopher's perceived need for cool, detached serenity. *Agapé*, in short, is the species of love symbolically represented by Christ on the cross. It's love gratuitously overflowing, from the strong to the less strong; benevolence flowing, from those with the reckless inner strength to make themselves vulnerable for their neighbour's sake, to all of their neighbours without exception; in the first instance, quite regardless of what those neighbours deserve.

Aelred, indeed, presents his Latin conception of divine *'spiritualis amicitia'*, 'spiritual friendship', as an unfolding of *1 John* 4:8, 16. And yet it really is very different, not only from Platonist, pagan *eros*, but also from New Testament *agapé* as interpreted by Nygren. Translated back into Greek, friendship is *philia*. And *philia*, unlike *agapé*, is *not* manifest in relationships between the strong, as such, and the less strong, as such. On the contrary, it's a radically egalitarian ideal. It's an egalitarian refinement of *eros*. *Spiritualis amicitia*, as Aelred conceives it, is God revealed in the corporate activity of individuals, bound together in solidarity as equals, frankly owning their need of one another. God as *agapé*; God as *amicitia / philia*: these are by no means incompatible notions of the divine. The full reality of God, surely, includes them both. Note, however, that *in terms of their aesthetic expression* they do each suit quite contrasting *media*.

The God whose reality is mediated to us most straightforwardly through *liturgy* is very much God as *agapé*; inasmuch as liturgy is ritualised thanksgiving, for divine generosity. Aelred, on the other hand, also glimpsed something else, in the wider communal life of his austere North Yorkshire monastic community: a spirit of defiant togetherness, in face of the fixed class distinctions and consequent injustices of the surrounding feudal order. But his world still lacked the ideal sort of artistic resource required, for intellectually exploring the full truth of God as *spiritualis amicitia*.

It lacked, precisely, novels! That's to say, novels evoking just such friendship, its authenticity made clear by being rigorously tested. To illustrate the point here: consider, for example, Colson Whitehead's celebration of embattled friendship in *The Nickel Boys*.

∽

Whitehead's novel originates from his shocked reaction to the uncovering of a particular negative-revelation scandal. The Florida School for Boys in Marianna, a small panhandle town, had at one point been the largest reform school, or boarding establishment for wayward children and adolescents, in the USA. (In 1967 it was renamed the Arthur G. Dozier School, after a former principal.) Founded in 1900, it had long had a fearsome reputation. And two years after failing a state inspection, in 2011 it was finally closed. The following year, responding to reports of suspicious deaths, a team of archaeologists and forensic anthropologists from the University of South Florida began surveying the grounds. And when legal action – by the nephew of a student who had died there – delayed the proposed redevelopment of the site into an office park, the research team was given permission to exhume bodies. The written records regarding burials at the school were remarkably sketchy. But by 2016, when the researchers published their initial report, they had discovered fifty-five graves; just thirteen of them inside the designated cemetery, the others scattered through the wooded landscape. Then, in 2019, during a pollution clean-up, a further twenty-seven graves were identified. There may well be more, still awaiting discovery. Some can be matched by DNA analysis to names; many can't.

The suspicion is that a considerable number of these unrecorded deaths were either due to outright murder, or else to excessive punishments inflicted by the staff. In 1967 corporal punishment was officially discontinued at the school. But prior to that time, it had often been savage. Up until the late 1960s the school was, of course, racially segregated. In between the two campuses, however, right at the heart of the school as a whole there was a small, single-storey building known as the 'White House'. According to the testimony of survivors, this was a suite of torture chambers. Many also speak of having been raped by staff. They describe a regime of terror; bad enough for the white boys, still worse for the black boys.

Whitehead first heard about this macabre place in 2014. In his novel it's renamed: the 'Nickel Academy'. The town of Marianna becomes 'Eleanor'; and so forth. Basically, though, he sticks close to the historical reality. Having in his previous work skipped, with easy flair, from genre to genre – 'speculative fiction', epic historical fiction, light comedy, semi-autobiographical fiction, zombie horror, magic realism – here he simply sets out, with maximum, quiet moral intensity, to bring a scandal to imaginative life.

He does so by telling the story of two black adolescent inmates, in the mid-1960s. They become close friends; the charm of their friendship is set over against the extreme *un*-friendliness, the cruelty, of the establishment in which they meet; thereby highlighting it.

And one of them, moreover, aspires to be a saint.

∼

Elwood Curtis is from the Frenchtown district of Tallahassee. His parents having abandoned him, and disappeared to California, he's brought up by his grandmother Harriet; which is more of a family than many of his eventual fellow-students have. For Christmas 1962 Harriet gives him a record of Martin Luther King speeches; which captivates him. Not that she's herself a keen civil rights campaigner. When she learns that he has actually participated in a demonstration, she's dismayed.

Thanks to the encouragement of a liberal teacher, Elwood enrols on an extra-curricular course for high-achieving high-school students at a 'colored college' seven miles outside Tallahassee. It's cycling distance. But his bike has been vandalised by kids aggrieved at his refusal to collude with their shoplifting from the store where he has a part-time job. So, the first day of the course, he hitches a lift there. Alas, it turns out that – quite unbeknownst to him – the car has been stolen. The police appear. He's found guilty of being an accessory to the theft. The judge sends him to the Nickel Academy.

At first sight, the place doesn't look so bad at all: no great perimeter walls, no barbed wire; but, on the contrary, lush well-tended lawns, cedars and beech.

He settles into the dormitory, and has already fallen asleep, when he's woken by a mysterious roar, from outside:

> a rush and a whoosh without variation. Forbidding and mechanical and granting no clue to its origin. He didn't know which book he'd picked it up from, but the word came to him: *torrential*.[3]

It's the following day that he meets his future friend Turner. And Turner explains to him what the roar is. Namely: a gigantic industrial fan installed in the White House, to drown out the noise of the punishment beatings administered there.

A day or two later, Elwood intervenes in a fight, seeking to protect a small boy against two much larger bullies. A 'houseman', as the warders are called, appears on the scene, and puts an end to the scuffle. Then, at one o'clock in the morning the authorities come round the dormitory with torches, to round up those involved and take them to the White House. They don't discriminate: all four are taken, and no one asks Elwood for his side of the story. In the gale, as the fan roars, first the two bullies are thrashed with a leather strap, twenty-eight licks for one, about sixty for the other; then their victim, about seventy licks; and finally, Elwood, who passes out before they're finished, so has no idea how many licks he received. He ends up in the school's hospital. There he meets Turner; who's malingering, having eaten soap powder to make himself sick, as he's done before. And it's at this point that their friendship is really sealed.

When Elwood's grandmother comes to visit, he can't bear to burden her with the knowledge of what has happened.

Then, even darker things transpire. There's a tradition of boxing matches, between the champion of the white boys' campus and the champion of the black boys' campus. The black half of Nickel is represented by Griff. It's generally supposed that he's likely to win. But Turner, napping one day unseen in a warehouse loft, happens to overhear Superintendent Spencer telling Griff to take a dive in the third of the scheduled three rounds. *Or else they'd take him 'out back'* ... Evidently, this is because Spencer has a bet to win. But what does 'out back' mean? Turner takes Elwood to a secluded corner of the grounds and shows him two oak trees, with iron rings fixed tight into their bark. The word is that black boys are from time to time spread-eagled against these trees and horse-whipped, to death. No one who's taken 'out back' returns to tell the tale.

In fact, Griff fails to take a dive; and is awarded victory by two rounds to one. From the ring, in all the hubbub, he screams at Spencer, 'I thought it was the second! I thought it was the second!' Turner and Elwood wonder: had the boy's brain been addled by a blow to the head? In any case, that night he mysteriously disappears.

When he was younger, Elwood used to haunt the kitchen of the Richmond Hotel in Tallahassee where his grandmother worked. And, as he was a studious child, the kitchen staff passed on to him a set of encyclopaedia volumes which some traveling salesman had carelessly left behind. In fact, the encyclopaedia was a bit of a disappointment. On closer inspection, only the first volume, *Aa – Be* was actually printed; in all the others, the pages were blank. Nevertheless, he does remember looking up *'agapé'* in it, after coming across the word in the great speech of Martin Luther King, 15th October 1962, at Cornell College, Iowa; where King, amongst much else, expounds a version of Nygren's argument for the moral primacy, in Christian terms, of *agapé*. In recording this, Whitehead is indeed giving a name to what Elwood paradigmatically represents. He also quotes some of King's splendid oratory at the climax of the Cornell address:

Throw us in jail, and we will still love you. Bomb our homes and threaten our children, and, as difficult as it is, we will still love you. Send your hooded perpetrators of violence into our community after midnight hours, and drag us out onto some wayside road, and beat us and leave us half-dead, and we will still love you. But be ye assured that we will wear you down by our capacity to suffer, and one day we will win our freedom ...[4]

Such is Elwood's exceptional inner strength that he's willing – in just this spirit of *agapé* – to risk his very life, with a view to non-violently bringing down the Nickel regime.

A little team of state officials is due to conduct an inspection of the school. It's meant to be a surprise, but the school authorities nevertheless get advance warning, and mobilise the students in a frantic effort to get everything looking good. So, Elwood also knows that the inspectors are coming. He decides to present them with a letter, opening their eyes to at least some of the abuses the authorities will be anxious to conceal. Not that he's quite so crazy as to charge them, straight out, with murder! But his idea is, at any rate, to establish some sort of real, initial contact with the inspectors by blowing the whistle on lesser forms of corruption, with regard to which he's in an excellent position to supply actual names and dates. For, he and Turner have been recruited into what is called the 'Community Service' team. That's to say: they've been helping deliver food and equipment allocated by the state to the black boys' campus, which the staff however have siphoned off and sold instead to their cronies in town. And likewise, they've been sent round town to do odd jobs, unpaid, as a special favour for the same sort of cronies. Evidently, Elwood's idea is that, once he's in conversation with the inspectors about these matters, he might also broach the topics of the White House, and of Griff.

But this scheme doesn't succeed.

～

136

If Elwood embodies a heroic aspiration to *agapé*, Turner by contrast represents sheer will-to survive. Meeting him for the first time, Elwood immediately senses his 'eerie sense of self':

> The mess hall was loud with the rumble and roil of juvenile activity, but this boy bobbed in his own pocket of calm. Over time, Elwood saw that he was always simultaneously at home in whatever scene he found himself and also seemed like he shouldn't have been there; inside and above at the same time; a part and apart. Like a tree trunk that falls across a creek – it doesn't belong and then it's never not been there, generating its own ripples in the current.[5]

Turner isn't a type who gets bullied. Nor is he a type that others are liable to find threatening. Thus, his whole demeanour is shrewd policy for survival. Unlike the other boys, he's known only by his surname. This, in itself, is a token of his strategic detachment.

The two boys quickly become inseparable. But Turner is, at times, irritated by Elwood. He says:

> 'You got to quit that eager-beaver shit, El.'[6]

He deplores Elwood's intervention in the incident leading to his punishment in the White House: the boy who was being bullied, he suggests, was actually complicit, in a masochistic way, with his sadistic tormentors.[7] As Turner sees the world the great thing is just to keep out of trouble. In general, he thinks, Elwood in his naivety fails to see how people tick; and is deluded by false hope.

Turner is jealous of Elwood's relationship with his grandmother. He himself has no real sense of family belonging. His father disappeared when he was three; his mother is dead, from alcohol poisoning. At one point he lived with his mother's sister. But then, when he was eleven, his aunt took in a boyfriend, who violently abused the pair of them. That he has developed a cagey attitude to life is only natural.

When Elmore confides to Turner his plan to turn whistle-blower, Turner's initial reaction is therefore scathing and appalled:

'You're getting along. Ain't had trouble since that one time. They going to take you out back, bury your ass, then they take me out back, too. The fuck is wrong with you?'

To which Elwood replies:

'You're wrong Turner ... It's not an obstacle course ... You can't go around it – you have to go through it. Walk with your head up no matter what they throw at you.'[8]

Turner then sulks.

Yet, when Elwood at the crucial moment is ordered to run an errand which will take him away from where the inspectors will pass, and so scupper his chance of handing over the letter he has written them, Turner instantly volunteers to hand it over for him. He does so against his better judgement. And he's by no means surprised when it grows clear that the inspectors aren't, after all, going to do anything serious in response.

His handing over of the letter is just a supreme act of friendship. The novel may very well be read as an extended parable, revolving around this moment.

∾

The plot then runs on right up until the time, half a century later, when the archaeologists and forensic anthropologists arrive on the scene. It has a poignant denouement. But what, at the end, are we the readers left with? On the one hand, we're shown Elwood, the saintly devotee of *agapé*, defeated. Defeated, yes – but still glorious in defeat. On the other hand, we're shown *spiritualis amicitia* – the friendship between Elwood and Turner – chastened, yet, insofar as the context allows, paradoxically triumphant.

To what shall we compare the kingdom of heaven? For

example: it's like Elwood's friendship with Turner. It's like Turner's friendship with Elwood.

---

1. Aelred of Rievaulx, *Spiritual Friendship*, trans. Mary Eugenia Laker SSND (Kalamazoo, Michigan: Cistercian Publications, 1977).

2. English translation by Philip S. Watson (London: SPCK, 1953).

3. *The Nickel Boys* (New York: Doubleday, 2020), p. 52.

4. Ibid. p. 170.

5. Ibid. p. 55.

6. Ibid. p. 53.

7. Ibid. p. 79.

8. Ibid. p. 172.

CHAPTER TEN

André Schwarz-Bart:
The Last of the Just

Yiyun Li, in *The Vagrants*, portrays sublime virtue against a background of (what I'm calling) sheer negative revelation.[1]

Colson Whitehead, in *The Nickel Boys*, portrays sublime virtue against a background of acute negative revelation, with some slight reference to tradition informed by positive revelation, in the form of Martin Luther King's preaching.

But now let's consider a novel portraying sublime virtue against a background of the most extreme negative revelation, mixed however with the prodigiously resilient positive-revelation tradition of Hasidic Judaism.

André Schwarz-Bart's 1959 magic realist epic *Le dernier des justes* (*The Last of the Just*) culminates in the Shoah; but it's also a study of sainthood, featuring a whole sequence of Hasidic saints. Here, Deutero-Isaiah's implicit argument is brought up to date. What shows the faith of Israel to be uniquely true? Answer: its exceptional capacity, at its best, to inspire a truly generous-minded steadfastness even under pressure of the most terrible disasters and persecutions; the virtue symbolised by the archetypal image of the Suffering Servant.

Schwarz-Bart describes a whole sequence of saintly characters, spanning eight and a half centuries: individuals collectively embodying the very essence of the Isaianic archetype. These are, precisely, latter-day Suffering Servants. Given the political marginality of the diaspora-communities in which the Hasidic tradition flourished, they lack the capacity to match this with any very public expression of the *Amos* impulse, beyond the sheer intransigence of their non-assimilation to the society around them. But in Schwarz-Bart's fiery writing the task of representing that impulse is largely transferred to the author himself.

◆

Schwarz-Bart himself had been fourteen when his parents, two brothers, and the great-aunt who lived with them, were all deported, in 1942, to their death in Auschwitz. The family was of Polish-Jewish origin, settled since 1924 in Metz, Alsace-Lorraine. He'd actually been born Abraham Schwarcbart, his first language was Yiddish; at this stage he still spoke very little French. As a young teenager, working as a farm labourer for his keep, he nevertheless joined the French Resistance. It was this that eventually qualified him for a bursary to study at the Sorbonne.

There he started to write. Dostoevsky's *Crime and Punishment* was a major early influence. *The Last of the Just* was his first publication. In 1959, the year it appeared, it was awarded the supreme French literary honour, the Prix Goncourt, amidst much excitement and controversy. Nothing that he wrote afterwards ever had anything quite like the impact of this first work. At that moment, it seemed, the French public was waiting for just such a book.

In 1961 he married Simone, who was subsequently to become a notable writer herself. She came from Guadeloupe in the Caribbean, and the couple ended up as residents of that island. There, they (more or less) co-authored four novels, the central characters of which are black and mulatto women of Guadeloupe and Martinique; novels reflecting the long after-effects, up to the present, of the trans-Atlantic slave-trade and its attendant trauma.[2] Also: a four-volume non-fiction essay series, translated into English as *In Praise of Black Women*.[3] In Guadeloupe he thus became very much a polemicist against white-on-black racism. And finally in 2009, three years after André's death, Simone Schwarz-Bart brought out another novel of his, *The Morning Star*, once again focused on Hasidic life in Poland and its genocidal annihilation; although, this time, curiously framed in science-fiction terms, as a matter of historical research by a post-human being, an extra-terrestrial immortal clone, at work sometime after the final suicide of our whole species in the year 3000.[4] However, *The Morning Star* is a much less substantial, and much less finished, work than *The Last of the Just*.

∿

Schwarz-Bart's masterpiece concludes in the most nightmarish fashion possible by taking us, with the herded new arrivals at Auschwitz, right into the gas chamber. It begins, some seven and a half centuries earlier, with the great pogrom of 1190 in York: the mass suicide of Jews on that occasion, besieged within the castle keep, to which they had fled for refuge. Book One then follows a particular dynasty through the following six centuries of Jewish history, around Europe; Book Two evokes the life of a Hasidic community in Poland, from the late eighteenth century to just after the First World War; Books Three to Five are set in a little Rhineland town, depicting the childhood of Ernie Levy and the coming of the Third Reich; Book Six begins with his family's flight, following Kristallnacht, to France; Books Six to Eight, as a whole, follow Ernie's final, slow descent into hell.

The novel as a whole is a great catalogue of antisemitic atrocities. So how does it work, as a piece of *literature*, as distinct from a simple indictment? It really is relentless. How, then, does Schwarz-Bart avoid driving his readers away, overwhelmed with 'compassion fatigue'?

This, surely, is the rationale of his magic realism. It's a sugaring of the bitter pill, a technique allowing readers – at any rate for the moment – to half-withdraw, wherever necessary, from the unbearably horrendous, not at all magic, historically actual reality being described, into another, enveloping realm of fantasy.

The primary element of 'magic' in *The Last of the Just* is Schwarz-

Bart's deployment of traditional Jewish legend concerning the *Tzadikim Nistarim*, the 'Hidden Righteous Ones'. This legend derives both from the celebration of exemplary suffering in *Isaiah* 52:13 – 53:12 and, also, from the story of Abraham's bargaining with God over the fate of Sodom, in *Genesis* 18:23—33. Here, seeing the prevailing wickedness of its inhabitants, God has resolved to destroy the city. But Abraham pleads for its preservation. If there are just fifty individuals in the city who are truly innocent, will God not spare it for their sake? God gives way to his prayer. And then Abraham starts to bargain further, trying to get the minimum number down. What if there are forty-five? Or forty? Or thirty? Or twenty? Finally, he gets the number right down to ten. In the event, alas, it appears that there aren't even that many innocent individuals in Sodom; and accordingly, the city is destroyed. But the legend nevertheless picks up on the basic principle of Abraham's bargaining, and extends it to the world at large. Notwithstanding the general sinfulness of humanity, so the story goes, just as long as there are thirty-six Just Men in the world, God will spare it for their sake. These Just Men are also, therefore, called 'thirty-sixers': *Lamed-Vof*.[5] In the wider tradition, the *Lamed-Vof* are supposed to remain as a general rule unaware of their identity, as such. But Schwarz-Bart imagines an exceptional family, surnamed Levy, who are widely known to produce a new one in every generation.

Were it not for the *Lamed-Vof*, he writes,

the sufferings of mankind would poison even the souls of the new-born, and humanity would suffocate with a single cry. For the *Lamed-Vof* are the hearts of the world multiplied, and into them, as into one receptacle, pour all our griefs. Thousands of popular stories take note of them. Their presence is attested to everywhere … In the seventh century, Andalusian Jews venerated a rock shaped like a teardrop, which they believed to be the soul, petrified by suffering, of an "unknown" *Lamed-Vof*. Other *Lamed-Vof*, like Hecuba shrieking at the death of her sons, are said to have been transformed into dogs. 'When an Unknown Just rises to Heaven,' a Hasidic story goes, 'he is so frozen that God must warm him for a thousand years between His fingers, before his soul can open itself to Paradise. And it is known that some remain for ever inconsolable at human woe; so that God Himself cannot warm them. So from time to time the Creator, Blessed be His Name, sets forward the clock of the Last Judgement by one minute.'[6]

The first fourteen generations of Levy *Lamed-Vof* are paraded before us; fathers and sons, in direct succession, one concise pen-portrait after another. This parade is a demonstration of just how many forms such Suffering Servant virtue may, in principle, take. There are rabbis, merchants, craftsmen. Intellectually, they range from expert lawyer to Kabbalist; to two barely literate simpletons. Most die violent deaths, as martyrs of one sort or another. The Kabbalist is enslaved, and packed off (perhaps) to China. Two are cut off from their family as children, and brought up as Christians, yet eventually return to the fold.

Chaim, the twelfth in line, is born in Kiev, but leaves to become a disciple of that greatest of Hasidic masters, the Baal Shem Tov; then becomes a travelling preacher; and finally, in the year 1792, settles in Zemyock, a town in the province of Bialystok. The incumbent rabbi there insists on Chaim taking his place. Unlike almost all his predecessors, Chaim has numerous children and, to his dismay, lives to a ripe old age. His direct descendants inherit the post of Zemyock rabbi, and likewise become old men, with sparkling eyes. The charismatic role of Levy *Lamed-Vof* becomes institutionalised. Even when the Jews of Zemyock are massacred by Cossack forces during the Russian Civil War, the incumbent *Lamed-Vof* is spared.

But then, it seems, the succession veers off along a different line of the same kin. Already as a child, Ernie Levy is recognised by his devout grandfather Mordecai as yet another *Lamed-Vof*. And the idea seizes hold of Ernie himself; indeed, with alarming consequences. Ernie, then, is 'the last of the Just' belonging to the Levy dynasty; as he finally goes childless to his death, along with all his relatives, in Auschwitz.

~~

It would be pedantic to complain about the inaccuracies, as such, in Schwarz-Bart's somewhat cavalier treatment of actual historical detail; and I have no particular desire to do so. Nevertheless, the way he fictionalises, especially, the opening scene of the novel – the infamous mediaeval pogrom in York – is, I think, quite significant.[7] He assigns a very specific false date to the event:11th – 17th March 1185. In fact, the pogrom occurred some five years later, and was over after just two days, 15th – 16th March 1190. He invents a historically non-existent eye-witness chronicler, 'Dom Bracton', whom he then purports to quote. But he makes no mention of the main actual source, the Augustinian Canon William of Newburgh (1135/6 – 1198). William describes the pogrom in his *History of English Affairs*, which covers the period from 1066 to his own day.[8] And, although he wasn't himself an eye-witness, his account is probably quite reliable, not only because he was writing so soon after the event, but also because he was resident at Newburgh Priory, just sixteen miles north of York, and so had plenty of eye-witnesses near at hand to consult.

Schwarz-Bart names the rabbi who persuaded most of his people, on this occasion, to commit suicide together, after the example of the sicarii of Masada, besieged by the Romans in 74 CE, as described by Josephus.[9] He tells us that he was called Yom Tov Levy. And, in the novel, this man then becomes the first of the Levy *Lamed-Vof*. William of Newburgh likewise attributes the role of leader amongst the besieged to an elderly rabbi; adding, moreover, the further information that this rabbi was from overseas. He was probably, in fact, the French-born rabbi and poet, Yom Tov of Joigny.

However, the main discrepancy between William of Newburgh's account and the account given in the novel has to do with the leadership of the mob. William is quite clear that prime responsibility lay with the local lord Richard de Malebisse, along with other 'conspirators' of noble rank, whom he doesn't name.

Richard de Malebisse was deeply in debt to the Jewish moneylender Aaron of Lincoln; and William reports how, once the pogrom was over, the 'conspirators' at once went to York Minster; demanded to be given the documents recording their moneylender-debts, which were stored there for safekeeping; and made a bonfire of them.[10]

Schwarz-Bart however, in the novel, attributes blame instead to the Archbishop of York: whom he describes as preaching a great rabble-rousing sermon against the Jews. He names the archbishop in question as 'William of Nordhouse'. The name is fictional – the actual archbishop, from 1181—91, being Geoffrey Plantagenet. And it should be noted that William of Newburgh, for his part, makes no mention of any such sermon as a trigger-event. True, William does mention that there were a number of priests participating in the mob. One particular Premonstratensian hermit evidently played quite a theatrical role, urging the Jews to come out of the castle and submit to Christian baptism. He was hit by a well-aimed, large stone launched from the castle wall, and killed; the one recorded casualty among the rioters. But, if William is to be believed, the real instigators of the pogrom were members of the secular aristocracy.[11]

Why does Schwarz-Bart prefer to tell it another way? He isn't opposing William of Newburgh; rather, he appears simply to be unaware of him. And, of course, plenty of rabble-rousing anti-Jewish sermons have as a matter of fact been preached in Christian churches down the ages, even at times by quite senior churchmen. Although, so far as we know, that wasn't what happened in this case, it easily could have been.

But I'm further inclined to associate the anticlerical slant he gives to the York story with his consistent practice, throughout the novel, of referring to the Jew-haters of Europe not as 'Gentiles' but as 'Christians'. This becomes especially pointed once the narrative has reached the period of the Third Reich: for, after all, Nazi antisemitism, with its pseudo-scientific veneer, was largely of a different species from that of mediaeval Christendom; and many of the leading Nazi ideologues explicitly rejected Christian faith, precisely on the grounds that it was still too Jewish in nature.

Nevertheless, Schwarz-Bart shows us Ernie Levy, as a schoolchild in 1933, for example, leading his younger brother Jacob through the back-streets of their German hometown, on the way to synagogue – by an indirect route so as to avoid the gang of Nazi S.A. men whose songs they can hear in the distance – anxiously 'looking around, *'gauging the Christian world'* ...[12] And again, in August 1942, the day before Ernie's girlfriend Golda is interned at the Drancy transit camp, he shows us the pair of them taking one last walk together through the streets of Paris. First, they go down to the banks of the Seine. There, in the shadow of a bridge, they stuff their jackets, with the yellow star on them, into a shopping-basket, and cover them with newspaper. Then, hand in hand, they stroll along to the Pont-Neuf where, 'in delicious anguish', they climb the steps *'to the surface of the Christian world'* ...[13]

Why does Schwarz-Bart begin his novel with a fictional archbishop's sermon? And why these repeated reminders, specifically, of the notional religious faith of the persecutors; even when it scarcely seems relevant? The novel is partly a great lament, addressed to God. Partly, it's a cry of prophetic fury, hurled in the face of humanity at large. At the same time, however, as a Christian priest and theologian I'm also conscious that Schwarz-Bart has a subordinate (but, yes, quite justified) desire to needle people like myself; to appeal to us; to confront us.

As they walk through Paris that fine autumn day, Golda turns to Ernie:

'O, Ernie,' Golda said, 'you know them; tell me why, *why* do the Christians hate us the way they do. They seem so nice when I can look at them without my star'.

Ernie put his arm around her shoulders solemnly. 'It's very mysterious,' he murmured in Yiddish. 'They don't know exactly why, themselves. I've been in their churches and I've read their gospel. Do you know who the Christ was? A simple Jew like your father. A kind of Hasid.'

Golda smiled gently. 'You're laughing at me.'

'No, no, believe me, and I'll bet they'd have got along fine, the two of them, because he was really a good Jew, you know, sort of like the Baal Shem Tov – a merciful man, and gentle. The Christians say they love him, but I think they hate him without knowing it. So they take the cross by the other end and make a sword out of it, and strike us with it! ... Poor Jesus, if he came back to earth and saw that the pagans had made a sword out of him and used it against his sisters and brothers, he'd be sad, he'd grieve forever. And maybe he does see it. They say that some of the Just Men remain outside the gates of Paradise, that they don't want to forget humanity, that they too await the Messiah. Yes, maybe he sees it. Who knows? ... You understand, *Goldeleh*, he was a little old-fashioned Jew, a real Just Man, you know, no more nor less than ... all our Just Men.'[14]

How is a Christian priest, such as myself, to respond? Elsewhere, Schwarz-Bart describes Jesus as the 'beautiful herald of an impossible love'.[15] Well, it's the role of the true Christian saint to demonstrate, in practice, that such love isn't *absolutely* impossible. But no doubt one does have to concede the impossibility of 'heralding' it, in the way that Jesus does, without *grave and ineradicable risk.*

Of course, there's risk with all religion: that the communal warmth it serves to generate will be corrupted into communal hostility towards outsiders. This risk is at least somewhat softened where God, the ultimate Intensifier, goes to work anonymously. But for God to be revealed *as* God has a twofold effect. On the one hand, it does indeed make possible an altogether more powerful confrontation with corrupt, gangster-authorities or with corruptly xenophobic herd-instinct, as such: in the name of God's forever higher authority, mediated through the *Amos* impulse and the Isaianic archetype. Yet, on the other hand, the resultant gain in confrontational intensity immediately entails the risk that the critical energy thereby generated will, after all, be defensively co-opted by the very corruption that it was, to begin with, intended to help overcome; and so be turned back on itself.

And yes: Christian faith proves, in this sense, to be the highest-risk strategy of all. Thus, there couldn't, surely, be a more vivid symbolic confrontation with xenophobic corruption than is, in principle, represented by the image of God incarnate as a crucified dissident; God's symbolic Resurrection of the Crucified. The Christian gospel really is God gambling for maximum stakes! But all symbolism is ambiguous – that's the price of multi-layered poetic outreach. And how does xenophobic corruption, masquerading as 'Christian', defend itself? It co-opts the symbolism, but transfers the blame. Instead of recognising the gospel story as critique of itself, it crassly blames – 'the Jews', instead. And to the extent that it succeeds in establishing that interpretation in people's minds, God's gamble fails.

(Was God's original gambling with the Christian gospel, then, a *mistake*? Maybe it was. But – be that as it may – it's too late now! We Christians just have to try and make it work.)

~

Although chiefly concerned with the short life of Ernie Levy, the narrative of *The Last of the Just*, as I've said, extends over eight and a half centuries of Jewish history.

Yet, note also some of the omissions. One conspicuous example: there's nothing here about the Sabbatean movement, that spectacular frenzy of excitement which raced through the Jewish world, radiating out from Smyrna, where in 1665 Sabbetai Zevi had been proclaimed as the Messiah. The movement soon subsided, after Sabbetai Zevi was arrested by the Ottoman authorities and, upon being offered the choice between death and conversion to Islam, chose conversion. But, nevertheless, it did leave an indelible memory. In the novel, that memory is covered up completely. The Levy *Lamed-Vof* of the mid-1660s is the 'crazy peasant' Nehemiah; a man, in general, only minimally aware of goings-on in the world at large. Moreover, he's in his dotage by that time, whilst his son and successor, the naturally reclusive Jacob, is still a child.

Why does Schwarz-Bart choose, in this way, to overlook such a momentous event in the history of the religious environment he's sketching? I think that this indicates his urgent concern to present the pre-Shoah world of traditional Hasidism in the most favourable light possible. And, it's true, there's so much in that world to celebrate! However, the Sabbatean movement is, surely, symptomatic of a certain basic weakness: the weakness, indeed, common to all intense religious cultures lacking any coherent overall institutional order. Insofar as authority in such cultures is simply supposed to derive from personal charisma, there's always going to be an unchecked possibility of charlatanism. In retrospect, Sabbetai Zevi does rather look like the charlatan of charlatans.

And then, a second example: there's only the very slightest of allusions to the early Zionist movement. Following his family's escape from the Zemyock pogrom, which occurs in the context of the Russian Civil War, Ernie Levy's future father Benjamin is conscious that, among the other survivors in Warsaw, some of his contemporaries, more or less abandoning their ancestors' Hasidic faith, have chosen either to join the Jewish General Union of Russian and Polish Workers (the 'Bund') or else to emigrate to Israel. But this is only a passing mention in the novel. And Benjamin himself opts for Germany instead.[16]

Schwarz-Bart, notwithstanding that he chose to settle in the Caribbean rather than in Israel, was certainly a Zionist. Only, he was a Zionist of the same general kind as Martin Buber for instance. That's to say: one whose patriotic sense of Israel's special vocation was very much bound up with an idealising love for the old religious world of the shtetl; the small-town world of Eastern Europe, in which Hasidism flourished.[17]

There's an all too obvious paradox in this. In general, a society may either be bonded together by a shared love of justice and peace, or else by a shared, competitive quest for corporate power in the world. Most cultures, of course, involve some uneasy mix of the two. But the special beauty of Hasidic tradition, the beauty which it also has in common with its 'Litvak' rival, largely derives from the way in which the pressures of diaspora-life effectively ruled out the second way, altogether.[19] This produced just about the most purely non-militaristic ethical culture imaginable; a purity, in that regard, sharply highlighted by the contrast with the surrounding Christianity, so deeply compromised, on almost every side, by its accommodation with coercive power. Buber in particular was, consistently, both a liberal intellectual celebrant of the old Hasidic tradition and also, in his politics, a Zionist who wanted above all precisely to minimise the element of militarism in the culture of the new Israel.[20] So he advocated a binational state; one which would pride itself on preserving absolute equality of status between Arabs and Jews, with a largely de-centralised political order, in which power was so far as possible devolved to an archipelago of collective farm communities, the kibbutzim. His 'Hebrew Humanism' was a utopian ideal, almost anarcho-pacifist in character; the vision of a unique state for a unique people, a people rendered unique just by virtue of their long-term history of diaspora. It's a beautiful vision. Yet, how *could* it ever have worked, with two peoples co-habiting the same space, each with their own, different history of urgent trauma; two peoples so damaged by their history? After all, notwithstanding all its virtues, traditional diaspora Judaism provided no real training for statehood. And one can well see why so many Israelis have, in effect, therefore chosen to disown that past, and adopt a casual secularism instead; so provoking, in turn, the neo-Hasidic / neo-Litvak reaction of the hard-line puritan 'Haredim'.

As for Schwarz-Bart: he, like Buber, belonged to neither of those two camps. And when *The Last of the Just* was first published it met with a great deal of fierce criticism from more aggressively secularised Zionists. (The Haredim, for their part, are simply not novel readers!) What these critics wanted from a novel about the Shoah wasn't so much Schwarz-Bart's lament for the destruction of the old, radically non-militaristic Jewish religious culture to which the Levy family belongs. They wanted something more along the lines of Franz Werfel's 1933 novel *The Forty Days of Musa Dagh*: Werfel's fictionalised account of events at the beginning of the Armenian Genocide in 1915, which celebrates the military resistance of one particular community; not Jewish, but comparably embattled.[20] In short, they weren't looking for the 'sublime of the saint', as in Schwarz-Bart's novel. Rather, they were looking for the 'sublime of the warrior-hero'.

There is one case of warrior-heroine Jewish resistance in *The Last of the Just*. Immediately after the Zemyock pogrom, as the Levy family – Benjamin, and his parents Mordecai and Judith – are hiding in the woods outside the town, a pursuing Cossack discovers them. The Cossack prods Mordecai with his sabre, and giggles. Whereupon, catching him entirely by surprise, the redoubtable Judith steps forward and punches him in the face; knocks him over; seizes hold of the sabre, and strikes blow after blow on his head and shoulders 'as she might have with a meat-cleaver ...'[21] But, of all the members of the family, Judith has always been the one least taken with the aura of the Levy legend. And the Levys don't otherwise counter violence with violence. This is very much the exception that proves the rule.

Thus, Ernie Levy in August 1942, suddenly left alone after the arrest of the last four members of the Association of the Elders of Zemyock in Paris, stretches out on his bed, shivering:

> Occasionally he thought he should go on downstairs and join one of the movements now forming in the ghetto and outside. There had been stories about the high deeds of certain young Jewish heroes. But all the Germans on earth could not pay for one innocent head, and then, he told himself, for him it would be a luxurious death. He had no intention of glorifying himself, of separating himself from the humble procession of the Jewish people.[22]

For that simply isn't the way of a *Lamed-Vof*.

∽

I remarked, above, that when (some eight years previously) the eleven-year-old child Ernie Levy is, first of all, intuitively recognised by his grandfather Mordecai as a *Lamed-Vof* – and Mordecai then reveals his intuition to Ernie himself – the consequences are 'alarming'. This is because of the way in which, for Ernie, the notion of being called to be a *Lamed-Vof* is so closely entangled with an impulse to *self-harm*.[23]

His very first night as a self-aware *Lamed-Vof*, he does serious damage to himself by applying a burning candle to the palm of his hand. Why? He explains to his grandfather that he's in 'training'. 'But training for what?' asks Mordecai. 'To die', Ernie replies. In his childish way, he has missed the point, Mordecai insists. A *Lamed-Vof* has no need to run after suffering like a spiritual athlete in training; as if to acquire the necessary mental strength for some heroic battle, to transform the order of the world. The death of a *Lamed-Vof* isn't redemptive in that sense. Perhaps, after all, it changes nothing in the world. Except, that is, for how the world looks, from God's point of view. A *Lamed-Vof* is, quite simply, one whose soul is opened up, in compassion, to the sheer influx of other people's grief, and who thereby helps justify the world's existence, to God; nothing more and nothing less.[24]

Then, shortly afterwards, Ernie runs away from home. This second act of self-harm is prompted by his sheer bewilderment as to his vocation; his not knowing how to proceed; his gaucheness. Stirred by waves of overflowing generosity – and not yet having learnt how, decently, to disguise the fact – he troubles his grandparents, and puzzles his mother. He gazes at a Gentile beggar in the street, a legless war veteran, so intently that the man bursts out in a rage: *"You all through staring at me or not?"*[25] He approaches the Gentile grocer's much-abused nine-year-old daughter, as she's minding her father's shop; but his innocent friendly overtures so scare her that she screams. And then the whole street is in an uproar. His grandmother defends him in public, but she's also scandalised; as is his mother. And so away he runs. He spends the night in a field, before being brought back home. Grandfather Mordecai admits to having been mistaken: 'You understand,' he says tenderly, 'if you were a true Just Man, things would certainly not have come to pass this way ...'[26]

Yet, Mordecai is wrong in this. His original intuition hadn't in fact been a mistake; Ernie *is* called to be a *Lamed-Vof*. And next we see him serially self-harming, in desperate bid after bid to deny, and so to escape, a vocation that's altogether beyond his strength to endure. As a *Lamed-Vof*, he has no moral-anaesthetic defences, to help him bear the weight of the world's woes. In the historic context of Jewish existence under the Third Reich, that weight is heavier than it has ever been. From now on, Ernie's persistent self-harming registers the pressure in microcosm. Already in 1933 Ernie had been compelled by a gang of his Gentile contemporaries to play the role of the wicked Jew in an antisemitic game, re-enacting Christ's passion. They nearly kill him then.[27] For a while he's protected by his kindly school teacher Mr Kremer. But then Mr Kremer is replaced by a Nazi sadist. The gang, now thoroughly integrated into the Hitler Youth, beat him up again. And Ernie finds himself betrayed by his one and only Gentile school-friend, Ilse Bruckner, with whom he'd been brought together, at little tea-parties, by Mr Kremer, entertaining his two star-pupils; Ernie, 'Mr First in German' and Ilse, 'Miss First in Music'.[28] His grief at this betrayal is what then triggers his next bout of self-harm. First, he engages in a vast slaughter of insects, catching them, squashing them, eating them. Earlier, when he had run away from home – growing lovingly aware of all the insects in the field where he'd made his bed – he'd vowed to be 'a Just Man for the flies'. Now he turns on them.[29]

And, next, he goes home and makes a very nearly successful suicide attempt.[30]

After two years recovering in hospital, he emerges as a fist-fighter, seeking to protect his younger brother Jacob. But in so doing he remains torn: 'he considered himself a traitor to the cause of the Levys', and hence to his own deepest calling.[31] Then, in November 1938, after Kristallnacht, the family flees to France. On the outbreak of war, Ernie impulsively, and without consultation with his family, has enlisted in the French army as a stretcher-bearer. As a result, when in May 1940 they're all interned, as emigrés from Germany and therefore 'enemy aliens', he's spared. He isn't around when they're sent to their deaths, but is in Provence, where he has fled following the French surrender. And there, again in deliberate flight from his intolerable vocation, he embarks on a further systematic campaign of *spiritual* self-harm. Abandoning life as a Jew – and changing his tell-tale surname to 'Bastard' – he resolves '*to become a dog*'.[32] (Like the ancient Cynics, such as Diogenes. The Greek word '*kynikos*' originally means 'dog-like'.) In Marseilles he gains a reputation for a sort of informal 'circus act': consuming raw meat. 'Bloody meats, sausages of all kinds, lumps of fresh blood, stuffed him to the ears'.[33] No one knows he's Jewish. But the whole point for him, of course, is to contravene kosher regulations in the most decisive fashion possible: desperate to escape his plight as a Levy *Lamed-Vof*, he's intent on rendering himself, in his own Jewish eyes, as unworthy as possible of the devout veneration accorded to his predecessors. As Schwarz-Bart puts it, 'his object, though unformulated, was to bar any infiltration of light into the hole.'[34] He just doesn't want to see what's truly going on – in the acute sense of *seeing* which applies to a *Lamed-Vof*. Afflicted by the all too visible suffering of the prostitutes in Marseilles, he therefore leaves; and goes on walkabout around the Rhône Valley, working as a farm-labourer. Eventually, he ends up on the farm of Madame Trochu, whose husband is a prisoner of war, and who, in his absence, now sleeps with all comers. 'As he did not love her in the least, the late Ernie Levy imposed a penance upon himself – to display a herculean passion, which she accepted without question'.[35] As a result, his self-abasement, in his own eyes, is absolute.

But not even these drastic measures are enough to keep his true calling at bay for long. The local blacksmith, a good man, recognises his Jewishness. This triggers a dream, playing on the heroic memory of grandfather Mordecai, on Kristallnacht, refusing to hand over the prayer books which the mob wants to burn:

He dreamed that he was a dog running along the boulevards of a great city, while passers-by pointed to him, surprised but nonchalant: Look, there, a dog with Jewish eyes! The hunt began without his knowledge, and already people were running towards him from everywhere, brandishing nets that covered the whole sky. A cellar sheltered him, and he thought he was safe until the sound of pursuers came through the door, demanding that he give them at least his eyes. My eyes? But that's silly. And suddenly screaming at the top of his voice:

'We won't! We'll never give up our eyes, never, never, never. *We'd sooner give up our lives*, arf, arf!'[36]

When he awakes, he at once bids farewell to Madame Trochu, and sets off for Paris, to re-join his people. On the way, as he goes, he starts bashing himself in the face with a stone: another gesture of penance. Here, self-harm has become ritual lament. And he, who'd been spared, has freely chosen, after all, to accompany his people to their death.

The Last of the Just is a novel built around a traditional mythic conceit, which however also pointedly subverts the original mythic rationale of that tradition. Clearly, the notion of the *Lamed-Vof* originates as a straightforward symbolic affirmation of Jewish community-pride. In the story of Ernie Levy, however, any element of boastful corporate egoism is seared away. Nothing remains but infinite anguish.

❧

At the end of the novel is a strange prayer: interlacing a simple fragment from the beginning of the Mourners' Kaddish with a sequence of place-names evoking the Shoah. The Yad Vashem 'World Holocaust Memorial Centre' has reproduced it, painted on a wall. It's one the last things the visitor sees there:

> And praised. *Auschwitz*. Be. *Maidanek*. The Lord. *Treblinka*. And praised. *Buchenwald*. Be. *Mauthausen*. The Lord. *Bełzec*. And praised. *Sobibor*. Be. *Chelmno*. The Lord. *Ponary*. And praised. *Theresienstadt*. Be. *Warsaw*. The Lord. *Vilna*. And praised. *Skarzysko*. Be. *Bergen-Belsen*. The Lord. *Janow*. And praised. *Dora*. Be. *Neuengamme*. The Lord. *Pustków*. And praised ...

In the novel, this prayer picks up from the prayers prayed in the gas chamber. Do those prayers represent a last clutching at consolation? To the extent that they do, the context cruelly refutes them. But prayer has other possibilities, which are here, as it were, being sieved apart from its consolatory function. It may, above all, also be an *intensifier of compassion*: insofar as the one praying is opened up, to become a participant in God's own, infinite love for the afflicted.

The consolatory function of faith in God is more immediately attractive. Evangelists have therefore always tended to emphasise it. And yet, the primary truth-potential of faith surely lies, far rather, with its opening-up-and-intensifying function. In the past, Jewish thought has, to a significant degree, been preserved – if only by oppressive lack of opportunity – from the evangelistic impatience that has so often disfigured Christian and Islamic preaching. Explicit, and systematic, critique of the malign consequences of evangelistic impatience, as such, actually seems to me to be *the* core task for the theology of the future. In relation to the great trauma of the Shoah, I find the same quality as in Schwarz-Bart's novel, also, for instance in the poetry of Nelly Sachs.[37]

Faith as: *allowing oneself to be forever opened up, to the sheer realities, simply, from which ordinary moral anaesthesia serves to close us off.* That's the essential virtue of the *Lamed-Vof*. But the *Lamed-Vof* are not only, therefore, the world's great grievers. They're, by the same token, the great affirmers; in God's eyes, the great vindicators of the world's existence. Come what may.

---

1. Again, for the concept of 'negative revelation': see Chapter 7, above.

2. *Un plat de porc aux bananes vertes* (1967) is explicitly a collaboration; as are *L'ancêtre en solitude* (2015) and *Adieu Bogota* (2017). *La mulâtresse solitude* (1972) was published in André's name alone; but may well have involved substantial input from Simone, nevertheless.

3. Original title: *Hommage à la femme noire* (1989); English translation by Rose-Myriam Rejouis and Val Vinokurov (Madison WI: University of Wisconsin Press, 2001—08).

4. Original title: *L'étoile du matin*. English translation by Julie Rose (London: Duckworth, 2011). The post-human researcher is named Linemarie: Simone Schwarz-Bart's middle name.

5. *Lamed* is the name of the letter 'l' which, in the code of gematria, also has the numerical value of 30; *Vof* (alternatively *Vaf* or *Waf*) is the name of the letter

'v', with the numerical value of 6. In the Vintage Classic edition of *The Last of the Just* used here, translated by Stephen Becker (London, 2001) the plural is simply rendered '*Lamed-Vof*', but other variants are: *Lamed-Vav[nikim]*, *Lamed Vav Tzadikim*.

6. *The Last of the Just*, p. 5.

7. Ibid. pp. 3—4.

8. See the translation in Richard Howlett, ed., *Chronicles of the Reigns of Stephen, Henry II, and Richard I: Containing the Four Books of the Historia Rerum Anglicarum* of William of Newburgh (London: Rolls Series no. 82, 1884-9); Book 4, Chapters 9—10.

9. *The War of the Jews*, Book VII, Chapter 9; in Josephus, *Works*, translated by William Whiston (Nashville TN: Thomas Nelson Publishers 1998).

10. The royal constable in charge of the castle keep (*not* 'an old disused tower at the edge of the town', as Schwarz-Bart has it!) at first admitted the Jews to that refuge; it seems, around 150 of them in all. For, after all, were they not protégés of the king? But they didn't trust him, and so, when he left them, they, perhaps foolishly, locked him out. He then summoned a military force, with siege engines.

11. William himself deplored the 'mental blindness' of the hermit; and of the mob as a whole. Christians, he argues, ought to tolerate the presence among them of 'the perfidious Jew, the crucifier of the Lord Christ', if only as a 'useful' reminder of proper Christian otherness, prompting a sort of competition in virtue. He explains the pogrom with reference to the prosperity achieved by leading Jews in the reign of Henry II, which had just come to an end: 'They had,' he remarks, 'impudently puffed themselves up against Christ and inflicted very many burdens on Christians'. Nevertheless, he certainly doesn't think that this *justified* the lawlessness of the mob. And he's especially distressed by the treatment of those few, amongst the besieged, who, to escape death, opted for baptism; only for Richard Malebisse to order their death, too.

    It seems probable that William's ambivalent attitude was widely shared, in respectable church circles.

12. *The Last of the Just*, IV:1, p. 147.

13. Ibid. VII:3, p. 321.

14. Ibid., pp. 323—24.

15. Ibid., III:8, p. 140.

16. Ibid. II:7, pp. 78—79.
    We do also learn that Ernie Levy, as a young man, likes to read the
    Zionist poetry of Chaim Bialik: Ibid. VI:3, p. 278.

17. Buber, *Tales of the Hasidim* (New York: Schocken Books, 1991.) Originally
    published in two volumes in 1947.

18. 'Litvak': originally, the majority Jewish religious tradition in Lithuania
    and surrounding regions. It differs from Hasidism in the more exclusive
    emphasis placed on scholarly study of the Talmud, as distinct from sheer
    intensity of devout enthusiasm.

19. See Samuel Hayim Brody, *Martin Buber's Theopolitics* (Bloomington:
    Indiana University Press, 2018). In 1902—4, when he was in his early
    twenties, Buber was editor of the weekly *Die Welt*, the main journal of
    the Zionist movement. Subsequently, he withdrew in order to pursue
    research into the history of Hasidism. In 1925 he joined the newly
    formed Brit Shalom (Covenant of Peace) Zionist group; and in 1942 was
    a co-founder of the Ihud (Unity) party. But neither of these ever gained
    much popular traction in Israeli politics.

20. Werfel, *The Forty Days of Musa Dagh*, trans. Geoffrey Dunlop (New
    York: Viking Press, 1934). Werfel's work was widely read in Jewish
    communities, as an inspirational text, during the Nazi period; not least
    where there were resistance organisations, in the Warsaw, Białystok,
    Częstochowa and Vilna ghettos. See Yair Auron, *Banality of Indifference:
    Zionism and the Armenian Genocide* (New Brunswick NJ: Transaction,
    2000), pp. 296—300.

21. *The Last of the Just*, II:7, p. 76—77.

22. Ibid., VII:2, p. 314.

23. The critical moment of revelation, to Mordecai, comes in ibid. IV:2, pp.
    161—64, when a mob of S.A. men are confronting a cowering Jewish

crowd outside their synagogue – crazy old Mrs Tuszynski steps out to protest – the Nazi leader, the local grocer, knocks her down – and Ernie leaps forward, to restore her fallen wig, and be knocked down in turn. Then, in IV:3, Mordecai has a talk to Ernie, which leads to the child asking the question (p. 166): "Tell me, Grandfather, what should a Just Man do in this life?"

24. Ibid. IV:4, pp. 171—77.

25. Ibid. p. 181.

26. Ibid. IV, 6, p. 201.

27. Ibid. III:8.

28. Ibid. V:2, 4.

29. Ibid. IV:6; V:5.

30. Ibid. V:5.

31. Ibid. VI:1, p. 261.

32. Ibid. VI:5, pp. 285—86.

33. Ibid. p. 289.

34. Ibid. VI, 6, p. 293.

35. Ibid. pp. 293—94.

36. Ibid. p. 300.

37. See Nelly Sachs, *Revelation Freshly Erupting: Collected Poetry*, translated by Andrew Shanks (Manchester: Carcanet, 2023).

D.

People Paid
to be Saints?

CHAPTER ELEVEN

Two Contrasting Takes on the Role of Pastor, or Priest

In the world of Hasidic Judaism, background to André Schwarz-Bart's classic novel, the traditional concept of the saint, the *tzaddik* or paragon of justice, combines sublime virtue with male leadership within the worshipping community (the *tzaddik* is typically a rabbi) and sometimes, although not always, miracle-working powers.[1]

In the world of Sufi Islam, the traditional concept of the saint, the *walí* or 'godfriend', likewise combines sublime virtue with male leadership within the worshipping community, and miracle-working powers; but is also shaped, after the death of the individuals in question, by the development of shrines dedicated to their memory, pilgrimage centres.[2] This latter practice has been deplored by various reform movements within the Islamic world: namely, from the eighteenth century CE onward, the Wahhabi movement originating in Saudi Arabia and the *Ahl-i-Hadith* originating in the Indian sub-continent; then, from the late nineteenth century CE onward, the Salafi movement and the more liberal Islamic Modernist movement, both originating in the wider Arab world.[3] Nevertheless, it persists in many places.

In Christendom, the traditional concept of the saint again tends to combine sublime virtue with leadership within the worshipping community – mostly male leadership, although also extending to the leadership of women in religious orders, especially visionaries. It features miracle-working powers, both in life and after death; and, as in Sufi Islam, is also associated with the development of local shrines, which the more radical Protestant churches deplore. But, in addition, the major saint-honouring institutions – Roman Catholic, Eastern Orthodox, Coptic, Lutheran, and Anglican – have systematically ordered the liturgical year, with official calendars of saints' days.

From the point of view of the hierarchical institutions officially licensing such calendars, the point is, not least, to *appropriate* – for themselves – as much as possible of the moral authority intrinsic to the memory of those whom they thus honour. In affirming the authority of its saints, each church hierarchy is also intent on boosting its own authority. However, this may become problematic in two ways. In the first place, it helps create the possibility of just that basic corruption of theology into mere sacred-ideological propaganda which I'm arguing we need the assistance of novelists to help put right.

But secondly, also, it helps generate an interesting paradox.

For it means that the authority of leaders within the worshipping community, at every level of the hierarchy, is officially associated with, and indeed grounded in, an ideal *calling*, at least, to sublime virtue; some measure of Christ-likeness. Stipendiary pastors and priests are, in principle, people paid to be saints! Yet, at the same time, they're also people who are paid to build up congregations; attract outsiders to become active insiders; and preserve peace between, perhaps, fractious sub-groups. In New Testament terminology, they're given charge over the 'flock', as such. See especially, from Paul's speech to the Ephesian elders, *Acts* 20:28—31; also, *1 Peter* 5:1—3.

How though, after all, does the 'flock' here differ from the 'herd' of herd-morality? Evangelistic success comes easiest when the evangelist skilfully flatters the herd, accommodating the gospel message to the herd's prejudices. And pastoral success comes easiest the same way. But the challenge of sublime virtue *by definition* terrifies the herd-animal within each one of us. It's only natural for us, in our capacity as members of the flock, to recoil from it; as the chorus initially recoils from the Suffering Servant.

Again: there's a blatant contradiction between being shepherd to the human 'flock' and bearing witness to Christ-like sublimity.

∾

It's a contradiction which cries out for novelistic narrative treatment. And in this section, I want to consider two contrasting attempts to supply what's required in this regard: on the one hand, the work of *Georges Bernanos*; on the other hand, that of *Marilynne Robinson*.

The context of Bernanos's work differs from that of Robinson's, in that he's writing about priests of the Roman Catholic church in 1920s France; whereas she's writing about a Congregationalist pastor, in Iowa, some thirty or so years later. And the tone of her work is also quite different from that of his.

I admire both. But the juxtaposition of the two seems to me to bring out the strength of Robinson's work, especially.

---

1. There are, to be sure, two feminine variants of the term '*tzaddik*': viz. '*tzadeikes*' and '*tzaddeket*'.

2. *Walī* is Arabic. Michael Sells suggests the English translation 'godfriend': in his book *Early Islamic Mysticism* (Mahwah NJ: Paulist Press, 1996), p. 8. In Farsi the nearest equivalent term is '*pir*'; in English, 'elder'.

3. Sometimes early representatives of what nowadays would be called 'Islamic Modernism' self-identified as '*salafi*' – 'back-to-basics' campaigners – the same as radical anti-modernist reformers did. The two tendencies were united precisely in hostility to Sufism. But the connotations of the term '*salafi*' have evolved, and now it belongs very much to the anti-modernists.

CHAPTER TWELVE

Georges Bernanos:
The Diary of a Country Priest

Georges Bernanos's father was passionate about photography. He took numerous pictures of his son. One shows the boy between two priests playing chess. Another one shows him dressed up in clerical garb himself. His mother, in particular, would doubtless have loved for him to be ordained.[1] But there's a letter that he wrote in March 1905, at the age of seventeen, to his old teacher, the abbé Lagrange, in which he explicitly disavows any such vocation. Already, it was clear to him: his calling – in his eyes, a no less holy one – was to be a writer, instead.[2]

Very largely, however, he was to be a writer *about* the priestly calling. *The Diary of a Country Priest* (1936) is widely agreed to be his best novel.[3] But it was by no means Bernanos's only extensive novelistic portrayal of a priest. Priests also play a prime role in each of his initial three major novels; not to mention his historical studies, *Saint Dominique* (1926) and *Jeanne relapse et sainte* (1929). In the first of the novels, *Sous le soleil de Satan* (1926), the central character is a priest, the Abbé Donissan, largely modelled on the Curé d'Ars, Saint Jean-Marie Vianney: a man of peasant origins, not especially intelligent, who however ends up becoming a renowned father-confessor.[4] The second, *L'Imposture* (1927), inverting this pattern, depicts a priest, the Abbé Cénabre, who's a leading scholar – a specialist in the study of mediaeval mysticism – who finds that he has lost his faith, supplanted by a demonic spirit of arrogance. He then engages in spiritual struggle of sorts with another priest: a timid saint, the Abbé Chevance.[5] In the third, *La Joie* (1928), Cénabre reappears, eventually to find redemption through trauma and death.[6]

These works are all celebrations of sublime virtue. But they're also advertisements for the Roman Catholic Church, at its best. That's to say: for the Roman Catholic Church as a privileged conduit for sublime virtue. They're celebrations of sublime virtue primarily in the form of celibate priesthood.

Bernanos was a political advocate of Roman Catholic interests, identified with fierce French nationalism; a man of the Right, in that sense. As a celebrant of sublime virtue, he was indeed highly critical of any corruption of the Church by what he saw as a spirit of banality; worldliness; lust for domination. His eye-witness response to the Spanish Civil War is a prime example. Here, he turns his fire on the Spanish bishops for their condoning of Phalangist atrocities. At the outbreak of the war, as it happened, he had been living in Majorca. Again, his immediate partisan inclination was, in general, to support the pro-Church Phalange; his son was actually a lieutenant in the Phalange militia. But what he witnessed sickened him: the widespread rounding-up, torture and murder of factory workers and peasants suspected of Republican sympathies; all manner of old scores being settled, gangster-fashion; and 'the person whom good manners suggest I should refer to as His Lordship the Archbishop of Palma' simply blessing it all, as so many other Church dignitaries, right across Spain, also did. He wrote an impassioned tract, in protest.[7]

But note what's still missing in his thought. He develops no critique of partisan narrow-mindedness, *in itself*. On the contrary: he affirms only what's loyally Roman Catholic, and at the same time patriotic. The sole proviso appears to be that such commitment should be *excitedly sincere*.

The greatest work by a theologian discussing the thought of any novelist is, surely, *Hans Urs von Balthasar*'s expansive study of Bernanos, originally published in 1950, just two years after Bernanos's death.[8]

Balthasar was, of course, one of the most significant theologians of the twentieth century. He was an encyclopaedic thinker: drawing, with great originality, on the Early Church Fathers, the Scholastics, the whole Roman Catholic tradition to which he belonged; but also, notably, on the Reformed dogmatics of his fellow-Swiss, Karl Barth, with whom he developed a close friendship; and on all manner of art and literature. Besides his interest in Bernanos, he was also a warm enthusiast for those other modern French Catholic writers, Péguy and Claudel.

What drew Balthasar to Bernanos was indeed, above all, his desire to do full justice, as a theologian, to the proper excitement of faith, which Bernanos for his part so effectively evokes as a novelist. Balthasar's whole interest in aesthetics, as a way into theology, was driven by a sense that Catholic theology needed fresh aesthetic stimulus. He wanted to try and rescue it from its hitherto all too prevalent dry-as-dust, scholastic self-enclosure; its aversion to intellectual adventure. To this end, he examines Bernanos's work as a whole, rolling it around on his tongue, savouring its intoxicating power.

Balthasar's book is indeed a fine tribute to Bernanos's undoubted strengths as a novelist. Only, he seems to me rather to overlook Bernanos's limitations.

~

The confrontational excitement informing Bernanos's critique of Church corruption reflects his passionate commitment to the countervailing ecclesiastical ideal represented, in his novels, by the Abbé Donissan, by the Abbé Chevance, and, in *The Diary of a Country Priest*, by the unnamed curé of the parish of Ambricourt. He also writes of saints who aren't priests: the young girl Chantal de Clergerie in *La Joie*; and the martyr-community of nuns, in his drama *Dialogues des Carmélites* (1949), set in the period of the French Revolutionary Terror.[9] But, clearly, he's fascinated by the specific tension shaping the role of a priest, between the purity of the gospel and the temptations deriving from the Church's nature as an institution.

For him, the problem appears, quite simply, to be a cooling of faith; a straightforward decay of sincerity. In his novels generally Bernanos wants to re-infuse gospel purity with excitement. At first, this leads him into melodrama. So, for example in *Sous le soleil de Satan* he describes the saintly Abbé Donissan wandering lost in the night: a 'little man' appears, they get talking; it turns out the 'little man' is really Satan, intent on tempting him to despair; a struggle ensues in which Donissan, just about, triumphs. Then, later that same night, he encounters a sixteen-year-old girl, Mouchette, who we already know has just murdered the man who seduced her and left her pregnant, a local aristocrat. They talk: Donissan wrestling with her despair. This time he fails. For afterwards, when Mouchette has returned home, she takes her father's razor and fatally slits her own throat. Yet, he doesn't fail altogether: having received the news, he hastens to her bedside; moved by his intervention, as she dies, she asks to be carried into church, and laid before the altar. He's a physically strong man. Battling off the immediate resistance of both her father and the doctor – and to the subsequent scandalised indignation of the higher ecclesiastical authorities – he fulfils her request.

Or, again, what could be more melodramatic than the Abbé Cénabre's final redemption in *La Joie*? He finds the saintly Chantal dead. She has been murdered. The shock of it leaves him unhinged. He asks the cook, who's with him, to recite the Lord's Prayer – for "*I can't*", he says. Then, as she begins (in French), he cries out in a 'superhuman' voice, "PATER NOSTER", and pitches forward on his face. A footnote informs us that he subsequently died in hospital 'without regaining his reason'.

Balthasar comments on this:

The early novels ... have to be interpreted with latitude in light of the later ones if they are not to appear distorted and exaggerated. The later works, in which sheer creative genius and immediacy are perhaps no longer so striking, nevertheless have undergone a steady process of clarifying the author's basic intent and have thus attained the balance for which he strove from the beginning. This masterful balance is most resplendently persuasive in *The Diary of a Country Priest* and in *Dialogues of the Carmelites*.[10]

Indeed: by comparison with the preceding novels, *The Diary of a Country Priest* is charged with an altogether more *smouldering* sort of excitement. The saintliness of the young Curé d'Ambricourt is much less of a melodramatic firework spectacle than that of the Abbé Donissan, in particular. Encountering it in diary-form, one feels its essential inwardness all the more.

∿

The curé inhabits the same unglamorous scenery as the Abbé Donissan in the earlier novel: the environs of a small village in the flat hinterland of the Pas de Calais. Like Donissan, he comes from poor peasant stock; the poorest of the poor. He differs, however, in being, if not a 'lettered' priest, nevertheless highly intelligent.[11] His writing, in his diary, is of the same quality as Bernanos's own. And then other characters respond to his obvious intellectuality by launching into their own general reflections on life, similarly pithy and thoughtful, although representing a kaleidoscope of different viewpoints. The most notable example is his mentor the Curé de Torcy, at length. But it's the same with the Curé de Torcy's friend, old Dr Delbende who commits suicide; also, the young soldier, M. Olivier; the morphia-addict, Dr Laville; even the conservative Dean of Blangermont, briefly. So many refractions of the same voice – this novel is in part a sort of symposium.

Intent on evoking the aesthetic excitement of sainthood, Bernanos begins by setting it in a context representing the purely banal, dull opposite. So, on the first page of the curé's diary, we read:

> My parish is bored stiff; no other word for it. Like so many others! We can see them being eaten up by boredom, and we can't do anything about it. Some day perhaps we shall catch it ourselves – become aware of the cancerous growth within us. You can keep going a long time with that in you.[12]

He doesn't realise it yet, but he's in fact, himself, quite literally dying of cancer. Not the metaphorical cancer of boredom, but a cancer that robs him of his appetite; afflicts him with pain that he can only bear by medicating himself with wine; causes him to vomit blood; and leaves him ever weaker. Out of pride, he seeks to conceal his condition. When he's found one night collapsed in a ditch, rumour spreads around the village that he has a drink problem. Finally, he catches a train to Lille, with a view to consulting a specialist. And the novel ends with his death, there.

The striking lack of concern, for this sick man, shown by his parishioners is itself symbolic of their bored indifference to religion. The boredom that afflicts them, he goes on,

> is like dust. You go about and never notice, you breathe it in, you eat and drink it. It is sifted so fine, it doesn't even grit on your teeth. But stand still for an instant and there it is, coating your face and hands.

No doubt the original 'seed' of it has always been there. The general human capacity for boredom is a basic aspect of original sin. But, he remarks,

> I wonder if man has ever before experienced [quite] *this* contagion, *this* leprosy of boredom: an aborted despair, a shameful form of despair in some way like the fermentation of a Christianity in decay ...[13]

The historical setting, here, is a little after the end of the First World War.

Ambricourt, the village, is not at all a grand place.[14] But it does have one aristocratically titled landowner: M. le Comte. He lives in the Château with his wife Mme. la Comtesse, their teenage daughter Mlle. Chantal, and the governess Mlle. Louise.[15] M. le Comte is a habitual philanderer, currently sleeping with the governess. Mlle. Chantal, a fiercely resentful young woman, has consequently developed an implacable hostility to Mlle. Louise; and is at the same time furious with her mother for complaisantly accepting the situation.

The curé performs his duties conscientiously, but, in his own eyes, clumsily; tripped up by hostility on every side. He reports, for instance, a conversation with little Seraphita Dumouchel, the star pupil of the catechism class:

> 'Aren't you longing to welcome Our Lord Jesus? Doesn't it seem a long time to wait till your first communion?'
> 'No,' she answered, 'why should it? It'll come soon enough.'
> I was nonplussed, but not greatly shocked, for I know the malice there is in children. So I went on:
> 'But you understand me, though. You listen so well.'
> Her small face hardened and she stared.
> 'It's 'cause you've got such lovely eyes.'
> Naturally I didn't move a muscle, and we came out of the sacristy together. All the other children were outside whispering and they suddenly stopped and shouted with laughter. They'd obviously planned the joke together.[16]

From then on, she pursues him 'with surreptitious oglings, grimacing, apeing a grown-up woman in a way that is very hard to bear'. Deep down, her attitude towards him is ambivalent; by no means as hostile as here it seems. But that only emerges later. At this point he simply cries out: 'Oh, why should these little girls be so full of enmity? What have I done?'[17]

His attempts to set up a Sports Club for young men are stymied by M. le Comte's reluctance to donate any land for the purpose. Still, he presses ahead with a Young Men's Guild, or Study-Circle.

A disappointingly few turn up; and only one of them seems really keen. This is Sulpice Mitonnet. Eventually, M. le Comte comes calling and warns him against Sulpice: it turns out that the young man has a reputation as a homosexual. He had, according to M. le Comte, only narrowly escaped a court martial, for homosexual behaviour, during the period of his military service. Sulpice, sensing that the curé has now been spoken to about him, disappears without a word. The curé doesn't reach out, in any way, to call him back.[18] And perhaps this also explains Mme. Pégriot's mysterious parting shot when resigning from the role of the curé's housekeeper. Her main reason for leaving was simply that there wasn't enough work for her at the presbytery. But she had, at the same time, spoken of "certain people" whom she had "rather not have to be meetin' here".[19]

Most distressingly of all, one day an anonymous hand-written letter arrives:

> *A well-wisher advises you to apply for a change of parish. And the sooner the better. When at last you open your eyes to what everyone else can see so plain, you'll sweat blood! Sorry for you but we say again: 'Get out!'*[20]

The curé's first thought is to suspect Mme. Pégriot. Later, however, he catches sight of the same handwriting on the fly-leaf of the governess, Mlle. Louise's prayer-book. Why does *she* want him out? It's, perhaps, an inverted tribute to his integrity. He doesn't yet know of her affair with M. le Comte. Yet, it seems that she is afraid of the shame she'd feel, especially, to have *such* a priest confront her with it.

In recurrent acute pain, insomniac and lonely, he is, as is only natural, tempted to self-pity. He likes to sit on a hillside, above the village:

> I look down, but it never seems to look back at me. Rather does it turn away, cat-like, watching me askance with half-shut eyes ... Sometimes I fancy the village has nailed me up here on a cross and is at least watching me die ...[21]

A series of torn-out pages tacitly record his very worst moments of near-despair. Prayer becomes difficult, so does pity for others. [22] Although he continues to go through the motions required of him, the corresponding spontaneous impulse dries up. But, just by virtue of his nonetheless sticking to the task, he becomes – at least to some extent – a true Suffering Servant according to the Isaianic archetype. His diary, itself, is the direct record of his taking upon himself the sins and the suffering of his people.

The *Amos* impulse, meanwhile, appears at two levels here: in the form both of theological theory and of pastoral practice. The curé is proud of his poor-peasant background. He remembers, as a child, reading the childhood memories of the Russian Marxist writer Maxim Gorky – Gorky's account of growing up in extreme poverty – and identifying with them. Ever since then, he writes, he has prayed for Gorky every day.[23] And theologically this counter-cultural pride is right at the heart of his Christian faith. It may have taken the greater part of two millennia for the radical incompatibility of gospel truth with the actual institution of slavery to have become apparent. However, that delay doesn't trouble him. For him, the key point is just that the germ of the development was there from the outset.[24] He discusses the matter with the Curé de Torcy; also, a man defiantly proud of his peasant origins. The Curé de Torcy is old enough to remember the immense enthusiasm with which Pope Leo XIII's 1891 encyclical 'Rerum Novarum' had originally been received, by 'democratic priests' and Catholics keen to build alliances with trade unionists. Jesus indeed says, "The poor you have always with you" (*Matthew* 26:11; *Mark* 14:7). The older priest absolutely shares Pope Leo's mistrust of revolutionary socialism, for its idolatry of coercive centralised power. He doesn't, for one moment, believe in the *abolition* of poverty as an ideal. But he's eloquent in his dedication to Christ as representative of the poor; Christ, in symbolic terms, rendering poverty holy; Christ revealing God's special love for the poor.[25] The friendship of the two curés is very largely founded on this basis, their shared theological openness to the *Amos* impulse.

And, pastorally, one may also see the *Amos* impulse in the

younger priest's remarkable gift of *parrhesia*; that is, his friendly, but uninhibited – even brutal – frankness, where he judges it necessary, towards his parishioners, including the gentry. Peasant he may be, but he gives it them straight! He's an eminently courageous pastor. We see this quality emerge above all in three conversations he has: the first with Mlle. Chantal at the end of Chapter 4; the second with Mme. la Comtesse – the long interview which fills most of Chapter 5; and the third with Mlle. Chantal again, briefly, at the end of Chapter 7.

The first conversation with Mlle. Chantal takes place in church, where she has waylaid him. She wants him to take up with her mother the matter of her father's adultery. He agrees to do so. But at the same time, he also reproaches her, in scorching words, for the hatred and jealousy by which she's driven, and for the class-pride all too apparent in her attitude towards himself. Refusing to be a mere instrument of her desire for revenge, he commands her to kneel. And then, prompted by an obscure intuition, cries: 'Give me that letter – that letter in your bag – at once.' '*You* must be the devil,' she replies – yet, nevertheless, hands it over. It's addressed to her father. He doesn't read it but, once he is home, throws it in the fire.

Then, the ensuing encounter with Chantal's mother is a magnificently dramatic set-piece. We watch as Mme. la Comtesse's soul is unpeeled, layer by layer like an onion, by the curé's eloquence. He begins by speaking of his encounter with Chantal. 'You're the dupe of a little intriguing girl,' says Madame. 'Don't drive her to despair,' he replies, 'God does not allow it.' ... The tension steadily escalates ... 'You don't love your daughter, Madame,' he says. She explodes: 'How dare you?' – However, she acknowledges the truth of what he says ... From her hatred of her daughter, the topic shifts to her hatred for her husband. And here again: a moment of class conflict. Why has she never at all seriously discussed these matters with her confessor? It is, she argues, a case of *noblesse oblige*; preserving the outer vestiges of respectability. 'This is a Christian household, father.' Whereupon, *he* explodes ... 'Madame, the most stupidly blind of all people are

175

the satisfied rich.' ... He gets up to leave. 'You're a queer sort of priest,' she says. 'I've never met another like you. Well, at least let's part friends.' ... The real climax, however, is yet to come. For it isn't only her daughter and her husband whom she has come to hate. Deep down, she also hates God: blaming God for the death of her infant son, some years ago. Once again, the curé protests against her attitude to Chantal, whom she plans to send away, as the guest, for a while, of friends in England:

> 'Madame, you turn your child out of doors and know that it will be for ever.'
> 'That depends on her.'
> 'I mean to oppose you.'
> 'You don't know her. She's too proud to stay here on sufferance. She wouldn't stand it.'
> My patience [he writes] suddenly gave out. 'God will break you,' I shouted. She uttered a kind of moaning cry. But not a cry of defeat imploring mercy – a sigh rather, the deep sigh of a creature gathering up strength for defiance.
> 'Break me! God's broken me already. What more can He do? He's taken my son. I no longer fear Him.'[26]

But what has happened to her grieving love for her son? Has it not been increasingly swallowed up and transformed into her egoistic resentful hatred, now, for those others close to her who fail, in her view, properly to share her grief; and for God, who commands her to abandon that hatred? The curé confronts her with the risk she therefore faces, of *hell*. Not the manipulative notion of hell, which functions as a mere motivational back-up for herd-morality, but the true hell which is definable as: 'not to love any more'. He delivers a great speech, at the end of which he's near to physical collapse. And she begins to give way ... 'Would you deign to show me my hidden sin? The worm in the fruit?' she asks. And he replies: 'You must resign yourself to – to God.' Gradually the truth of what he has been saying begins to sink in ... She unclips and opens a medallion containing a lock of her dead son's hair ... 'It's to you I surrender,' she says. To which he responds: 'I'm too insignificant and stupid. It's as though you were to put a gold coin in a pierced hand.' But she has made up her mind ... She throws the medallion with the hair into the fire. This was by no means what he intended, and he scrabbles to retrieve it, blistering his hand. In vain!

The next day he receives a letter from her, brim-full of gratitude and a sense of having been released. And almost immediately afterwards – her heart was weak – she dies.

It turns out that Mlle. Chantal had been spying on their conversation. Maliciously, Chantal spreads word that he'd *forced* her mother to throw the locket into the fire, as a symbolic gesture. M. le Comte is outraged, and vows that he'll complain to the bishop, in the strongest terms. Intent on preserving pastoral confidentiality, the curé won't defend himself. The novel ends with his death from cancer; but had he lived, he'd no doubt have been sent away in disgrace. Yet, Chantal – waylaying him this time at the presbytery – confesses:

'When you talked to mother I was hiding under the window. And suddenly her face became so – so gentle. I hated you then. I don't believe much in miracles, not any more than I believe in ghosts, but I did think I knew my mother. She cared no more about pretty speeches than a fish for an apple. Have you a secret, yes or no?'

'It's a lost secret ... You'll rediscover it, and lose it again, and others after you will pass it on, since your kind will last as long as the world.'

'My kind? Whatever do you mean?'

'Those whom God sends on and on for ever, who will never rest while the world remains.'[27]

∿

'The saints', Bernanos writes, 'are not sublime ... They are not heroes, at least not in the manner of Plutarch's heroes.'[28] And yes, if 'sublime' virtue is simply what that all too conventionally pagan celebrant of 'great' men admires – then it's simply a truism that *Christian* saints aren't 'sublime'. So, the curé writes in his diary: 'Nothing is farther removed from me than stoic indifference, so how can I hope for the death of a stoic? Plutarch's heroes both terrify and bore me. If I were to go to heaven wearing such a mask, I think even my guardian angel would laugh at me...'[29]

But now let us return, once again, to the basic distinction that I have sought to draw – in a quite different, not at all Plutarchan sense – between the 'sublimity of the saint' and the 'sublimity of the hero-as-holy-warrior.'[30]

The 'sublimity of the saint': virtue framed as a maximally thoughtful, devout transcendence of one's *own* culture's religious herd-morality; its gangster codes; and its mob passions.

The 'sublimity of the hero-as-holy-warrior': virtue framed, far rather, as supremely heroic resistance to an *outside enemy*.

Bernanos's ideal – represented in the characters of Donissan, Chevance and the Curé d'Ambricourt – is effectively an amalgam of the two, without any recognition of the difference. Certainly, these priest-saints are critical of the institutional Church to which they belong. But they're critical just to the extent that the Church has sold out to the secular world, properly considered as an enemy. They're by no means critics of ecclesiastical aggressive zealotry as such. For, as I've said, the mischief which such zealotry may do, on its own account, is simply not an issue for Bernanos.

The Curé d'Ambricourt is a zealot by conviction, just as Bernanos was. But he lives and dies in obscurity, so that his zealotry remains concealed. He lacks any opportunity, or temptation, to express it, grand show-man style. This is perhaps fortunate!

Yet, just as ardently as Péguy, Bernanos reveres Joan of Arc, that great heroine-as-holy warrior; and show-woman genius. His little book about her, *Jeanne relapse et sainte* (*Joan, Apostate and Saint*), focuses on her trial, before a church court. Here, as Balthasar puts it, 'Bernanos spoke for Joan herself, uttering statements [he imagined] she longed to hurl at her judges but had instead to leave unsaid'.[31] And so too towards the end of *The Diary of a Country Priest* there's a vivid scene in which her name comes up again.[32] Here the curé encounters Mlle. Chantal's cousin M. Olivier, a soldier on leave, who takes him for an exhilarating, blissful spin on a motor-bike. When they stop and talk, M. Olivier is eloquently cynical about the decadence of modern soldiering, as contrasted with what St. Joan represents. He speaks of her as 'the last real soldier'. In M. Olivier, the curé feels that he has met a true friend, a kindred spirit.

Moreover, in another major work, the tract entitled *La Grande peur des bien-pensants* (*The Great Fear of the Politically Correct*), published in 1931 five years before *The Diary of a Country Priest*, Bernanos celebrates the 'sublimity of the hero-as-holy-warrior' in the modern secular form of a campaigning show-man journalist.[33]

This is a work of somewhat indeterminate genre. Partly, it's history: a study of French politics in the decades following the great national trauma of 1870. Partly, it's biography: celebrating the life of a man whom Bernanos presents as a great political warrior – in a non-Plutarchan sense, one might well say, a great rhetorical evoker of the sublime. And partly, it's a speculative novel-like sketch of that man's inner life. It's written with all of Bernanos's usual verve; full of great energy and excitement.

But the ghastly fact is that the central character here, whom he's celebrating, is actually a man whose whole career revolved around *vitriolic – demented – antisemitism!*

Édouard Drumont (1844—1917) had been a major pioneer of modern right-wing populist politics. He made his name with a two-volume book, a best-seller, *La France Juive* (*Jewish France*) published in 1886. A series of other books then followed; all of them, like the first, dedicated to antisemitic propaganda. In 1890 he was the leading spirit involved in the founding of the Antisemitic League of France; and in 1892 he launched a journal, *La libre parole* (*Free Speech*), again ferociously antisemitic. Drumont's career as an elected politician was brief, and not so notable: he entered the Chamber of Deputies as representative for Algiers in 1898, but lost the seat just four years later. As a journalist, however, he played a key role in establishing a mass antisemitic movement in France. His bravado led to him being fined, for libel; on one occasion, also, to his spending three months in prison; and to his being involved in two duels. The Panama Canal Company Scandal of 1892—3 provided him with a major opportunity, when a list of all the Deputies whom the Company had bribed, to vote for government grants to it, was leaked to *La Libre Parole*. The Dreyfus Affair, from 1894—1906, provided another. He was strenuous in his attempts to translate the accusation levelled against one Jewish officer into an accusation against Jews in general.[34]

Bernanos remembered, as a child, listening to his father read aloud from Drumont's writing. Drumont had died in reduced circumstances; and, fourteen years after his death, was already a largely forgotten figure. There was an element of defiance in Bernanos's attempt to revive his memory. Bernanos had long been a supporter of right-wing populism in the form of the *Action Française*, led by Charles Maurras. But Maurras, although he valued the Church as a political phenomenon, was not himself a practising Catholic; and in 1926 Pope Pius XI had condemned the movement. Bernanos, the loyal Catholic, was interested in Drumont not least as an alternative historic role model to Maurras. Not that Drumont's attitude to the Church was all that different from Maurras's. However, as a freelance man of letters like Bernanos himself, he represented a form of populism, at any rate, far less constrained than that of Maurras by the dictates of party discipline; unlike Maurras, Drumont wasn't leader of a well-drilled organisation, out of the Church's control. Let's be fair: Bernanos was not primarily attracted to Drumont by the latter's antisemitism, for its own sake. Rather, he admired Drumont's sheer effectiveness as a critic of the role played by big money in politics; and his strategic use of antisemitism, then, for the popularising of that critique, in a context where the business of banking was, as it happens, largely run at the highest level by Jews.

The timing of *La Grande peur des bien-pensants*, in the early 1930s, was certainly unfortunate. Would Bernanos still have wanted so brazenly to celebrate the memory of this French literary antisemite after Hitler's brand of antisemitism had come to power in Germany? Probably not. His contempt for Nazism was unwavering from the outset; as was his contempt for Italian

Fascism. I've already noted his response to Franco's version, in Spain. Having emigrated in 1938, to Brazil, he wrote scathingly of the Vichy regime, and resolutely supported the resistance of the Free French Forces under De Gaulle.

However, Bernanos honours Drumont, crucially, as a literary stylist, another like himself, a past-master in the art of polemic. He includes great chunks of quotation from Drumont in his text. Commenting on the novelistic aspect of the work, Balthasar remarks: 'Bernanos by no means intends to make a Christian hero out of this antisemitic journalist'; but, to a large extent, he nevertheless 'portrayed Drumont in his own image and likeness.'[45] In short, *La Grande peur des bien-pensants* is very much a book in which *one zealot salutes another zealot* as his *alter ego*.

And so, what does Balthasar make of Bernanos's choice of Drumont in this role? He deplores the antisemitism, of course.[36] But, further, he diagnoses what he calls *'the temptation of a heroic cult of death'* at work.[37] So he remarks:

> The fundamental thought underlying this astonishing book is
> … that a life should be constructed that the power of death
> steels for anything and everything.[38]

In other words, one might well describe the book as a systematic attempt imaginatively to inhabit the 'sublimity of the hero-as-holy-warrior' in a civilian context; grounded, as such sublimity is, in a life-or-death defiance of risk. The figure of Drumont, in effect, becomes for Bernanos a cipher for this attempt. In Balthasar's view, the result is certainly quite a disastrous deviation from his authentic Catholic faith. I agree!

One might, perhaps, argue that the matter isn't so grave. Bernanos, after all, is an admirer of Drumont but is also a no less ardent admirer of Péguy, the militant *Dreyfusard* and *philosemite*. Yes – but, by the same token, he's an admirer of Péguy who also admires Drumont! What Péguy and Drumont, notwithstanding all their differences, have in common – what Bernanos treasures in both of them alike – is just their shared taste for the 'sublimity of the hero-as-holy-warrior', flamboyantly expressed. And here, I'd suggest, we see two things:

(a) the moral ambiguity intrinsic to any celebration, theological or otherwise, of the 'sublimity of the hero-as-holy-warrior', considered simply in itself;

(b) the theological ambiguity of any approach to faith which fails adequately to distinguish the 'sublimity of the saint' from the 'sublimity of the hero-as-holy-warrior', and to rank the former, quite decisively, above the latter.

In describing Bernanos as a 'zealot', I mean that he's addicted to an ardent self-certainty, unfortunately excluding any real interest in the philosophical discernment of such ambiguity.

Nor do I think that *Balthasar* actually goes anything like far enough in criticising this. Thus, although he deplores Bernanos's dalliance with 'a heroic cult of death', he fails, as I'd see it, properly to *generalise* the key, underlying point at issue. For isn't that cult, also, absolutely present in the *Book of Revelation*? Doesn't it, then, to a disturbing degree pervade the Early Church's glorification of its martyrs? And later on, as well – quite apart from Joan of Arc – isn't it a core ingredient in every form of the 'crusader' ethos, both military and civilian? Balthasar doesn't pursue these resemblances.

Moreover, as he sees it, the weakness here is one that Bernanos eventually overcame. Balthasar writes:

> The temptation of a heroic cult of death is strong, and it will take Bernanos a long time to overcome it completely.[39]

Nevertheless, in the end – he suggests – that overcoming *is* completely accomplished.

But *when*, exactly, does he think this happens?

To me, on the contrary, it seems that Bernanos's dedication to 'a heroic cult of death' is intrinsic to his thinking right from beginning to end. For isn't it also there in the *Diary of a Country Priest*? As the curé wrestles, so heroically, with his cancer, isn't that by implication presented as a metaphorical vindication of Bernanosian zealotry, sublimely warring against all its foes? Bernanos's zealotry prompts him to go in search of theological *excitement-devices* of every kind. And he repeatedly mobilises the thought of death to this end.

In the end, I think, Balthasar fails properly to see the deeper cautionary lesson to be learnt from the all too obvious folly of Bernanos's collusion with antisemitism. His own view of theology still remains so one-sidedly skewed towards *endorsing the proper sheer passion of faith*, as such – rather than theology's other, no less crucial role in *discerning faith's ineradicable ambiguities* – that, when faced by the shortcomings of such an impassioned religious writer as Bernanos, he pulls up short.

---

1. Hans Urs von Balthasar, *Bernanos: An Ecclesial Existence* (1954), trans. Erasmo Leiva-Merikakis (San Francisco: Ignatius Press, 1996), p. 58.

2. Bernanos, *Oeuvres romanesques (Paris: Pléiade*, 1961); p. 1727. This is the second of a series of letters to the Abbé Lagrange, printed here as an Appendix.

3. *Journal d'un curé de campagne*; first published 1936. English translation, *The Diary of a Country Priest*, by Pamela Morris (New York: Carroll & Graf, 2002.)

4. The original English translation was entitled *The Star of Satan*; but this has since been superseded by J. C. Whitehouse's version, *Under Satan's Sun* (Lincoln NE: University of Nebraska Press, 2001).

5. *The Impostor*, trans. J. C. Whitehouse (Lincoln NE: Bison, 1999).

6. *Joy*, trans. Louise Varese (Providence RI: Cluny Classics, 2017).

7. *Les grands cimetières sous la lune*, translated by Pamela Morris as *A Diary of My Times* (London: Boriswood, 1938).

8. See note 1. The title of the German original is *Gelebte Kirche: Bernanos.* The 1996 English translation is of the third edition (1988).

9. His last work; published posthumously. English translations: (a) by Gerald Hopkins, *The Carmelites* (New York: Fontana, 1961); (b) by Michael Legat, *The Fearless Heart* (Westminster MD: Newman Press, 1952). Made into an opera by Francis Poulenc.

10. Balthasar, *Bernanos*, pp. 27—8.

11. C.f. *The Diary of a Country Priest*, p. 4:

> By nature I am probably coarse-grained, for I confess that I have always been repelled by the 'lettered' priest. After all, to cultivate clever people is merely a way of dining out, and a priest has no right to go out to dinner in a world full of starving people.

12. Ibid. p. 1.

13. Ibid. pp. 2—3. My italics.

14. C.f. Ibid. pp. 1—2: 'It was drizzling. The kind of thin, steady rain which gets sucked in with every breath, which seeps down through the lungs into your belly. Suddenly I looked out over the village, from the road to Saint Vaast along the hillside – miserable little houses huddled together under the desolate, ugly November sky. On all sides damp came steaming up and it seemed to sprawl there in the soaking grass like a wretched worn-out horse or cow. What an insignificant thing a village is ....'

15. A curious discrepancy: at the beginning of Chapter 2 (p. 25) there's also mention of 'two little boys'. (This would help account for the continuing presence of a governess.) But by Chapter 5 (pp. 153—55) they've been forgotten: there, it appears that Mme la Comtesse has only ever had one other child besides Mlle. Chantal; a boy who died in infancy.

16. Ibid. pp. 27—8.

17. Ibid.

18. Ibid. pp. 120—21. Sulpice is described as a somewhat creepy character. C.f. Balthasar, 1996; pp. 392—4: on homosexuality as 'a kind of

sacramental sign of evil' in Bernanos's work, generally; citing the novel *Monsieur Ouine* (1943) as the prime case. (Balthasar himself evidently approves of such a view. It seems lamentable to me. But, of course, the prevailing state of theological debate on the issue was very different in the mid-20th century, when Balthasar was writing, from what it is today.)

19. *The Diary of a Country Priest*, pp. 85—6.

20. Ibid. p. 102.

21. Ibid. p. 40.

22. See for example Ibid. p. 111.

23. Ibid. pp. 51—2.

24. Ibid. pp. 46—7.

25. Ibid. pp. 53—63.

26. Ibid. p. 162.

27. Ibid. p. 256.

28. Bernanos, 1953; p. 286.

29. *The Diary of a Country Priest*, p. 294:

30. See above: Chapter 5.

31. Balthasar, *Bernanos*, p. 187.

32. *The Diary of a Country Priest*, pp. 233—48.

33. This remains untranslated. (It was published in Paris by Bernard Grasset.)

34. On the background: c.f. Hannah Arendt, *The Origins of Totalitarianism* (New York: Schocken Books, 2004), pp. 124—30.

35. Balthasar, *Bernanos*, p. 337.

36. I say 'of course', in view of the post-Shoah context. But c.f. Paul Silas Peterson, *The Early Hans Urs von Balthasar: Historical Contexts and Intellectual Formation* (Berlin / Munich / Boston: De Gruyter, 2015), on the traces of antisemitism in Balthasar's own early work: Chapter 7, 'The anti-modern anti-Semitic complex'; focussing especially on Balthasar's doctoral dissertation, *Die Apocalypse der Deutschen Seele*, published in three volumes 1937—9.

37. Balthasar, *Bernanos*; p. 465.

38. Ibid. p. 464.

39. Ibid. p. 465.

CHAPTER THIRTEEN

Marilynne Robinson:
Gilead, Home and *Lila*

Bernanos depicts a saintly zealot-priest, whose saintliness essentially consists in his courageous sincerity, as such.

Marilynne Robinson, by contrast, depicts a saintly pastor, whose saintliness essentially consists in his radical honesty; as honesty transcends sincerity, and opens towards deep empathy for the outcast, in general.

The Curé d'Ambricourt, in Bernanos's novel, is himself very much an outsider in his parish. But the novel doesn't afford him much opportunity to display solidarity with other outsiders. (The one exception: Sulpice Mitonnet. Whom, alas, he fails!) Robinson's portrait of the Congregationalist minister John Ames, on the other hand, is absolutely focussed on this very matter.

Her novel *Gilead* consists of Ames's memoirs. And he also plays a central role in her subsequent books, *Lila* and *Home*.[1] He's pastor of a small-town church in the south-western corner of Iowa. In fact, he pays fulsome tribute to *The Diary of a Country Priest*:

> I remember reading that book all night by the radio till every station went off, and still reading when the daylight came.[2]

This must have been in the late 1930s, when the English translation first came out. Ames is writing in 1956. He's now, himself, seventy-six. Some years previously, as a widower in his late sixties, he met and married a much younger second wife, Lila; and they have a young son. The memoirs Ames is writing are intended to be a posthumous gift, for his child to read once he has grown up.

Although a devout and eminently serious-minded man, and an admirer of Bernanos's book, Ames is very definitely *not* himself a zealot, of the kind that Bernanos celebrates. This is underlined by the contrast with the way he remembers his grandfather, who was one: a zealot, namely, for the abolition of slavery. The Ameses are a dynasty of Congregationalist ministers. Ames's father (John Ames II) was a minister, in the little town of Gilead; and so was his father (John Ames I), before him. But the memoirist, John Ames III here remembers this grandfather as something altogether more than just a normal pastor. Namely: as a tragic figure, somewhat in the mould of an Old Testament prophet.

'I am not by any means a saint', John Ames III writes, 'My life does not compare with my grandfather's.'[3] But is 'saint', really, the right term for John Ames I? If so, then it's a form of 'sainthood' oddly akin to what many good Christians would regard as criminality! As the memoirist recalls:

> I got up the courage to ask my father once if my grandfather had done something wrong and he said, 'The Good Lord will judge what he did,' which left me believing there had been some sort of crime for sure. There is one photograph of my grandfather around the house somewhere, taken in his old age, that might help you understand why I thought this way. It is a good likeness. It shows a wild-haired, one-eyed, scrawny old fellow with a crooked beard, like a paintbrush left to dry with lacquer in it, staring down the camera as if it had accused him of something terrible very suddenly, and he is still thinking how to reply and keeping the question at bay with the sheer ferocity of that stare.[4]

John Ames I, indeed, represents the *Amos* impulse at maximum intensity, in the service of the Abolitionist struggle. But he also represents a complete mix between the 'sublimity of the saint' and the 'sublimity of the hero-as-holy-warrior'. And, already before the outbreak of the American Civil War, the suspicion is that he may have killed a man, or even several; quite unrepentantly.[5]

He's a visionary. Here we have the opening of a short speech he delivers, in his old age, at a civic event on the Fourth of July:

> Children –
> When I was a young man the Lord came to me and put His hand just here on my right shoulder. I can feel it still. And He spoke to me, very clearly. The words went right through me. He said, Free the captive. Preach good news to the poor. Proclaim liberty throughout the land. That is all Scripture, of course, and the words were already very familiar to me at the time. But it is clear enough why He would feel they needed special emphasis. No one lives by them, unless the Lord takes him in hand. Certainly I did not, until the day He stood beside me and spoke those words to me ...[6]

That vision had led to his becoming a participant in John Brown's paramilitary anti-slavery campaign during the 'bleeding Kansas' struggle of 1854—59. His son, the memoirist's father, was a child of ten when John Ames I returned home, to his parish in Kansas, from some secretive expedition, with two bloodied shirts and a gun. Years later, the remembered shock of the event is still vivid:

> It was the very next Sunday the old devil preached in one of those shirts, with that gun in his belt. And you would not have believed how the people responded, all the weeping there was, and the shouting.

Afterwards, too, John Ames I was regularly away for several days at a time. And

> there were Sundays when he would ride his horse right up the church steps just when it was time for service to begin and fire that gun in the air to let the people know he was back. They'd find him standing in the pulpit, with his eyes red and his face

pale and dust in his beard, all ready to preach on judgment and grace.[7]

Then the Civil War broke out; and his fervent preaching persuaded many from the town of Gilead to enlist. He himself served as a chaplain. That was when he lost an eye, in battle. Numerous others from Gilead lost their lives. John Ames II (who'd also fought) recalls that, following the war, there was hardly anyone left in his father's congregation besides war-widows and orphans, and mothers who'd lost their sons. Yet, 'there was his father, preaching every Sunday on the divine righteousness manifested in it all.'[8] People were turning away to the Methodists, with their outdoor meetings down by the river. John Ames I was no doubt saddened by the decline of his own congregation; but, as mere church growth was never his goal, he took no offence. He opened the doors and windows of his church, to let the sound of the Methodist singing in.[9]

John Ames III has his own strong memories of his grandfather, in later life:

[He] seemed to me stricken and afflicted, and indeed he was, like a man everlastingly struck by lightning, so that there was an ashiness about his clothes and his hair never settled and his eye had a look of tragic alarm when he wasn't actually sleeping. He was the most unreposeful human being I ever knew; except for certain of his friends. All of them could sit on their heels into their old age, and they'd do it by preference, as if they had a grudge against furniture. They had no flesh on them at all.[10]

Notoriously, John Ames I had a complete disregard for property rights. In order to give to the poor, he'd ruthlessly thieve from his own family; from well-to-do members of his congregation; even from the members of other churches of which he approved.[11] He's remembered, it appears, among African Americans with great respect.[12] But that Fourth of July address ends on a melancholy note:

What is left here in Gilead? Dust. Dust and ashes. Scripture says the people perish, and they certainly do. It is remarkable. For all this His anger is not turned away, but His hand is stretched out still ...[13]

The crowd titters. 'Thank you, Reverend,' says his daughter-in-law. He shakes his head. 'I doubt it did much good.' And then, a little later, he leaves. To the great distress of his family, he goes to spend his final days in Kansas, revisiting his glorious memory of raids and ambushes. Some years after his death, his son and young grandson make a difficult expedition to locate his grave. They find a dustbowl semi-wilderness; an overgrown graveyard; a rough wooden marker, with nails driven in, spelling out 'REV AMES'.[14]

Another childhood memory of John Ames III: one Sunday, five minutes into his father's sermon, his grandfather rises and walks out of the church. He comes home after dinner.

My father said, 'Did my sermon offend you in some way? Those few words you heard of it?

The old man shrugged. 'Nothing in it to offend. I just wanted to hear some *preaching*. So I went over to the Negro church.'

After a minute my father asked, 'Well, did you hear some preaching?'

My grandfather shrugged. 'The text was "Love your enemies"' ...

My father said, 'You sound disappointed, Reverend.'

My grandfather put his head in his hands. He said, 'Reverend, no words could be bitter enough, no day could be long enough. There is just no end to it. Disappointment. I eat and drink it. I wake and sleep it.'

My father's lips were white. He said, 'Well, Reverend, I know you placed great hope in that war. My hopes are in peace, and I am not disappointed. Because peace is its own reward. Peace is its own justification.'

My grandfather said, 'And that's just what kills my heart,

Reverend. That the Lord never came to you. That the seraphim never touched a coal to your lips –'[15]

When it comes to his leaving them, not long after this, his only farewell is a note left on the kitchen table, saying:

> No good has come, no evil is ended.
> That is your peace.
> Without vision the people perish.
> The Lord bless you and keep you.[16]

John Ames III, for his part, remembers his father John Ames II as a good man; a conscientious father; certainly, an altogether more successful pastor, in conventional terms, than John Ames I had been. And yet, at the same time, he doesn't altogether dismiss his grandfather's verdict. For he too feels that – 'with all respect' – there was, deep down, something 'disappointing' about his father's life.[17]

In his old age, John Ames II settles into a comfortable retirement on the Florida coast. The contrast with the last days of John Ames I could scarcely be more striking! But as John Ames III, in turn, draws near to the end of his life, he chooses to remain in Gilead: wrestling there, not least, with their joint legacy.

~

Whereas Bernanos excitedly celebrates a Roman Catholic ideal of the zealot-priest, Robinson, by contrast, invites her readers to ponder the ineradicable moral ambiguities attendant upon even the sincerest actual practice of organised Christianity, in any form.

Thus, we're not only vividly confronted, in *Gilead*, with the essential moral ambiguity intrinsic to the one-sided 'sainthood', the zealotry, of John Ames I. But then there are also the moral ambiguities (already adumbrated in Chapter Eleven, above) intrinsic to the pastoral role itself; as this is, by its very nature, more or less entangled in the conventional prejudices – whether zealous or merely banal – of devout herd-morality. We're shown the pastoral role performed with true saintly thoughtfulness by John Ames III. And, just by virtue of the thoughtfulness here, we see something, not only of the moral opportunities opened up by the role, but also of the limitations on true saintliness that it's, at the same time, always liable to impose, *even when* ideally performed: as the pastor is expected to reinforce the mere respectability-code of the flock; forever tempted, or obliged, to collude with the associated closed-mindedness, more or less endemic in their congregation.

The dialectical inter-relationship of the three novels in which Ames is a protagonist is fundamentally designed to draw attention to the resultant moral ambivalence: as first, in *Gilead*, we see things through Ames's own eyes, just as we see things through the curé's eyes in the *Diary of a Country Priest*; but then, in *Home* and *Lila*, an external, minimally obtrusive narrator takes over; and Ames is seen, objectively, responding to the challenges presented both by his prodigal godson Jack Boughton – who's also the central character of *Jack*, the fourth novel in this four-novel sequence[18] – and by Lila, the stray young woman who, to Ames's astonishment, becomes his wife. It's these challenges which serve to highlight the ambivalence in question. And – the basic situation having already been set out in *Gilead* – more or less everything in the narratives of *Home* and *Lila* then goes towards intensifying the effect, by awakening the reader's sympathy, already engaged for Ames, now as well for Jack and Lila. We're being made to *feel* the difficulties that they each of them have in trusting this pastor, *as such*. In Jack's case the problem arises from an intense sense of guilt; in Lila's case, from a radical sheer vulnerability – due to her never really having *belonged*, anywhere, before. His guilt and her vulnerability: here are two major blockages to trust, in view of all that Ames, in his role as pastor, inevitably represents.

Ames's saintliness is, in the first instance, a matter of his approximation to the Isaianic archetype of the Suffering Servant who 'bears' the affliction of others. Although his character is largely shaped by decades of grief-stricken loneliness, following the death in childbirth of his first wife and their infant child, he's admittedly not himself a social outcast, the way the original Servant, pictured by Deutero-Isaiah, is. But Jack and Lila are outcasts. And Ames shares in their outcast-perspective – still brings it, after all, vicariously into the mix – by way of his intimately engaged compassion.

Jack and Lila are, both of them in their different ways, complete outsiders to the herd, or flock, morality normally framing the pastor's role. Ames looks decisively beyond the constraints of such convention – as the curé of Ambricourt, also, does. The difference is just that in Robinson's work there's far greater emphasis on the difficulty experienced by the social outsider, then, in reciprocally managing to receive the grace on offer; to open up, in turn, even to this particular pastor's convention-dissolving generosity.

~

Thus: Jack's the son of Ames's oldest and closest friend, the Reverend Robert Boughton, long-term pastor of the Presbyterian Church in Gilead. His full baptismal name is actually John Ames Boughton; originally chosen as a surprise tribute to that friendship.

The Boughton family includes eight brothers and sisters. Jack is 'not the eldest or the youngest or the best or the bravest, only the most beloved.'[19] But – quite unlike any of his siblings – he has been in trouble all his life. For no obvious reason, it so happens that he has never fitted in. And he's loved by his now very doddery father all the more, because of the anxiety he therefore provokes. In *Home* we see things chiefly from the point of view of Glory, Jack's younger sister, who has come back home to care for their father. (All the other siblings are away, well settled; only Glory remains unmarried, with a broken relationship behind her.) And then Jack too returns; mysteriously, after twenty years of absence, during which his family have heard nothing from him, other than occasional requests for financial assistance. Nor does he say anything at first, to anyone, of where he has been all that time, or what he has done. *Jack* – the heart-breaking fourth novel, tells *us* what he's concealing; but the psycho-drama of *Home* essentially

194

revolves around his acute difficulty in trusting anyone, even Ames, enough to make confession.

Ames remembers him as a child: 'always alone, always grinning, always intent on some piece of devilment.'[20] He was forever stealing things, not least from Ames. Once, to Ames's fury, it had been a little photograph of his dead wife, taken when she was a child. True, the picture reappeared eventually, as the other things did. But – 'the sheer meanness of it!' On another occasion, at dusk, Jack had stuffed Ames's mailbox, and then set fire to it. So many gestures of mockery: in the first instance, directed against everything that his father, as a pastor, stood for; but frequently deflected into a tacit taunting of his father's pastor-friend, the man after whom he had been named. The older Jack had grown, the more the mischief started to escalate into matters of actual concern to the police: stealing liquor, joyriding, theft of a rifle. It was a sort of game, Jack testing what he could get away with, by virtue of the general respect in which his father was held. Then, as a young man – the last act of his early years in Gilead – he in turn had fathered a child. Whom he'd abandoned! The mother, in fact, was scarcely more than a child herself; dirt poor; from a farm nearby. To escape the consequences, Jack had left town, leaving it to his father to try and make peace with her family. They, however, had rejected every advance. Eventually, the child had died. And yet, the trauma remains. Here, at last, Jack saw that he'd done something his father could never, really, forgive.[21]

When Jack reappears, in 1956, he's a man in his early forties: shabby, pale, unshaven, with the nick of a scar under his eye, which he has a habit of touching whenever he's embarrassed. In manner, he's painfully polite; weary; and guarded. Glory soon realises that he has become a recovering, but not entirely trustworthy, alcoholic. He has, we learn, spent time in prison. Glory, at one point, prepares a meal to which the Ameses are invited: 'dinner with Lazarus', he suddenly remarks – the revenant scrubbed up perhaps, but still 'disreputable'.[22]

It's Glory who initially encourages Jack to approach Ames:

She said, 'Ames has mellowed a little. At least he's not as abstracted as he used to be. So much of that was loneliness, I think. And it would please papa if you paid a call on him.'[23]

The first meeting doesn't go well. 'You know', he says to Glory, 'after all these years he still can't stand the sight of me.'[24] Ames isn't overtly hostile; but Jack is hypersensitive. As time passes, on the other hand, he grows increasingly anxious to mend the relationship. He does want to be forgiven. Unable to confide in his father, he hopes that eventually he'll be able to confide in Ames. By way of a beginning, he befriends Ames's little six-year-old child, Robby, with baseball-play. Then, he resolves to attend Ames's church. His initial attempt fails: at the last minute, he loses his nerve. The second time, he succeeds in getting through the door. But it's a disaster!

'What happened?' asks Glory. Jack says:

'He preached. The text was Hagar and Ishmael [*Genesis* 21:8—21], the application was the disgraceful abandonment of children by their fathers [viz. as Abraham abandoned Ishmael]. And the illustration was my humble self, sitting there beside his son with the eyes of Gilead upon me. I think I was aghast. His intention, no doubt. To appal me, that is, to turn me white, as I am sure he did. Whiter.'[25]

In *Gilead* we have Ames's account of that sermon.[26] It had been prepared several days earlier. And, Ames writes, he never would have chosen that text had he known that Jack was going to be there. But the trouble is, he'd extemporised far more than usual, and had found himself saying things that he now very much regrets; not explicitly, or at all consciously, aimed at Jack in particular; but nevertheless, as he now acknowledges, all too easily liable to be taken that way, by Jack.

Everything, with the word of God, depends on context. There's a sense in which Ames's error has just been a *mis-timed* effort to balance, in his preaching, the two prime elements of sainthood, the Isaianic archetype and the *Amos* impulse. The main thrust of the sermon, he writes, had been to affirm God's more than fatherly love – as manifested in the person of the Suffering Servant on the cross – not least for those (like Ishmael) whose own experience of childhood, in the literal sense, renders the metaphor of divine fatherhood largely inoperative. Here, in other words, we have a preacher's appeal to the Isaianic archetype. Then, however, he'd sought to balance this with a second thought:

> I have always worried that when I say the insulted or the downtrodden are within the providence of God, it will be taken by some people to mean that it is not a grave thing, an evil thing, to insult or oppress. The whole teaching of the Bible is explicitly contrary to that idea. So I quoted the words of the Lord: 'If anyone offend these little ones, it would be better for him if a millstone were put around his neck and he were cast into the sea.' That is strong language, but there it is.[27]

And in this we have something of his grandfather's old *Amos*-spirit resurgent.[28]

The consequences of the sermon aren't, after all, entirely malign. As he grows more and more worried about the effect it must have had on Jack, Ames eventually decides to write him a letter of apology, with an offer to talk further.

Jack is now drinking again. His first attempt to take Ames up on his offer is abortive. He makes a suicide attempt; and then begins to make arrangements to leave Gilead. Yet, on the eve of his departure, he does finally manage to have the conversation with Ames that he'd been hoping for. At long last, all his secrets spill out. And Ames, in response to his anguished honesty, is moved to embrace him. 'You are a good man,' Ames says.[29] Even though everything else in Jack's life remains wrapped in sadness, there's at least this moment of pastoral breakthrough.

∾

Both Jack and Lila are vividly realised characters, in themselves. Yet, they may also be seen as representative figures: standing, as they do, for two very different types of obstacle to the reception of pastoral love, on contrasting levels of intellectual sophistication. Jack, by virtue of his upbringing, knows the Bible well; is aware, for instance, of the writing of Karl Barth; engages Ames (much to the latter's irritation!) in discussing the traditional notion of predestination, with particular implicit reference to his own plight. Lila, on the other hand, has had a bare minimum of formal education: no more than a single year's schooling, just enough so that she can read and write. She's no fool. But, whereas Jack's resistance stems from rebellion, hers is, quite simply, an outcome of never having been accustomed to a church context, or to any sort of truly settled life whatsoever. The third novel of the trilogy gives us Lila's story.

It begins at the moment when, as a toddler, she's rescued – by being stolen – from her highly dysfunctional birth-family. Her rescuer/abductor, 'Doll', then becomes her *de facto* mother. They tag onto a group of itinerant farm labourers. Apart from the one year of schooling, Lila's whole childhood is actually spent in vagrancy. Things might have been different: at one point, without warning, Doll just disappears for a few days. Whereupon, the group's leader, Doane, just abandons Lila on the steps of a church. But Doll returns and, after some searching, eventually finds her; brushes aside the concern of the church's pastor; and re-joins the group. Then (it's the 1920s) the economy starts to fail. The soil of the prairies is crumbling into windblown dust. Well-paid temporary farm jobs grow ever rarer. And at length the group dissolves, when Doane is arrested for theft.

At school Lila has accidentally acquired the Norwegian surname Dahl: 'Doll', mis-heard. What's Doll's proper name? Lila never learns. Doll has a savage burn-mark on her face, memento of some fight. And she carries a sharp knife which, once upon a time, she'd used to sever a belligerent man's hamstring. She lives in constant wariness, lest her enemies from the past catch up with her. As soon as Lila is old enough to fend for herself, Doll, anxious to spare her this burden, leaves her. But then – all of a sudden

– she's back. There has been a violent fracas somewhere. A man, who may or may not have been Lila's father, lies dead. Arrested for murder, Doll escapes. But she dies, of exposure, whilst on the run. In shock, Lila moves to St. Louis, where she spends a number of desolate years – which end with her virtually having lost the habit of speech.

She decides to head west. A woman, a stranger who turns out to belong to the puritanical Church of the Nazarene, offers her a lift deep into Iowa. Being a nervous driver, in a rickety car, this woman says she's glad of the company.

> Lila could feel her wondering, and she almost said, I was working in a whorehouse because the woman who stole me when I was a child got blood all over my clothes when she came to my room after she killed my father in a knife fight. I've got her knife here in my garter. I was meaning to steal a child for myself, but I missed the chance and I couldn't stand the disappointment, so I got a job cleaning in a hotel. You can't say dang or go to movies, and look who you got sitting next to you hour after hour. Look who you been offering half of your spam sandwich. She was laughing and the woman glanced at her. So she said, 'You can try bringing me to Jesus if you want to. Might pass the time.'
>
> The woman was quiet for a while. The windshield wipers were groaning and the rain was pounding the glass. She said, 'I'd better not. I'd better be trying to see the road.' She said, 'You've got to come to it in the right frame of mind. Otherwise it's just talking for the sake of talk. Passing the time. I might be making excuses here. Lord forgive me if I am. But you strike me as a woman with a lot of bitterness in her soul. I don't mean any offense. I might just make things worse.'
>
> Lila said, 'I doubt you could do that.'[30]

She imagines continuing: 'I was bad at whoring …' Which would be true, since she could never disguise her distaste for the clients. But, again, she thinks better of it.[31]

199

A truck driver gives her another lift on from where the woman drops her. And he, in turn, drops her just outside Gilead.

She spots a derelict shack, across some fields, by the riverside. And thinks, why not pause here for a while? Then, of a Sunday morning, exploring the town, she's surprised by a rainstorm; and seeks shelter in a nearby church. Ames sees her enter, in the middle of his sermon. And here begins their curious love affair. He's thirty years older than she. Yet, he's fascinated by her strangeness, to him; and by her bewilderment. As she, for her part, is reciprocally fascinated by his strangeness, to her; and by his kindness. His presence in the town becomes a reason for delaying her departure. Where else does she have to go, anyway? He discreetly encourages the congregation to employ her for odd jobs, and to sort out second-hand clothes for her. She takes to working in his neglected garden; then, also, to tending the Ames family graves in the cemetery. If she comes to church, she makes sure that she's last in and first out. But, after a while, she starts to consider being baptised. She quickly gives up on the regular baptism preparation classes: anxious lest she expose her ignorance. Never mind, though! Meeting her in the street one day he promises, if she'd like it, to baptise her even so. He thanks her for her work in the cemetery: 'I wish there were some way I could repay you.' And then –

> she heard herself say, 'You ought to marry me.' He stopped still, and she hurried away, to the other side of the road, the flush of shame and anger so hot in her that this time surely she could not go on living. When he caught up with her, when he touched her sleeve, she could not look at him.
>
> 'Yes,' he said, 'You're right. I will.'[32]

So, it comes to pass. He baptises her alone, by the river bank, without the embarrassment of any crowd. After which, Boughton marries them, in the parlour of his house.

Nevertheless, the underlying problem remains: 'I just can't trust you, at all,' she says to him, early on in their relationship.

He said, 'Is there anything I can do about that?'
And she said, 'Nothing I can think of. I don't trust nobody.'
He said, 'No wonder you're tired.'
She thought, That's a fact.[33]

Nothing in her previous life has prepared for any sort of serious adult commitment to another person. Her immediate reaction when Ames agrees to marry her is to start planning her departure: now she really must be off, she thinks – to California, or somewhere – could be anywhere. Even after the marriage has actually taken place, she's all the time expecting him to change his mind, and reject her. He gives no sign, whatever, of doing so. Nonetheless, she keeps day-dreaming, plotting her exit. He knows that she's doing so; but also recognises that there's really nothing he can say, or do, to put her mind, once and for all, at rest. Even after she has become pregnant, it turns out that she still has a tidy sum of money set aside, hidden, enough at any rate for a long-distance bus fare out of town.

Again, as with Jack, the deep-seated ambivalence of her attitude towards Ames largely derives from his professional role. The church people evidently respect him enough to accept his eccentric marriage, without too many eyebrows raised. But still she says, 'I hate it when they look at me.'[34] She appreciates the usefulness of what, at his prompting, they cheerfully do for her. Yet, she can't bear to be in receipt of charity; hates it, with a passion. Doane, the itinerant gang-leader of her childhood, had also been a proud man, always scathing in his contempt for churches: those folk just want your money, he'd say. And Doll, likewise, had never had anything but mockery for the respectable world at large.

Doll used to say, 'No cussing!' and they would laugh because of all the things they knew and nobody else did. But if you're just a stranger to everybody on earth, then that's what you are and there's no end to it. You don't know the words to say ...[35]

Lila is anxious lest her being baptised is, after all, an implicit betrayal of Doll, and of 'Doane's people' generally. For, what do the people who don't 'cuss' truly think of those who do? Are they, perhaps, of the opinion that those who 'cuss' are liable to be damned? Ames's friend Boughton is distinctly less wary of pious self-righteousness than Ames himself is; some of the things that Boughton, especially, lets slip do trouble her. And so, a little while after Ames has baptised her, she goes back down to the river with the idea of, so to speak, washing the baptism off. She reads biblical texts – choosing at random *Ezekiel* and *Job* – with the most vivid intensity. The words glow for her, charged somehow with the strangeness of this lonely man's love, and thereby rendered, authentically, 'good news to the poor'. But how does that intensity relate to the regular life of his congregation – as a gathering, merely, of good people who don't 'cuss'?

Like Jack, in other words, she recoils from what herd-morality, at work within respectable congregations, tends to make of the pastor's role.

~

In *Isaiah* 52:13 – 53:12, and in the gospel portrait of Jesus, the two personas of sin-'bearer' and vindicated outcast are united in a single figure. Robinson's novels split them apart: depicting Ames as sin-'bearing' pastor, Jack and Lila as (in the reader's eyes) vindicated outcasts. It's, essentially, by virtue of this refraction that these novels become such rich studies in ambiguity: as Ames's professional role as pastor both helps and hinders in bridging the gap here.

As for the *Amos* impulse, on the other hand: Jack's sister Glory certainly has a sardonic view of church life in her home town:

> Granting the many perils of spiritual complacency, and her father did grant them as often as Pharisees figured in the text, complacency was consistent with the customs and manners of Presbyterian Gilead and was therefore assumed to be justified in every case. Christian charity demanded no less, after all. Among the denominations of Gilead, charity on this point was

not granted by all and to all in principle, but in practice good manners were usually adhered to, and in general the right to complacency was conceded on every side.[36]

In other words, the usual decorum of herd-morality, unremarkably, prevails.

Nevertheless, the politics of race, in particular, continue to be a haunting off-stage presence. Gilead, after all, had been founded in the mid-nineteenth century by Abolitionists from New England, like Ames's grandfather, intent not least on helping runaway slaves from over in Missouri escape. Jack remembers, in his childhood, there still being a substantial black community in the town. But the blacks had always worshipped in a separate church of their own. And then, one day, there had been an arson attack on that building. This was one of the factors prompting Ames's grandfather to leave, as he did, in disgust. The fire had been swiftly extinguished, with little actual damage done, physically. Yet, over the following years the black folk had, one after another, drifted away, to Chicago and elsewhere; until none remained.

In 1956, when Jack comes home, the news media are filled with stories of racial tension. The Montgomery Bus Boycott is in full swing. There's major rioting at the University of Alabama in Tuscaloosa, as the first black student is enrolled, then forced out again. And the lynching of Emmett Till remains recent news. One day Glory finds Jack standing on the pavement, transfixed, watching the television in a shop window: news reports from Montgomery. She buys the television, for him. Over the following days he watches events there unfold, obsessively. To his father's dismay, he's moved to 'cuss': 'Jesus Christ!'

The old man doesn't share Jack's agitated fury at the spectacle of white racism, at all. On the contrary, he blames the blacks, squarely, for all the trouble: even though the protests in themselves are nonviolent, they provoke violence, he remarks; and, whilst the police may seem brutal, the bottom line is, the law must be enforced.[37] 'So much bad blood,' he says. 'I think we had all better just keep to ourselves.'[38] Ames, not least because he honours his grandfather's memory, naturally sides with Jack here.[39] But Boughton is a man altogether more at ease in the pastor-role. On the one hand, his piety is exemplary: such fluency in extempore prayer! On the other hand – the unfortunate flip side of such piety – his moral outlook is, in effect, simply swallowed up into what is no doubt the natural consensus of those whose pastor he has been.

And how then can Jack ever confide in him? For, as Jack finally does manage to tell Ames, the crucial secret behind his present troubles is that he's in love with a black woman, Della; and has a son by her. (This is the story recounted in *Jack*). She herself is the daughter of a pastor, who deeply disapproves of the relationship. And as Jack's affairs have gone from bad to worse, Della has been compelled, for their son's sake, to return to her father's care. Jack writes letter after letter to her, without reply – until eventually a batch comes back, unopened, and marked 'Return to Sender'. This is what triggers the final crisis of his stay in Gilead.

Jack had come 'home' – it turns out – half-wondering if it would be possible to begin a new life there, with Della. And might not Ames perform the marriage formalities that had been impossible under the anti-miscegenation laws of Missouri, where he'd first met her?[40] Indeed, he fantasises about a wedding in the dead of night – a wild dream! More soberly, however, he asks Ames whether Gilead might be ready to accept them, a white man and a black woman, as a couple.

In all honesty, Ames has to admit he is unsure. And the following day, after further reflecting on that question, Ames writes in his journal:

> I woke up this morning thinking this town might as well be standing on the floor of hell for all the truth there is in it, and the fault is mine as much as anyone's.

He recalls all the disasters to have befallen America in general, and Gilead in particular, during his lifetime: the wars, the influenza pandemic, the droughts and the Depression. A preacher, he remarks, is properly a prophet, someone called to 'find meaning in trouble'; converting trauma into fresh intensities of moral commitment. That's what the Old Testament prophets did; but, sadly, not – to any great effect – the preachers of modern America, or of Gilead.

What did all that suffering mean? The trouble is,

> we didn't ask the question, so the question was just taken away from us. We became like the people without the Law, people who didn't know their right hand from their left. Just stranded here.[41]

Certainly, there's a sort of excess in the classic writings of the prophet Amos, and his successors: an excessive rage, licensed by the notion that God wanted to *punish* his people. Again, this excess is just what prompts the corrective represented by the Suffering Servant, in *Isaiah* 52:13 – 53:12; as that text proposes a conception of sainthood involving absolute cancellation of even the most righteous vindictiveness. But the 'meaning', as Ames puts it, to be 'found in trouble' doesn't have to be conceived in punitive terms. *At its core, it's simply the gift of a moral 'question'.* That's to say: an all-questioning spirit. John Ames I had once represented that gift – with *Amos*-like excess – as a living reality in Gilead. His grandson grieves for the loss of it.

Two days after Jack has left, without a forwarding address, Della actually arrives in Gilead, with their young son; a reluctant sister has driven them all the way from Memphis. Disappointed not to find Jack, she only has time for the briefest of conversations with Glory: "We have to get back down to Missouri before dark," she says. "Especially the way things are now. We have a place to stay down there." Glory observes how she carries herself 'with the tense poise of a woman who felt she was being watched, wondered about.' To melancholy Glory, a native of the place, this is 'worn, modest, countrified Gilead, Gilead of the sunflowers.' To Della, the black outsider, however it's clearly 'a foreign and a hostile country.'[42] In the poignancy of this scene all the charm, for us, of Gilead's dreamy, backwater homeliness simply dissolves.

1. *Gilead* (London: Virago, 2005); *Home* (London: Virago, 2008); *Lila* (London: Virago, 2014).

2. *Gilead*, p. 52.

3. Ibid. pp. 44—45; and c.f. p. 36.

4. Ibid. pp. 92—93.

5. See Ibid. pp. 119—25.

6. Ibid. p. 200.

7. Ibid. p. 125.

8. Ibid. p. 100.

9. Ibid. pp. 101, 110, 114.

10. Ibid. pp. 56—57.

11. Ibid. pp. 36—39, 199. The Boughtons remember him once visiting their church for a service, and when the collection plate came round, he emptied it into his hat: Ibid. p. 259.

12. So Jack Boughton for instance discovers, in conversation with his black fiancé Della's father, the AME bishop, in Memphis: Ibid. p. 259.

13. Ibid., pp. 200—01.

14. Ibid. p. 13.

15. Ibid., pp. 95—96.

16. Ibid. p. 97.

17. Ibid. pp. 7—8.

18. *Jack* (New York: Farrar, Straus and Giroux 2020).

19. *Gilead*, p. 82.

20. Ibid. p. 206.

21. *Home*, p. 289.

22. Ibid. pp. 192—3; alluding to *John* 12:2. And c.f. also p. 250.

23. Ibid. p. 81.

24. Ibid. p. 92. Also, p. 132: 'When he looks at me he still sees a scoundrel. The other day I had the terrible feeling that he wasn't quite wrong. So I began to be charming, you know. A little oily ... I called him Papa. He deserved it, too. He hadn't even mentioned to the wife that my father had honoured him with a namesake. Can you imagine?' C.f. *Gilead*, pp. 91—4: the same encounter from Ames's point of view.

25. *Home*, p. 215.

26. *Gilead*, pp. 146—50.

27. Ibid. p. 148: quoting *Matthew* 18:6; *Luke* 17:2.

28. There's a basic theological difference on this score between Ames and Boughton. Glory remembers countless arguments over the years: 'her father asserting the perfect sufficiency of grace with something like ferocity, while Ames maintained, with a mildness his friend found irksome, that the gravity of sin could not be gainsaid.' *Home*, pp. 230—31. Ames's sermon on Hagar and Ishmael is certainly clumsy. But Boughton's line by contrast appears, in actual practice, to be a theological vindication of generalised passive aggression!

29. *Gilead*, p. 264; *Home*, pp. 321—22.

30. *Lila*, p. 216.

31. Ibid. p. 217.

32. Ibid. pp. 80—81.

33. Ibid. p. 58.

34. Ibid. p. 86.

35. Ibid. p. 79.

36. *Home*, p. 116.

37. Ibid. pp. 99—104, 162—4, 213—4.

38. Ibid. p. 153.

39. Ibid. p. 227.

40. Missouri was one of sixteen states that continued to have such laws in force right up until 1967; as was Tennessee, where Della's family lived.

41. *Gilead*, pp. 266—67.

42. *Home*, pp. 332—9.

E.

Paradoxical Martyrs

CHAPTER FOURTEEN

Beyond the Sacralisation of Truth-as-Correctness

The first saints to be honoured by the Christian Church were naturally enough its martyrs, under the pagan Roman Empire; from Saint Stephen onwards (*Acts of the Apostles* 6:8 – 8:3). For here was sublime virtue in its most dramatic expression; most directly aligned with the example of the Saviour himself. Indeed, long after the conversion to Christianity of the Emperor Constantine in the early fourth century – and the consequent ending of that first era of persecution – Christian sainthood continued to be pre-eminently associated with martyrdom. So there, in the later fourth century Latin hymn the *Te Deum*, stands 'the noble army of martyrs': alongside 'the glorious company of the apostles' and 'the goodly fellowship of the prophets'. And, even where properly historic narratives were lacking, it was in any case presumed that all of the apostles had themselves ended up as martyrs.

Not all of those who die for their faith, however, can exactly be called 'saints'.

For, after all, Jihadi suicide bombers are also called 'martyrs' by those who admire them! *Their* courage, however, is surely an altogether debased form of the 'sublimity of the hero-as-holy-warrior', as I've been using the term; as opposed to the authentic 'sublimity of the saint'.

Or, consider that massive sixteenth-century work, *Foxe's Book of Martyrs* (more properly known as *The Actes and Monuments*).[1]

Here's a book primarily glorifying one set of martyrs, victims of the old Roman Catholic regime in England; serving however as propaganda for a later regime – that of the Elizabethan Anglican Church – which was now itself engaged in the savage persecution of another set of martyrs, English Roman Catholics.[2] The sheer courage shown by those who died, on both sides, was no doubt in many instances quite remarkable. But, in this case as well, it appears to have been a courage belonging only to the 'sublimity of the hero-as-holy-warrior', dressed up in zealot-ideology.

True Christ-like martyrdom is surely quite another matter. For might one not say that Christ died upholding an ideal of perfect *truth-as-openness*; which is, in fact, the polar opposite to rigid zealotry, or fanaticism, dedicated to some notion of supposedly sacred *truth-as-correctness*?

Christ represents a vivid renewal of the *Amos* impulse: a sublime openness, in other words, towards the plight of the poor and the oppressed, purely and simply as such. Yet, equally, this is the *Amos* impulse modified by approximation to the Isaianic archetype of the Suffering Servant: representing a sublime openness, also, towards all and sundry, even including one's worst enemies; a non-resentful 'bearing' of their sins. There can, in principle, be no greater *moral* threat to tyranny as such than the twofold openness of spirit here. Let me repeat: Christ's crucifixion represents the natural reaction of tyranny, here at its most flamboyant, to that threat. And what's the point of Christ's Resurrection? It's God's poetic vindication of the openness he represents. In it, we're shown the triumph of that openness – in the perspective of eternity – over the very worst that tyranny can do.

And yet, evangelistic impatience is as old, in Christian tradition, as what it tends to distort; forever re-introducing closed-mindedness where Christ stands for openness, because closed-mindedness is what appeals to the herd, the gang and the mob. Whereas gospel truth is a pre-emptive outpouring of unconditional divine love, evangelistic impatience is, on the contrary, a project of expansive control: the building, ultimately, of a religious empire. And such a project involves nothing less than a whole other *species* of truth-claim.

Thus, in general: gospel truth is surely, through and through, a poetic expression of the proper claims of truth-as-openness. That's to say: the highest truth-ideal governing (neuro-typically) the right hemisphere of the brain. But the 'truth' to which evangelistic impatience lays claim is no longer a pure expression of truth-as-openness. On the contrary: what's sacralised here, in general, is just a form of purported moral, metaphysical and historiographical truth-as-correctness; the highest ideal of the *properly subordinate* left hemisphere! It's an idolatry of supposedly correct propositions, occluding the authentically higher truth which transcends all propositions. Occluding that higher species of truth which can never be *captured* in 'correct' formulations, *alone*; but always depends on the manner of their *appropriation*.[3]

Borrowing the terminology of Martin Buber, one might well say that, whereas the highest truth-ideal of the right hemisphere, generally, involves the skills designated by 'the primary word *I-Thou*', the *only* truth-ideal within the specialist scope of the left hemisphere involves the skill-set designated by 'the primary word *I-It*'.[4] So 'the primary word *I-Thou*' is Buber's name for the truth that consists in sheer openness towards the other person, whoever that other may be. On the other hand, 'the primary word *I-It*' includes everything involved in the basic, purely technical mastering of language; in the systematic organising of concepts, developing logical arguments; in the accurate mapping and analysis of the world; in the consistent application of law; in the shrewd exploitation of useful resources as such: in short, all the various skills of control. We need to grasp the world correctly, in analytical thought, if we're to control it. And yes, all truth, including authentic truth-as-correctness, is of God. But what we call 'original sin' – in the deepest sense – is surely nothing other than the ineradicable tendency of the associated will-to-control, again and again, to over-reach its God-given bounds: thereby reifying the '*Thou*'; treating the '*Thou*' as just another '*It*'; effectively nullifying the proper truth-claims of 'the primary word *I-Thou*'.

Indeed: to understand the nature of a thing correctly is to be, so far as possible, enabled to control that thing; to understand the nature of a situation correctly is to be, so far as possible, enabled to manage that situation; to understand the animal nature of other people correctly is to be, so far as possible, enabled to manipulate them. But to be *open* to the other person is, quite simply, to abandon all manipulative ambition. It's pure '*I-Thou*' purged of any tincture of '*I-It*'.

And this purity is just what's properly *sacred*. For true Christian faith, Christ surely dies as a representative of all martyrs engaged in resistance to the universal over-reach of the 'fallen' will-to-control; participants in the perennial struggle to defend truth-as-openness. Christ dies to set us free – from the controlled, and controlling, banality of mere herd morality at one level; from manipulative zealotry and fanaticism, the ethos of the sacralised gang, prodding mobs into action, at another.

Yet, the trouble is, Christian evangelistic impatience remoulds faith into a discipline by which one's saved precisely by being subjected to control: whether it be according to a 'Christian' version of ordinary herd morality, or according to a 'Christian' form of zealotry. Because 'faith' misunderstood in terms of control is always so much easier to assimilate, so much more immediately attractive therefore to the majority of folk, so much more suited to propagandistic dissemination.

I'm a particular admirer of the philosophy of Hegel: not least because of the pioneering way in which he begins systematically to distinguish between the two primordial species of truth-claim involved here. Thus, what I'm calling 'truth-as-openness' Hegel calls the work of *Geist*, or Spirit. And what I'm calling 'truth-as-correctness' he calls the work of *Verstand*, or (technical) Understanding.[5] In Hegelian terms: evangelistic impatience reduces faith to a mere counterfeit simulacrum of its real truth, a front for what Hegel calls the 'Unhappy Consciousness'.[6] In Hegel's lexicon, the 'Unhappy Consciousness' is a general term for *Geist* blocked by the hubris, the arrogant ideological self-assertion, of dogmatic *Verstand*. Note: this mentality is by no means necessarily unhappy at the conscious level. It's *objectively* unhappy, in the sense of being pitiable. But, if the ideological correctness in

214

question demands a show of joyful assent, well then, the 'Unhappy Consciousness' grins, whoops and applauds. *Subjectively*, it rejoices. In fact, it can only persist insofar as it remains unconscious of its own true objective condition. In Hegel's day, the conceptual distinction between 'the conscious' and the 'sub-conscious' hadn't yet become commonplace. But (considered as a stable condition) the 'unhappiness' of the 'Unhappy Consciousness' is, after all, necessarily *sub*-conscious. As soon as it starts to become conscious of its unhappiness, the process of healing has begun.

Basically, the 'Unhappy Consciousness' is the self-defeating state of inner servitude underlying *any* sort of rigidified closed-mindedness. It isn't just a Christian phenomenon – although Hegel primarily illustrates the concept with allusions to Christianity, for the simple reason that he himself is a Christian thinker. But it may appear in all kinds of self-expression. It's a disease which threatens every sort of religious culture, and every sort of irreligious ideology, alike. However, there clearly is a particular risk inherent in biblical/qur'anic monotheism, where the internalised will-to-control shaping the 'Unhappy Consciousness' is projected onto the tremendous figure of the misconceived, all-controlling Lord God. Everything in biblical/Qur'anic tradition is, as a result, rendered profoundly liable to ambiguity, a radical truth-potential intertwining with a no less radical falsehood-potential; as, specifically in the Christian context for example, Christ the revelation of perfect truth-as-openness more or less disappears, in actual practice, to be supplanted by 'Christ' the projection of church-ideological 'truth'-as-correctness. On the surface, the propositional belief-content of faith may remain unchanged. Yet, deeper down, its actual meaning has been hollowed out. It has gone rotten, within.

And hence, then, the need for philosophical theology: the essential calling of which, in my view, is none other than to disambiguate the whole tradition along these lines. *But that need is most urgent of all when it comes to martyrdom: inasmuch as the inner value of one and the same outward act of ultimate self-sacrifice may, in different cases, actually be quite opposite. So, on the one hand, there's* the Christ-like martyr, whose motivation is the *Amos* impulse modified by approximation to the Isaianic archetype. But, on the other hand, there's the fanatical martyr, the zealot, whose courage is stoked, *instead*, theoretically by notions of an eternal reward in heaven, but more effectively perhaps by the imagined prospect of posthumous glory on earth, amongst their co-religionists. This prospect may well be further enhanced by apocalyptic dreams of eventual vengeance; as in *Revelation* 6:10, and passim. Such dreams are quite incompatible with the Isaianic archetype!

The Church's official canonisation procedures have never focussed in any systematic fashion on the basic difference between these two opposing types of motivation. However, novels can. It's clear that they have great potential for going deeper into the matter: probing what it *truly* means to keep faith with the ideal demands of truth-as-openness *in extremis*.

~

So, for example, one type of narrative serving this purpose shows us a martyr willingly surrendering their life in obedience to the most intransigent demands of truth-as-openness – inasmuch as they do what they do for sheer love of an oppressed body of people; a martyr however who, quite clearly, cannot be motivated by any dream of posthumous glory, due to the all too obvious 'incorrectness' of their behaviour, according to the Church's official criteria, in other respects.

Here, I want to consider two such novels: *The Devil's Advocate* by Morris West, and Graham Greene's *The Power and the Glory*.

And, then, another variant: Shusaku Endo's *Silence*, in which we're shown a central character who sincerely yearns for glorious martyrdom, yet who's placed by his captors in a situation where steadfast continuing resistance actually becomes the egoistic option, tragically to be renounced for reasons of conscience, in view of the damage liable to ensue for others. Thus, the central character of Endo's narrative is guilty, in the end, of what, according to the official criteria, is the ultimate theological 'incorrectness' – namely, outright (apparent) apostasy. But that very 'incorrectness', *itself*, is absolutely motivated in this case by the intransigent demands of truth-as-openness; sheer love of the oppressed!

West, Greene and Endo are all Roman Catholic novelists; imaginatively trampolining, as it were, from the rules that govern the Vatican's bureaucratic governance of saint-cults.

---

1. John Foxe's grand survey of church history as a whole, viewed from a militantly Protestant point of view; with a particular emphasis on persecutions generally, from pagan Rome to the reign of Queen Mary in England. The first edition was published in 1563; the second, much revised and expanded, in 1570; the fourth, the most imposing, in 1583. This fourth edition was almost four times the length of the Bible!

2. In 1571 it was ordered that *The Actes and Monuments* should be chained up next to the English-language Bible in all cathedrals, and also major churches. During Elizabeth's reign, it wasn't unusual for selected passages to be read from the pulpit, just as if it were an extension of Holy Scripture.

3. See Iain McGilchrist, *The Master and his Emissary: The Divided Brain and the Making of the Modern World* (New Haven and London: Yale University Press, 2009); *The Matter with Things: Our Brains, Our Delusions, and the Unmaking of the World* 2 Vols. (London: Perspectiva Press, 2021).

4. Martin Buber, *I and Thou* (1923), translated by Walter Kaufmann (New York: Charles Scribner's Sons, 1970).

5. Hegel himself refers to the ultimate goal of *Verstand*, the ideal representation of the world in concepts, as the 'Absolute Idea'. He refers to the ultimate goal of *Geist* as 'Absolute Knowing'. But what is it that 'Absolute Knowing' absolutely knows? One might well say: it knows what it means, in practice, to acknowledge the supreme sacredness of 'truth-as-openness', in every relevant area of thought. So it transcends the domain of the 'Absolute Idea'. It's an ideal mode, not of re-presentation, but of presence.

6. Hegel, *Phenomenology of Spirit*, translated (a) by Michael Inwood (Oxford University Press, 2018); (b) by Terry Pinkard (Cambridge University

Press, 2018); paragraphs 206—30. I've discussed this concept of Hegel's in various places: *Hegel's Political Theology* (Cambridge University Press, 1991); *Hegel and Religious Faith* (London and New York: T. & T. Clark, 2011); *A Neo-Hegelian Theology: The God of Greatest Hospitality* (Farnham: Ashgate, 2014); *Hegel versus 'Inter-Faith Dialogue: A General Theory of True Xenophilia* (Cambridge University Press, 2015).

CHAPTER FIFTEEN

Morris West:
The Devil's Advocate

Morris West's novel *The Devil's Advocate* was right from the outset a best-seller; and largely established West's reputation.[1] I think it's an ingenious, rather than a great novel; an efficiently, rather than a brilliantly written one. But it plays upon the glamour, the mystique of the Vatican system. And it has, at its core, the natural attraction of a nagging puzzle; as in a detective novel. Except that here – in place of the detective – we have an inquisitor; who isn't attempting to solve a crime, but instead to investigate an enigmatic claim to sainthood, with regard to a man who has died some fifteen years earlier.

West was a devout Catholic; who however had his disagreements with the church institution. An Australian, he had been educated by the Christian Brothers; and at the age of fourteen entered a Christian Brothers Seminary; spending twelve years there, before finally deciding that that life was not for him. After the breakdown of his first marriage, on the other hand, he remarried, in defiance of canon law; and was then excluded from communion, a penalty with which he strongly disagreed.

The resultant ambivalence in his attitude to his church clearly does much to energise his portrayal of an irregular saint, in this work.

∾

After a brief beginning in Rome, most of the story is set in rural, desperately impoverished, late 1950s Calabria. Monsignor Blaise Meredith is an English priest employed by the Sacred Congregation of Rites. He's assigned to examine the burgeoning local cult of an alleged saint known by the name of 'Giacomo Nerone', there. Is this, or is it not, the sort of thing that Rome ought officially to endorse?

The Roman canonisation system has evolved over approximately a millennium.[2] The first clearly attested case of a Pope officially canonising someone is John XV's canonisation of Ulrich of Augsburg in 993.[3]

In 1170, Pope Alexander III wrote to King Canute of Sweden, insisting on the principle that no one in future should be venerated as a saint without authorisation from the Roman Church; and in the Decretals of Pope Gregory IX in 1234 this was then formally established as canon law. A bureaucratic regime systematically dealing with the causes of saints, along with other liturgical matters, the Sacred Congregation of Rites was created in 1588 by Pope Sixtus V. This regime gave a primary role to the 'Promoter of the Faith' ('Promotor Fidei'), also more informally called the 'Devil's Advocate' ('Advocatus Diaboli'), as a sort of investigating magistrate, charged with close examination of possible objections to canonisation in each particular case.[4] The classic work setting out the rules according to which the Devil's Advocate ought to operate was written by Cardinal Prospero Lambertini, who had filled the role for some twenty years before becoming Pope Benedict XIV in 1740.[5]

In West's novel, Monsignor Meredith is delegated to draft a preliminary report, in fulfilment of these rules. He's the Devil's Advocate of the title.

The other *dramatis personae* include, first, other clergy. Cardinal Marotta, the Prefect of the Congregation of Rites, is the one who selects Meredith for this job – Marotta is a possible future pope; although opponents would argue that, although clever enough, he lacks holiness. Aurelio, the local bishop, befriends Meredith when he arrives in Calabria, and briefs him. It's Bishop Aurelio who has requested the investigation; very much in the hope of a swift decision allowing him to close the burgeoning cult of 'Giacomo Nerone' down. For the Bishop is a northerner, keen to invest in sensible agricultural and social welfare projects, rather than a new pilgrimage church and hostel. Also, there's the village priest, Father Anselmo. But he's little help; as he's an aged and demoralised alcoholic who, to the bishop's dismay, shares a bed with his housekeeper.

Indeed, it isn't the clergy who are pressing the cause of this supposed saint. Rather, it's the peasants. There are two villages in question: Gemello Minore, 'little twin', and Gemello Maggiore, 'big twin'; together, Gemelli dei Monti, 'twins-of-the-hills'. It was in Gemello Minore that 'Giacomo Nerone' had actually lived, albeit for no more than ten months, at the end of the Second World War; and where he'd been martyred, shot by Communist partisans. However, it's the mayor of Gemello Maggiore who's the prime mover in pressing for his beatification.

A crucial witness is the local doctor, Aldo Meyer: a Jew from the north originally exiled to Gemello Minore by the Fascists (like Carlo Levi in real life, although, unlike Carlo Levi, he has opted to remain after the War).[6] He'd been a particular friend of 'Nerone'. And then, as well, there are two English expats, who – in addition to the English Devil's Advocate and as it turns out the, in actual fact, English 'saint' – help the novel connect with its original Anglophone readership. One is the somewhat pathetic figure of the Contessa; a middle-aged widow, resident in Gemelli dei Monte's one big house. The other is a guest of hers, a dilettante artist called Nicholas Black, who's also a homosexual predator, especially interested in the adolescent Paolo Sanduzzi.

It was Paolo Sanduzzi's mother, Nina, who'd originally given the 'saint', 'Giacomo Nerone', shelter, when he first arrived in the village: a man in his early thirties, gravely wounded and on the run, at the end of August 1943. That 'Nerone' spoke their language so well – albeit with, to the Calabrians, a curious, hard to place, northern accent – allowed him to pass amongst the villagers for an Italian. But he told no one at the time where he really came from.

He and Nina soon became lovers, and Paolo is in fact the 'saint's' son.

It had also quickly become apparent that this outsider had a natural flair for leadership. So, he began selflessly assisting whoever was in need amongst the villagers, and organising them: building up communal reserves of food; encouraging co-operative ventures, in preparation for any trouble to come. When, not long after his arrival, the retreating Germans arrived, it was in fact he who negotiated with them; successfully managing to deflect the potential threat that they represented to the village. Meanwhile, early in 1944, he'd left Nina's house and gone to live in a little hut that he'd built for himself. There he spent hours in prayer.

Then – the Germans having departed – the Communist partisans arrived. Dr Meyer joined them; and still remains deeply conflicted about what ensued. They ordered 'Nerone' to leave. He, however, refused. In late June 1944, they arrested him; summarily tried him, on a trumped-up charge of having collaborated with the Germans; and executed him.

~

Of course, it's clear what the mayor of Gemello Maggiore's motivation is in promoting the cause of 'Giacomo Nerone'. He's thinking of the potential economic benefits deriving from an influx of pilgrims to his village. But, underlying this, one can well see what makes 'Nerone' a plausible candidate for veneration from the peasants' point of view. For, doesn't he embody just the sort of religiously framed *leadership* that they ideally look for, and all too seldom actually receive, from the official church authorities?

On the other hand, there's plainly no way that the Sacred Congregation of Rites, which Monsignor Meredith represents, can endorse this 'saint'. The institutional Church works, in such matters, according to quite different criteria from those that determine the peasants' judgement. Granted, there might be some crude electoral benefit for the Christian Democratic Party in celebrating the memory of a devout Catholic so recently martyred by the

Communists. Catholic propaganda versus Marxist propaganda: the Communists remain, at this point, the Christian Democrats' chief electoral rivals in Calabria. Nor is there a lack of supposed miracles; a key factor for the Devil's Advocate to consider. One in particular strikes Meredith as certainly quite remarkable. When Paolo Sanduzzi was born, he was blind – his mother Nina had contracted rubella during the pregnancy. But 'Nerone', in his last days, assured her that the infant would be cured. And so it had then turned out – not least, to the very great surprise of the atheistic Dr Meyer.

Yet, how can the church authorities consider beatifying a man like 'Nerone' who, having fathered a child out of wedlock, did nothing then to regularise his relationship with the child's mother? Naturally, Meredith asks Nina about this. She replies that 'Nerone' would no doubt have married her had she wanted it. Only, the whole world was in chaos. He was very uncertain of his own future; and, for his part, didn't want to bind her – suppose he were to disappear, or be incarcerated – with the result that she'd then be prevented from finding another husband.

And still more serious than this casual attitude towards the sacrament of marriage is the fact that he was, in reality, a deserter from the British army. He'd kept this a secret, after his arrival in the village, for several months. But eventually, in January, he did confide in Dr. Meyer how it had happened. An officer, he'd been involved in the final assault on Messina; the Fascists' and Nazis' last stand in Sicily. A sniper was holding his men back, and had hit one of them. So, he shouted out a warning to surrender; and, when that was ignored, tossed in a grenade. It turned out that the sniper had been an old fisherman; gruesomely killed there, by the explosion, along with a woman and a nursing child. For 'Nerone' (we never do learn his English name) this was a decisive moment of truth. He knew that he could no longer continue.

The Roman Catholic Church however, as a global evangelistic enterprise, has no interest in unnecessarily antagonising military authorities, in general. How can it afford to recognise as a saint someone who was a deserter; especially from an army engaged in –

if ever any was – such a just war? The peasant devotees of 'Nerone' aren't concerned with this. But the Devil's Advocate has to be.

Nevertheless, there remains a final twist. The novel begins with Meredith being informed, by a surgeon, that he has inoperable cancer, and will be dead within six months or a year. This expedition to Calabria is the last action of his life; at the end of the novel, he dies. Having always hitherto been a somewhat unbending ecclesiastical functionary, simply focussed on following proper procedure, as he approaches death he begins to take a larger view of things. In his official role, he acknowledges the extreme improbability of 'Nerone's' cause being successful, in Rome. Yet, writing to Bishop Aurelio, he remarks that the judicial issue as such, according to canon law, now seems to him, after all, to be quite insignificant, beside the actual *human reality* of the matter. On the evidence of those who knew 'Nerone', plus what little survives of the man's writing, he's convinced that the alleged saint truly was a man of inspiring faith, who'd moreover died a genuine martyr's death. The system that Meredith serves lays down the official criteria not only for the liturgical veneration of saints; but also, in effect, for the literature of conventional hagiography. However, the whole theological point of this novel, as it shows the Roman system at work, is to gesture beyond the basic limitations intrinsic to that literature. So, in general, it depicts regular church order essentially as a doomed attempt to constrain, and tame, the boundless actual sheer freedom of the divine.

---

1. First published, in London, by William Heinemann Ltd., in 1959.

2. For the earlier background: see Peter Brown, *The Cult of the Saints: Its Rise and Function in Latin Christianity* (University of Chicago Press,1980.)

3. There's some evidence to suggest that Pope Leo III had already canonised St Swibert in 804, but this is uncertain.

4. The actual phrase 'Advocatus Diaboli' had first appeared in 1524, with reference to the case of St. Lawrence Justinian (1381—1456).

5. The five volumes of his *De Servorum Dei beatificatione et de Beatorum canonizatione* (1734—38) contain an exhaustive study of precedents.

6. Carlo Levi was the author of a celebrated memoir, first published in 1945: *Christ Stopped at Eboli: The Story of a Year*. English translation by Frances Fenaye (New York: Farrar, Straus and Giroux, 2006).

CHAPTER SIXTEEN

Graham Greene:
The Power and the Glory

A s for Graham Greene's thematically comparable – albeit tonally very different – novel *The Power and the Glory*: here, in Part One, Chapters 2 and 4, and again at the very end of the book, a mother appears, reading to her children from a work of hagiography, a celebration of contemporary martyrs. She has no other role to play in the narrative. But she's introduced simply as a representative devotee of pious kitsch, to highlight the bitter polemic contrast Greene intends, between the idealised martyr-stories that she so loves and the not at all idealised martyr-story he himself is telling.[1]

The Power and the Glory is set in Mexico, specifically the state of Tabasco, during the 1930s.

Mexican governments had by that time been embattled with the Church, harassing and persecuting it on and off, for a century or so. The first major eruption of militant governmental anticlericalism had occurred in 1833—34; under the leadership of the then Vice-President, Valentín Gómez Farías. Subsequently, there'd been a more sustained period of such anticlerical 'Reform' beginning in 1855. This was largely associated with the leadership of Benito Juárez. President from 1858 until his death in 1872, Juárez had to deal with two major challenges to his power: the Catholic rebellion leading to the 'Reform War' of 1857—1860, and the French-sponsored attempt to establish a pro-Catholic regime under the Emperor Maximilian I, from 1861 to 1867. Yet, he prevailed against both. And this second 'Reform' period only really came to an end with the rise to power of Porfirio Díaz in 1876; whose regime, whilst it didn't rescind the anticlerical laws, at any rate ceased for a while to enforce them.

Then, a third phase had begun with the outbreak of the Mexican Revolution in 1910; lasting until the election of the moderate Manuel Ávila Camacho in 1940. The prime mover of militant 'Reform' during this period was the fanatically atheist Plutarco Elías Calles: President from 1924 to 1928, but continuing to be a dominant influence in national politics right up until 1934. Calles's energetic implementation of the anticlerical provisions of the 1917 revolutionary Constitution provoked the 'Cristero War', a Catholic uprising across Central Mexico which lasted from 1926 to 1929. That uprising, however, failed to dislodge him from power.

And one of Calles's most enthusiastic supporters was Tomás Garrido Canabal, the dictatorial ruler of the south-eastern state of Tabasco for most of the period 1919—35.[2]

Stage by stage, the 'Liberal' Reformers had confiscated church property. They'd secularised church schools; restricted and eventually prohibited church charitable work; banned, first, all foreign missions, and then all religious orders without exception. Benito Juarez had begun his work by strictly subordinating the church courts to those of the state. The registration of births, marriages and deaths was taken out of the Church's hands; and the clergy were forbidden to charge fees for any services. The Constitution of 1917, then, had denied the vote to church officials, and had prohibited them from any involvement in politics. According to the Constitution, the clergy weren't allowed to wear clerical garb on the streets; no out of doors religious celebrations were permitted; the ringing of church bells was restricted. And, most provocatively of all, Article 130 required all clergy to be registered by the state authorities. The 'Liberals' were also keen de-centralisers; each state was allowed to determine its own rules for this. In 1925 Garrido Canabal's regime in Tabasco had decreed that all clerics had to be Mexicans by birth, with at least five years residency in the state; that they had to be over forty years of age, with adequate education, no reputation for moral scandal, no involvement past or present in any lawsuit; and – crucially – that they had to be *married*!

There had been approximately 3,000 priests in Mexico prior to the outbreak of the Cristero War in 1926. In 1934 there were just 334 licensed by state governments. At least forty had meanwhile been martyred. Another 2,500 were either in hiding or in exile.[3] Tabasco was one of seventeen states, out of thirty-one, with no licensed priests at all. In Tabasco, moreover, the persecution of religion in every form was greatly enhanced by the presence of Garrido Canabal's personal militia, the Red Shirts; whilst, at the same time, the dictator engaged in an energetic programme of school-building, the new schools being intended not least as propaganda centres for the 'Rationalist' cause. (He also campaigned against alcoholism; banned the wearing of corsets; outlawed the erection of tombstones ...) In 1934, Garrido's patron ex-President Calles was beginning to lose power; and, following a scandal relating to murders committed by members of the Red Shirts, Garrido himself was actually dismissed from office by President Cárdenas; then sought refuge in Costa Rica. Nevertheless, in Tabasco the policy that he'd pioneered went on.

Graham Greene visited Tabasco in the spring of 1938. Here's how he describes his first impressions. He'd sailed, he tells us, for some 'forty-one hours from Veracruz, in an appalling heat' ...

And then round a bend in the river [we arrived at the port of] Frontera ... the Presidencia and a big warehouse and a white blanched street running off between wooden shacks – hairdressers and the inevitable dentists, but no cantinas anywhere, for there is prohibition in Tabasco. No intoxicant is allowed but beer, and that costs a peso a bottle – a ruinous price in Mexico. The lily plants floated by; the river divided round a green island half a mile from shore, and the vultures came flocking out, with little idiot heads and dusty serrated wings, to rustle round the shrouds. There was an election on: the name Bartlett occurred everywhere, and a red star. The soldiers stood in the shade of the Presidencia and watched us edge in against the river bank.

This was Tabasco – Garrido Canabal's isolated swampy state. Garrido – so it was said – had destroyed every church; he had organized a militia of Red Shirts, even leading them across the border into Chiapas in his hunt for a church or a priest. Private houses were searched for religious emblems, and prison was the penalty for possessing them. A young man I met in Mexico City – a family friend of Garrido's – was imprisoned three days for wearing a cross under his shirt; the dictator was incorruptible. A journalist on his way to photograph Tabasco was shot dead in Mexico City airport before he took his seat. Every priest was hunted down or shot, except one who existed for ten years in the forests and the swamps, venturing out only at night; his few letters, I was told, recorded an awful sense of impotence – to live in constant danger and yet be able to do so little, it hardly seemed worth the horror.[4]

It was the thought of this priest that inspired *The Power and the Glory*.

A little further on in Greene's account of his Mexican expedition, he records a conversation with a Mexican doctor of Scottish descent, resident in Villahermosa, the state capital of Tabasco:

> I asked about the priest … who had fled. 'Oh,' he said, 'he was just what we call a whisky priest.' He [the doctor] had taken one of his sons to be baptized, but the priest was drunk and would insist on naming him Brigitta. He was little loss, poor man … but who can judge what terror and hardship and isolation may have excused him in the eyes of God?[5]

Greene's novel tells the tale of an unnamed 'whisky priest' who's martyred. It's by no means a historically accurate account of Padre Macario Fernández Aguado, the actual priest in question. For one thing, Padre Macario hadn't, in fact, been martyred; but when the Tabascan state authorities finally caught him, in 1935, he had simply been deported to Guatemala, instead. On the other hand, he very well might have been martyred – as so many others were. His being spared was just a contingent tactical decision on the part of his pursuers; largely, a matter of fortunate historic timing.

And Greene does pick up on the curious little detail of his wanting to baptise a boy-child with the girl's name of 'Brigitta'. In the novel, 'Brigitta' is the name of the seven-year-old child that the fictional priest himself has fathered.[6]

~

Greene conjures up, in implacable prose, the steamy, rank, dishevelled landscape of Tabasco. And, framed within it: a bitterly realised cast of characters – through the midst of whom the priest, the Suffering Servant, moves, quite *un*-embittered.

The spirit of Garrido Canabal, '*garridismo*', is represented above all by the young lieutenant who is charged with hunting, capturing and executing him. We see the lieutenant on the streets of Villahermosa, his home town:

> There was something of a priest in his intent observant walk – a theologian going back over the errors of the past to destroy them again.

He arrives at his lodging:

> In the light of a candle it looked as comfortless as a prison or a monastic cell.

It's the hour of prayer, evensong:

> Black-beetles exploded against the walls like crackers. More than a dozen crawled over the tiles with injured wings. It infuriated him to think that there were still people in the state who believed in a loving and merciful God. There are mystics

230

who are said to have experienced God directly. He was a mystic, too, and what he had experienced was vacancy – a complete certainty in the existence of a dying, cooling world, of human beings who had evolved from animals for no purpose at all. He knew.

He lay down in his shirt and breeches and blew out the candle. Heat stood in the room like an enemy. But he believed against the evidence of his sense in the cold empty ether spaces. A radio was playing somewhere: music from Mexico City, or perhaps even from London or New York, filtered into this obscure neglected state. It seemed to him like a weakness: this was his own land, and he would have walled it in if he could with steel until he had eradicated everything which reminded him of how it had once appeared to a miserable child. He wanted to destroy everything: to be alone without any memories at all. Life began five years ago.[7]

The lieutenant is an incorruptible Robespierre; in sharp contrast to two other members of the ruling clique, the Governor's cousin and the *jefe*, the Chief of Police. Thus, when the priest, disguised in a drill suit, is seeking to replenish his supply of communion wine – difficult in this state, where the drinking of wine is illegal – it's the Governor's cousin to whom he's introduced, as a potential supplier. The Governor's cousin has just one bottle of wine available, but offers some (equally illegal) brandy as well; and insists that they have a celebratory drink together, as he puts it, 'to toast our business'. Then the *jefe* turns up – and joins in. 'It's good beer', the *jefe* says of the wine – (beer still being legal) – 'very good beer'. And the priest weeps to see the last of his wine disappear down the *jefe*'s throat.

On another occasion, we see the lieutenant walking with the *jefe*:

They passed the new hall built for the Syndicate of Workers and Peasants: through the window they could see the big bold clever murals – of one priest caressing a woman in the confessional, another tippling on the sacramental wine. The lieutenant said, 'We will soon make these unnecessary.' He looked at the pictures with the eye of a foreigner: they seemed to him barbarous.

'Why? They are – fun.'

'One day they'll forget there ever was a Church here.'[8]

His utopian dreams are an inverted parody of Christian hope for the Kingdom of God.

The Governor gives him *carte blanche* to adopt whatever methods he chooses for the pursuit of the last fugitive priest. He decides to take hostages from all the villages; and to shoot these hostages whenever he has reason to believe that the priest has been secretly in their village. Several are in fact shot. So, the net closes in. Twice the priest, incognito, encounters the lieutenant, before he's finally captured. The first time is in a little village, part of his original parish, where he has just finished celebrating mass when the lieutenant arrives with his men. Under pressure of persecution, it seems, the faith of these villagers is running almost on empty. But when they're rounded up in the plaza, with the priest, in peasant dress, amongst them, still no one betrays him. When the lieutenant says he's going to take a hostage, the priest volunteers. The lieutenant, however, chooses another man. And then the second encounter is in Villahermosa, when the priest, emerging from his unfortunate drinking session with the Governor's cousin and the *jefe*, is detained by a Red Shirt who discovers the not yet empty brandy bottle in his pocket. As a result, he's locked up overnight in jail. The lieutenant briefly interviews him when he is released; and, noting that when arrested he hadn't had the money to pay for his fine, gives him five pesos. Astonished, the priest responds: 'You're a good man.'

Other characters include several English-speaking expatriates: again, as in West's novel, these are, by virtue of their foreignness in this environment, proxy for the original readers of the novel. They're more or less indifferent to the persecution of the Catholic Church proceeding around them; their indifference representing the prevailing attitudes of the wider world. Mr Tench the English dentist is a hapless loner, lured to this out-of-the-way place by chance, and then trapped here by a fall in the exchange rate. He gets talking with the priest on the quayside, where he has gone to see if the ether cylinder he was expecting has arrived:

'Did you see what the peso stands at in Mexico City? Four to the dollar. Four. O God. *Ora pro nobis.*'

'Are you a Catholic?'

'No, no. Just an expression. I don't believe in anything like that.' He said irrelevantly, 'It's too hot anyway.'[9]

Captain Fellows the banana plantation agent is a happy man – his wife is miserable. What they have in common is 'a kind of diffidence'.[10] When the Captain returns home to find that his pubescent daughter Coral has hidden the priest in their barn, and then brazenly deflected the pursuing lieutenant, he's terrified. Nor has Coral thought it at all wise to confide in her mother. And, finally, the German-American brother and sister, Mr and Miss Lehr – Lutheran farmers over the border in Chiapas who give temporary refuge to the priest – for their part remain locked within an anaesthetic outlook of narrow-minded Protestant anti-Catholicism.

Representing faith defeated, meanwhile, is Padre José. He's the only other priest left in the state. But he has submitted to the regime, married his housekeeper, and accepted a pension. Padre José's despair, his contempt for himself, is total. Children mock him. Accosted in the cemetery by a grieving family who ask him for a simple prayer, he refuses. For how can he trust them not to tell? When his brother priest turns up, begging for shelter, he panics and slams the door. Even when the lieutenant himself arrives, after the final capture of the other, and offers as an act of clemency to sanction Padre José's hearing the condemned man's last confession, he still says no. 'Poor man', says the other, when informed of this – in no way condemning Padre José's fear.[11]

How successful, though, is the *garrridistas'* propaganda, as distinct from their reign of terror? When the priest is arrested, for possession of brandy, he's shoved into a cell crammed full of people, invisible in the pitch dark.[12] Voices intermingle. A murderer tries to justify his crime. In one corner a couple are noisily copulating. An old man, arrested for possession of a crucifix, nevertheless curses 'the priests'. Why? Before the Revolution, they had taken his illegitimate daughter away, and then poisoned her mind, against him. – The priest deplores this. A pious woman attacks him: 'You don't know what's right', she says. 'The priests know.' – After a momentary pause, he responds: 'I *am* a priest'. Suddenly, there's whispering everywhere.

'You shouldn't have told us. Father, there are all sorts here …'

Yet, a voice says: 'Nobody here wants their blood money.' And, notwithstanding the substantial monetary reward on offer, such is the general resentment of authority amongst these particular jailbirds that, in the event, none of them does betray him.

True, he's betrayed in the end. But even then, there's no element of *garridista* fervour involved. It's quite clear that his betrayer, an impoverished 'half-caste', is solely motivated by the money. This 'half-caste' is an unscrupulous man; and, also, very shrewd. He first conceives his suspicion of the priest when the latter, disguised as a peasant riding on a mule, stops in his village to ask directions. At once, the 'half-caste' dashes after him; volunteers to guide him; swims across a river in pursuit, and catches a fever as a result – which allows the priest to shake him off; but only after he has, at any rate, established that the priest is headed for Villahermosa. In Villahermosa, he reports to the police, who send him through the streets, hunting for their prey. As he's lodged in the jail, he actually encounters the priest there. Fearing however lest others, in these circumstances, might take credit for the arrest, he opts to turn a blind eye, and let the priest, for the time being, escape.

In the event, the priest manages to cross the border, into Chiapas, before the 'half-caste' catches up with him again, at the Lehrs' farm. There's nothing, therefore, to prevent him getting away for good. But the 'half-caste' spins him a tale. An American bandit is on the run – the priest has, indeed, already witnessed some of the havoc this Yankee has left in his wake. According to the 'half-caste', the bandit has been shot and mortally wounded. He now lies dying in an Indian hut, high up on the mountain ridge along the Tabasco/Chiapas border. And he's a Catholic; he has been calling for a priest. The half-caste shows the priest a note, scribbled in English, as evidence. It reads: 'For Christ's sake, father ...'

Nothing could be clearer than that this is a trap. But the priest is tired of life. Moreover, he's also dutiful. The story of the dying Yankee, in itself, is plausible enough – the note looks genuine – even if the messenger lacks credibility. Therefore, he accepts the pretext. And deliberately opts for martyrdom, after all.

∾

What are we to make of this? The lieutenant's new policy of taking hostages means that the priest's fugitive existence can scarcely be maintained. When he learns of it, and hears that one of the hostages, a man he knows, has been shot, he gives 'a little yapping cry like a dog's'. And says: 'Why don't they catch me? The fools. Why don't they catch *me*?'[13] On the other hand, the prospect of escape – to Mexico City, say, where at least the vestiges of normal church life still continue – doesn't seem so very enticing, either. During his time with the Lehrs, in Chiapas, he negotiates with the peasants: five pesos for a mass, one peso per baptism. 'He could feel the old life hardening around him like a habit, a stony case which held his head high and dictated the way he walked, and even formed his words.'[14] The fact is: he no longer really *likes* his old, returning, clerical self. And, besides, how – if restored to freedom – will he be able to contain his alcoholism? Already, a salesman accosts him: offering, in view of his prospective income from the baptisms, to sell him a dozen bottles of brandy. The future life that the priest renounces, in his acceptance of martyrdom, doesn't, after all, to him seem such a great loss.

But let's go back to the beginning. As, after his capture, he and the lieutenant sit together, by the corpse of the Yankee, the lieutenant asks him why, when so many of his colleagues had run, he – 'of all people' – had originally decided to stay.[15] In the first instance, he says, it had simply been a misjudgement, a failure to recognise the true gravity of the situation. And then

> 'Do you know I suddenly realized that I was the only priest left for miles around? The law which made priests marry finished them. They went: they were quite right to go. There was one priest in particular – he had always disapproved of me. He said – quite rightly – that I wasn't a firm character. He escaped. It felt – you'll laugh at this – just as it did at school when a bully I had been afraid of – for years – got too old for any more teaching and was turned out. You see, I didn't have to think about anybody's opinion any more. The people – they didn't worry me. They liked me.'

Moreover, as he now sees it, he'd begun to take a sinful pride in his predicament. And the critical colleague had been proved right:

> 'Pride was what made the angels fall. Pride's the worst thing of all. I thought I was a fine fellow to have stayed when the others had gone. And then I thought I was so grand I could make my own rules. I gave up fasting, daily Mass. I neglected my prayers – and one day because I was drunk and lonely – well, you know how it was, I got a child. It was all pride. Just pride because I'd stayed. I wasn't any use, but I stayed. At least, not much use. I'd got so that I didn't have a hundred communicants a month. If I'd gone I'd have given God to twelve times that number. It's a mistake one makes – to think just because a thing is difficult or dangerous ...'

The lieutenant 'in a tone of fury' says: 'Well, you're going to be a martyr – you've got that satisfaction.' 'Oh no,' the priest replies, 'Martyrs are not like me ...'[16]

We, the readers, however, are surely meant to protest. Never mind the mere numbers given communion. The significance of this priest's continuing presence in the danger zone can scarcely be reduced to that. And to us it's clear: there was much more than mere sinful pride involved in his continuing defiance. To be sure, he had grown lax in some things. But what of that scrupulous sense of pastoral duty which had helped lead him into this final trap? We've seen it before. Right at the beginning of the novel, when he's waiting on the quayside in the hope of getting a place on the boat out of Tabasco, to Veracruz, a child arrives, and asks him to come quickly: the child's mother, who lives six leagues away, is dying. Of course, the journey will mean missing the boat. Moreover, the priest very much doubts whether she's truly as sick as the child says. Nevertheless, it's his priestly duty to go. So he does.

It's also his duty – as he explains to young Coral – no matter how much he may long to get caught, to stay on the run.[17] In this regard, he's stubbornly dutiful. Yet, he can never enjoy the usual reward of the dutiful, their moral self-satisfaction. There may, as he says, have been some element of pride involved at an earlier stage of his staying on. But by the time that we see him all trace of that original pride has disappeared. It has, as it were, been burnt away over the years. Certainly, he doesn't strike any sort of heroic pose. On the contrary, when he's nervous, he giggles; he flaps his hands.

And so, how's he sustained? After all, his motivation is only intelligible in terms of love. He's ministering to impoverished peasants, in little villages: these are his people. They remain loyal to the Church – out of a mix of inertia, superstition, but also, one may presume, at least some sense of God's love for them. Serving that love, he reciprocates their loyalty. 'The people liked me.' However, he remains at the same time utterly alone; and all the more so now that the lieutenant has resorted to taking hostages. When he comes to the settlement where his ex-housekeeper Maria lives, mother of their now seven-year-old daughter Brigitta, he finds the peasants there in a sullen mood. Maria herself is sour towards him. At first, he doesn't recognise little Brigitta. When he tries to speak with her, she sniggers; sticks out her tongue. Her attitude towards him is a distressing mixture of precocious flirtatiousness, and contempt. (Is this a detail borrowed from Bernanos: the character of little Seraphita?)

In short, it's no longer for any particular emotional reward that this priest loves his people. It isn't needy *eros* at work here. It's pure *agapé*, part of an all-embracing Christ-like love for humanity at large. After all, he feels that he has forfeited the right to any other sort of love. Witness his conversation with the pious woman in the dark and crowded cell of Villahermosa jail. She's eager to revere him, as a prospective martyr. He tells her that he's a whisky priest; that he has fathered a child; and that he doesn't really repent of having done so. 'I don't know how to repent,' he says.[18] Nevertheless, she's irrepressible; still asks him to hear her confession. He protests: it's impossible, in this place. Sacramental confession requires secrecy. He suggests that she simply say an Act of Contrition for her sins. But then the couple in the corner start to copulate again, and she explodes with rage. Such animals! The priest says,

'What's the good of your saying an Act of Contrition now in this state of mind?'
'But the ugliness ...'
'Don't believe that. It's dangerous. Because suddenly we discover that our sins have so much beauty.'
'Beauty,' she said with disgust. 'Here. In this cell. With strangers all round.'
'Such a lot of beauty. Saints talk about the beauty of suffering ... Well, we are not saints, you and I. Suffering to us is just ugly. Stench and crowding and pain. *That* is beautiful in that corner – to them. It needs a lot of learning to see things with a saint's eye: a saint gets a subtle taste for beauty and can look down on poor ignorant palates like theirs. But we can't afford to.'
'It's mortal sin.'
'We don't know. It may be. But I'm a bad priest, you see. I know – from experience – how much beauty Satan carried down with him when he fell. Nobody ever said the fallen angels were the ugly ones. Oh no, they were just as quick and light and ...'
Again the cry came, an expression of intolerable pleasure.

The woman said, 'Stop them. It's a scandal.' He felt fingers on his knee, grasping, digging. He said, 'We're all fellow prisoners. I want drink at this moment more than anything, more than God. That's a sin too.'

'Now,' the woman said, 'I can see you're a bad priest.'[19]

Now *we*, on the other hand, can see just how deeply he has been transformed – thanks to the long 'dark night of the soul' through which he has passed – from the all too conventional 'good priest' that he once had been.

He loves Brigitta; he condemns no one; he loves God.

How's he sustained, in the absurdity of his plight? Patently, given the falling away of any other possible moral prop, it can only be by the sheer extravagance of that love for God; which Greene's novel thus distils.

---

1. *The Power and the Glory* was first published in 1940. In what follows I cite the Penguin edition of 1962.

    In 1953 Greene was indeed summoned by the Cardinal Archbishop of Westminster, who read him a pastoral letter from the Holy Office in Rome, deploring the book. But no further disciplinary action was taken.

2. Garrido Canabal was Governor of Tabasco for some months in 1919, then from 1920 to 1924, and again from 1931 to 1934; but he effectively controlled the state government in the interim, as well. In 1934 he briefly served as Minister of Agriculture in Mexico City.

3. These are the figures given in the Baltimore Catholic Review of August 23rd 1935. See Brian Van Hove SJ, 'Blood-drenched altars: Archbishop Michael Joseph Curley, Oklahoma's Bishop Francis Clement Kelley, and the Mexican Affair 1934—6' in *Faith and Reason,* Summer1994.

    The most celebrated martyr was the Jesuit Fr Miguel Pro (1891—1927). The Calles government had published photographs of his death by firing squad, hoping this would serve as a deterrent to the Cristero rebels; however, it appears to have had very much the opposite effect. Miguel Pro was beatified by John Paul II in 1988. The pious work which the mother reads to her children in Part One, Chapters 2 and 4, and Part Four of *The Power and the Glory* tells of a latter-day martyr named 'Juan';

but this 'Juan' appears to be very much modelled on Fr Pro.

4.   Greene, *The Lawless Roads* (Harmondsworth: Penguin, 1971), pp. 105—6.

5.   Ibid. p. 122.

6.   *The Power and the Glory*, Part Two, Chapter 1.

7.   Ibid. pp. 24—5.

8.   Ibid. pp. 55—6.

9.   Ibid. p. 10.

10.   Ibid. p. 33.

11.   Ibid. p. 205. And c.f. his memory of Padre José in the old days, p. 95: 'At the Elevation of the Host you could see his hands trembling – he was not like St. Thomas who needed to put his hands into the wounds in order to believe: the wounds bled anew for him over every altar. Once Padre José had said to him in a burst of confidence, "Every time … I have such fear." His father had been a peon.'

12.   Ibid. Part Two, Chapter 3.

13.   Ibid. p. 63.

14.   Ibid. pp. 167—8.

15.   Ibid. p. 195.

16.   Ibid. pp. 195—6.

17.   Ibid. p. 40.

18.   Ibid. p. 128.

19.   Ibid. pp. 130—31.

CHAPTER SEVENTEEN

Shusaku Endo: *Silence*

As for Endo's novel, *Silence*: this represents yet a further distillation of the element of sublime virtue, out of traditional notions of martyr-'sainthood'.[1]

Thus, the setting here is mid-seventeenth-century Japan. Endo describes the brutal persecution of Japanese Christians in that period, and of the European missionaries sent out to minister to them, for the most part quite realistically. But he modifies the historic actuality in one crucial respect – which suddenly opens up to quite a dizzying abyss of theological paradox.

The history of Christianity in Japan had begun in 1549, when the great Jesuit missionary St. Francis Xavier arrived, with two colleagues and an interpreter. Europe's first gift to Japan had been the matchlock rifle; carried on a Portuguese trading ship, blown off course on its way to China, some six years earlier. And Christianity was the second. With the charm of an exotic import – and a ready willingness, on the part of the Jesuits, to train up, and then trust in, indigenous leaders – it spread at first quite rapidly. The south-western island of Kyūshū, where ships from China initially made landfall, was the main area where it took root. In 1580 the little fishing village of Nagasaki was donated to the Jesuits as a trading colony. It grew, and became known as the 'Rome of Japan'; with no less than eleven churches before – the donation having been revoked – the truly serious persecution began some thirty years later. But there were also other Christian communities scattered far and wide. During the decades immediately following Xavier's arrival, it had in fact become quite widely fashionable for local lords (*daimyō*), baptised or not, to act as patrons of the new religion. (A notable incentive was the reciprocal offer of preferential trading terms with Portuguese merchants, especially for the purchase of saltpeter, a crucial ingredient in the manufacture of gunpowder.) The most notable example of such a patron is the ruthless warrior-ruler Oda Nobunaga, the first of the three great 'Unifiers' of Japan at the end of the Sengoku, or 'Warring States' Period. Unfortunately, however, for the missionaries, the two subsequent 'Unifiers' – Toyotomi Hideyoshi and Tokugawa Ieyasu – didn't share this attitude.

In 1587, after having finally conquered Kyūshū, Hideyoshi decreed the expulsion of all missionaries from the island. This edict wasn't all that stringently enforced. Nevertheless, it marks the beginning of serious hostility to the Church on the part of the central state authorities.[2] And ten years later Hideyoshi had twenty-six Christians (six Franciscan missionaries, three Japanese Jesuits and seventeen Japanese laymen including three young boys) crucified in Nagasaki, as a major statement of intent. After his death the following year, there was something of a lull. But in 1614 his successor Ieyasu, alarmed by what was perceived as the threat of Spanish expansion from the Philippines, issued another edict, completely banning the practice of Christianity. This initiated an all-out attack. Eventually, in the 1630s, Ieyasu's grandson Tokugawa Iemitsu proceeded to develop a systematic *sakoku*, that is 'closed country', policy: expelling almost all Europeans from Japan; drastically restricting trade with Europe; and prohibiting any Japanese from overseas travel. Meanwhile, between 1614 and 1643, the year in which Endo's novel is set, some five or six thousand Christians are said to have been martyred.[3] And this doesn't include the apocalyptic mass-slaughter at the end of the 1637 – 38 Shimabara Rebellion in the hinterland of Nagasaki; an uprising which had begun as a protest not only against over-taxation in time of famine, but also very much against the government's persecution of Christians. When the stronghold of the rebels, Hara Castle, finally fell, perhaps as many as thirty-six thousand rebels perished in the mayhem.[4]

Magistrates seeking to identify undercover remaining

Christians would typically require suspects to trample on images of the Virgin Mary or of Christ, called *fumie*, in symbolic token of contempt. This inquisitorial technique plays a key role in Endo's novel. As also does the ultimate form of torture deployed, in order to persuade prominent Christians to apostatise: 'the pit'. Victims subjected to this would be tightly bound and suspended from a wooden frame, upside down, their heads in a darkened pit lined with excrement. To prevent them dying too soon, from excessive accumulation of blood in the head, an incision was made behind their ears, allowing the blood to drip slowly away. And, if they didn't surrender, they would then over the following days die a protracted death, in agony.

The historic chain of events which most immediately forms the context for Endo's fiction begins in 1633 with the scandalous apostasy of Father Christóvão Ferreira, the acting Provincial of the Jesuit Order in Japan. Ferreira had been working in Japan from 1609 onwards; after 1614, in secret. But then, during an intensive fresh wave of persecution in Nagasaki, he'd been caught, and subjected, along with seven others, to what was, at that time, the brand-new punishment of 'the pit'. The seven others had held out, and died as martyrs. After five hours, however, Ferreira had given way. For the remaining seventeen years of his life, he was paid a stipend by the government; given a house, a wife, and the Japanese name of 'Sawano Chuan'; took to wearing Japanese clothes; and, when he wasn't working as an interpreter, spent most of his time writing. He produced notable treatises drawing on European developments in astronomy and surgery; but also, a denunciation of Christian faith.[5]

A number of attempts were made, by other Jesuits, to restore the honour of the Order; seen as having been lamentably besmirched by Ferreira's defeat. In 1637, Father Marcello Mastrilli arrived in Japan, hoping, if possible, to find and reconvert Ferreira. He was instantly arrested; subjected to the 'pit' for three days and afterwards beheaded. Two years later the remarkable Japanese Jesuit Father Petro Kibe followed, with the same end in view. Kibe had spent sixteen years in exile; during which time he'd walked all the way from Goa to Jerusalem, before settling in Rome. Accompanied by two colleagues, on his return, he'd ministered to the underground churches for a while; then, following his capture, as a prisoner in Edo, actually encountered Ferreira. His two colleagues, subjected to 'the pit', both apostatised – but Kibe died a martyr. And, finally, in 1643 two further groups arrived: the first including five priests, the second including four more. Both groups were captured almost as soon as they landed. Again, they encountered Ferreira in his role as interpreter, at their interrogation; and the first group's leader, Father Antonio Rubino – who'd come with a document of reproach for Ferreira already prepared – is said to have confronted him furiously. The members of Rubino's group were all then heroically martyred in 'the pit'. The second group, on the other hand, apostatised. And they, then, went on to live out the remainder of their lives incarcerated in what was known as the 'Christian Residence', in Edo, present-day Tokyo.

Endo's fiction replaces these latter four apostate priests with just one such: the central character of his novel, Father Sebastian Rodrigues. Presumably for the sake of economy, he omits any reference to the expeditions of Mastrilli and Kobe; and makes only brief reference to Rubino's group. He depicts the fictional Rodrigues as having originally belonged to a group of three young Portuguese Jesuits.[6] One of his colleagues, however, falls ill with malaria in Macao, which was the main base for all Jesuit operations in Far East. And so, Rodrigues eventually sets sail with a single colleague, a Father Francisco Garrpe. They also take with them a stray Japanese called Kichijiro, who says that he wants to return home. Kichijiro, from the outset, seems highly shifty and unreliable; but they need a guide, and there's no one else.

After a Prologue, setting the scene, the first four Chapters consist of first-person narrative, supposedly a series of letters written by Rodrigues, the first from Macao, the next three smuggled out of Japan, recounting his adventures prior to capture. These are scarcely plausible as the seventeenth-century epistolary texts they're meant to be. But never mind. They serve to bring the reader into intimate relationship with him. The core psycho-drama is then reported by an omniscient narrator. And at the end we have passages from the diary of a Dutch clerk, stationed in Nagasaki; also, in an appendix, entries in the diary of a Japanese official, working at the 'Christian Residence' for apostates, which conclude with Rodrigues's death in 1674.

The persecutory genius behind the anti-Christian campaign as a whole – the grand inquisitor, as it were – was Inoue Chikugo-no-kami [Governor of Chikugo] Masashige. Endo pictures him as a 'smiling little plump samurai'; he was, at the time he appears in the novel, in his late fifties.[7] Rodrigues first encounters him, without realising who he is, shortly after being betrayed by Kichijiro and captured on the Gotō Islands: the capture of a Portuguese priest is an event important enough for Inoue immediately to have dropped everything and made the sea voyage out from Nagasaki. Then, after Rodrigues has been transferred to a prison just outside the city, Inoue reappears as one of a group of five samurai interrogators. They're seated in a row, with him in the middle. He's smiling benignly. And he gazes at Rodrigues 'with the curiosity of a child who has been given a new toy.[8] As Rodrigues speaks, he keeps absent-mindedly rubbing his hands and nodding his head as if in sympathy.

They're sitting in the courtyard of the prison, with a group of Japanese Christians looking on from the cells, around them. Rodrigues speaks defiantly. What's the point of this interrogation? he asks. His interrogators have already made up their minds, haven't they? They aren't open to persuasion. And neither, he insists, is he. A surge of emotion seizes him, as he senses the encircling presence of the Japanese Christians, in their cells, hearing his words. Now, he's performing for them; playing his prescribed part, determined to inspire them with his heroic example.

'No matter what I say I'll be punished,' he exclaims. The 'old man', however, looks at him 'as though … soothing a naughty child'.

'We will not punish the fathers without reason,' he said.
'That is not the idea of Inoue. If you were Inoue you would punish me instantly.'

At these words the officials laughed heartily as though they had been told a joke.

'What are you laughing at?'

'Father, this is Inoue, the Governor of Chikugo. He is here in front of you.'

Stupefied he gazed at the old man who, naïve as a child, returned his glance still rubbing his hands. How could he have recognized one who so utterly betrayed all his expectations? The man whom Valignano [the Rector of the Jesuit College in Macao] had called a devil, who had made the missionaries apostatize one by one – until now he had envisaged the face of this man as pale and crafty. But here before his very eyes sat this understanding, seemingly good, meek man.[9]

And, indeed, Inoue is consistently courteous towards him, also in their subsequent encounters. 'I have never thought of Christianity as an evil religion,' he says.[10] It's just, he thinks, a religion unsuited to Japan.

Endo's key departure however from what's known of the historical actuality is with reference to the strategy which Inoue has, in the novel, developed for persuading missionaries like Ferreira and Rodrigues to apostatise.

Thus, Rodrigues is never, directly, subjected to torture. He witnesses terrible violence inflicted on Japanese Christians. For example: crucifixion on crosses planted by the sea shore, so that at high tide the victims are almost, but not quite drowned; or a man quite casually decapitated, without warning, in the prison courtyard. But, as for himself, up until the decisive final night he's held in quite comfortable conditions. He's given three meals a day, rather than the two that other prisoners receive; and mats to sleep on, another privilege. Also, he's permitted to socialise with the other prisoners.

Only, Inoue tells him that, until he apostatises, *others* will be tortured and martyred in his place. 'Peasants are fools,' Inoue says. 'It all depends on you whether or not they are to be set free.'[11] Whether the peasants live or die is neither here nor there for such a grand aristocrat as Inoue. But what really counts, for him, is the propaganda value of publicly breaking the resistance of priests. And he sees the compassion of the latter for their converts as a key weakness to be exploited.

Rodrigues, at first, can't quite grasp that Inoue really means what he says: that there's no prospect of the heroic martyrdom for himself that he'd anticipated; only, to the extent that he holds out, appalling punishment for the peasants. And so, Inoue arranges a demonstration. Without being told where he's going, or why, Rodrigues is transported to a pine grove overlooking an inlet of the sea. Down below, figures appear on the beach: four prisoners and their guards. He recognises three as the peasants he has got to know in the prison where he's held; and with them is his colleague Garrpe. Following a raid by the authorities on the village in which they'd at first found shelter, he and Garrpe had split up, so as not to both be captured at once – but, clearly, in vain. The three peasants are trussed up in matting 'like basket worms'; loaded onto boats which are rowed out to sea; then tossed overboard, to drown. The interpreter who's with Rodrigues, a familiar figure, tells him that they had in fact finally apostatised, and trampled as was required on the *fumie*, the sacred Christian images. But Garrpe had not. Therefore, they must die, notwithstanding their own submission. Garrpe runs desperately into the sea and swims out after them – there he is, his head bobbing 'like a piece of black dust, buffeted by the waves' – until he too is lost.[12] And now Rodrigues *does* know the score.

After that, weeks pass; time for the lesson truly to sink in. At length, he's taken off to meet Ferreira, now employed by the authorities as a persuader. Then, two days later, he's paraded on horseback through the streets of Nagasaki, to experience the derision of the people. On return, he's locked into a pitch-black, urine-soaked cell – he's convinced that Inoue has changed his mind, and that he's about to die. Somewhere nearby a guard is snoring:

Here he was in this dark cell overwhelmed with the emotion of a man who faces death, while another man snored in this carefree way – the thought struck him as utterly ludicrous.

Why is human life so full of grotesque irony, he muttered quietly to himself.[13]

Eventually, the persistent snoring becomes a torment to him. He hammers on the wall of his cell. The interpreter appears, accompanied by someone else. Snoring? The interpreter is amazed: no one's snoring! 'Sawano,' he says – that's Ferreira's Japanese name. 'Sawano, tell him what it is.' Then Rodrigues hears Ferreira's voice:

'That's not snoring. That is the moaning of Christians hanging in the pit.'[14]

Three victims: who depend entirely on him for their release. It's enough – he surrenders.

∿

As Endo reconstructs history, Ferreira himself had withstood three days in the 'pit', unbroken; before being exposed to the sort of psychological torment which – Inoue having experimentally refined his method – is now re-applied to Rodrigues, without any such preamble. So, he had, in the end, been broken the same way. Yet, of the two, Ferreira appears to be the more completely defeated. And the comparison is surely telling.

When they're brought together, Ferreira, seeking to justify his apostasy and persuade Rodrigues to follow suit, actually argues that the whole missionary enterprise in Japan is futile. It would still be futile, he contends, even if the Japanese Church weren't persecuted, but allowed to flourish. For, the problem is that Japanese culture is by nature a 'swamp', in which the 'sapling' of the gospel will never be able to put down real roots. Suppose all constraints were lifted, the more the Church in Japan became authentically Japanese, and grew, the less it would be truly Christian.

Rodrigues naturally protests. With his own eyes he has seen the martyrdom of Japanese Christians, their extraordinary courage!

'They did not believe in the Christian God.' Ferreira spoke clearly and with self-confidence, deliberately emphasizing every word. 'The Japanese till this day have never had the concept of God; and they never will ... The Japanese are not able to think of God completely divorced from man; the Japanese cannot think of an existence that transcends the human ... The Japanese imagine a beautiful, exalted man – and this they call God. They call by the name of God something which has the same kind of existence as man. But that is not the Church's God.'[15]

There is, of course, an immediately obvious rejoinder to this: what of the Incarnation? It's true that Christian theology, right from the outset, was engaged in a Trinitarian attempt to reconcile the straightforward picture-thinking faith of the masses, focussed on God incarnate – and infused by the Holy Spirit – with the more sophisticated faith of the exegetically and philosophically trained elite, distinguished by its greater stress on divine transcendence: picture-thinking, *in isolation*, being all too ambiguous, just as purely abstract theology, *in isolation*, is all too exclusive in conversational scope, too narrowly confined to intellectuals. At the level of picture-thinking, though, is there really any intrinsic difference in quality between the faith of illiterate Japanese peasants and the faith of illiterate European peasants? And whilst, at the more sophisticated intellectual level, Japanese culture lacks any exact equivalent to the twin heritage of Hebrew prophecy and Greek philosophy which first fed Christian theology – is that really irremediable?

Indeed, might not interaction with the traditions of Japanese Buddhism actually *enrich* global Church tradition?

To think otherwise is surely to risk muddling true Christian evangelism with mere European cultural imperialism. Ferreira's despair actually appears to be a symptom of continuing enslavement to this sort of muddle: a confusion of gospel truth in itself, as testimony to perfect truth-as-openness, with what a particular Christian culture, aggressively asserting its particularity, deems to be truth-as-correctness. Isn't he, after all, in effect suggesting that Japan can never be truly Christian, just because it can never become European enough, Portuguese enough? Note how his argument is echoed by Inoue, in conversation with Rodrigues after the latter's apostasy:

> 'Father, you were not defeated by me.' The Lord of Chikugo looked straight into the ashes of the brazier as he spoke. 'You were defeated by this swamp of Japan.'[16]

Perhaps Inoue has learnt to speak in these terms from conversations with Ferreira? At any rate, here we have the self-same chauvinist spirit that seemingly continues to haunt Ferreira's thinking; as it were, reflected back from the other side.

And this serves to prompt the question: what then actually *did* motivate the resistance of Japanese Christians to their persecutors? The original Jesuit evangelistic strategy was to try, first and foremost, to impress the feudal overlords, the *daimyō*, where necessary with the missionaries themselves putting on a great show of wealth and prestige. Peasant farmers were often then more or less coerced by their newly Christian *daimyō* to follow suit. By the 1640s, however, when there were no more Christian *daimyō* left and the only remaining Christians were, for the most part, poor peasants, it's quite remarkable how tenacious their faith was; how deeply it had evidently penetrated the collective psyche.[17] In the areas affected by the 1637 – 38 Rebellion (the Shimabara Peninsular and the Amakusa Islands) the hitherto largely Christian population, having been slaughtered, was replaced by non-Christian incomers; in Nagasaki and other major towns rigorous police measures had, by that time, effectively extinguished the last traces of Church life. But in more marginal places such as the Gotō Islands (where in the novel Rodrigues is arrested) or on the little island of Ikitsuki small communities of *Kakure Kirishitan*, 'hidden Christians', somehow persisted right through the following two centuries and beyond; undercover and completely cut off from the outside world. As they lacked Bible, prayer books, or any explicitly Christian artefacts whatsoever, naturally their tradition became, by orthodox standards, somewhat garbled. Inoue, as it were gazing into the far future, already taunts Rodrigues:

> 'If the root is cut, the sapling withers and the leaves die. The proof of this is that the God whom the peasants of Gotō and Ikitsuki secretly serve has gradually changed so as to be no longer like the Christian God at all.'[18]

Well, maybe so. But, still, one can't help wondering: what was it that inspired their rather wonderful obstinacy?

In fact, it appears to have been inspired by a primitive species of Liberation Theology. The very fact that Christianity had been excised, with such violence, from the world of the rich served to associate it all the more closely with the defiant self-assertion of the poor.[19] The explosive events of 1637 – 38 were in this regard just the most spectacular manifestation of a general tendency. Already before the arrival of the first Christian missionaries there had been other peasant uprisings, across central Honshu, appealing to religious authority: a whole series of them, spanning the fifteenth and sixteenth centuries, the work of *ikkō-ikki* rebels associated with the populist *Jōdo Shinshū Hongan-ji* Buddhist sect. The leading sage of this sect, Rennyo (1415 – 99) deplored the violence involved in the *ikkō-ikki* uprisings; nevertheless, shared religious loyalties were clearly vital for drawing together a diversity of local groups, each with their own particular grievances, into a larger movement. In Kyūshū, Christianity clearly came to play the same role. Of course, the imagery of Good Friday further helped; as peasant rebels identified their own suffering with that of their crucified Saviour. And the memory of the martyrs became a major inspiration. It seems that the faith of the *Kakure Kirishitan* increasingly evolved into an unconventional ancestor cult, dedicated to honouring their martyred ancestors.

Rodrigues, writing home, describes the wretched plight of the Christian peasants who first give him and Garrpe shelter. These aren't prosperous rice farmers. On the contrary, their land is good only for little fields of potatoes and wheat, extending half-way up a mountain, beside the sea. There they toil, in a constant struggle just to survive. The rents they have to pay the authorities in Nagasaki are ruinous. It seems that their overlords simply despise them.

He has a very simple explanation for the durability of their faith:

> The reason our religion has penetrated this territory like water flowing into dry earth is that it has given to this group of people a human warmth they never previously knew ... It was the human-kindness and charity of the fathers that touched their hearts.[20]

In this context, the missionaries represented a form of faith no longer contaminated by association with established power, as so much Christianity had been contaminated in Europe, and Buddhism in Japan.

> These people who work and die like beasts find in our teaching a path in which they can cast away the fetters that bind them.[21]

Namely: the mental fetters of self-contempt.

Rodrigues is a saintly figure from the outset, and surely remains so. At one level, he's defeated; as Ferreira had been. And yet, at another level, isn't it rather the case that his faith has been purified, by way of his defeat: the core element of authentic truth-as-openness in it separated out, in the most decisive fashion, from its original confusion with conventional Church ideology, deriving from evangelistic impatience?

Of course, the conventionally devout are liable to say that – 'of course' – he ought not to have given way in the end. 'Of course,' they may add, we who've never been exposed to such a test are scarcely in a position to judge. Nevertheless, they'll conclude that, even with all allowances made, 'of course' his ultimate surrender has to be seen as an all too human failure of courage. But how much emptier the novel becomes if one insists on reading it this way! Surely, he gives way, not at all for lack of courage, but rather for pitying love of those who are being tortured, and will otherwise continue to be tortured, in his place. Which is quite a different matter.

Ferreira by contrast, with his talk of 'the swamp', has inwardly appropriated the world-view of the persecutors, Inoue's gang. Or, rather, his thinking appears to remain, fundamentally, trapped within a mere Portuguese-Christian cultural imperialist equivalent to their Japanese exclusivist gang-ethos. The way in which both he and Inoue speak of 'the swamp' brings this latent affinity, of one gang-ethos with another, to light. To all practical intents and purposes, the two of them are here setting out the terms of an agreement between two gangs: that one should from now on keep off the turf of the other. Rodrigues, however, is different. He neither gives way, in argument over principle, to gangster-boss Inoue; nor does he flinch when he's ceremonially led through the streets of Nagasaki, to be exposed before the anti-Christian mob. Right from the outset his sense of missionary vocation already represents a radical determination to escape the limitations of normal, easy-going Portuguese moral herd-existence. And, at the end, his outward apostasy may well be seen as yet a further decisive stage along the same trajectory. So, he prays to Christ:

> 'You underwent every kind of insult; if you alone now understand my feelings, that is enough. Even if the Christians and the clergy look upon me as a blot on the history of the mission, that no longer matters to me.'[22]

In Rodrigues it seems to me we have a model of moral courage absolutely dedicated to the struggles of truth-as-openness: against mere gang-ethos, mere mob-ethos, mere herd-morality, the whole gamut.

Inoue tells Rodrigues that he has been defeated by 'this swamp of Japan'.

'No, no …' Unconsciously the priest raised his voice as he spoke. 'My struggle was with Christianity in my own heart.'[23]

In what sense is this so? I'd suggest that he was, precisely, struggling with the prevalent fetishising of theological truth-as-correctness, in the culture he represented, at the expense of authentic truth-as-openness. He'd come to Japan as an envoy of Jesuit truth-as-correctness; representing the usual confused amalgam between the two species of truth. But, once he'd arrived, he found himself exposed to the sheer humanity of Japanese Christians. He began to attach far more importance to evangelism through simple 'human warmth' – as expressing the primordial demands of truth-as-openness – than to the defence, no matter how heroic, of mere truth-as-correctness, in itself. In other words, he grew increasingly wary of orthodox zealotry, the 'sublimity of the missionary hero-as-holy-warrior', as such.

This development is already underway well before the final crisis of his apostasy. The first sign of it occurs after Inoue, with his retinue, arrives in the village where Rodrigues and Garrpe had originally taken refuge, and were hiding. An informer, Inoue says, has indicated that there are Christians in the village. The villagers deny it. But he demands that they select three hostages, and send them to Nagasaki. After he has left, the men who have volunteered to go as hostages – Kichijiro, Ichizo and Mokichi – come to the priests and ask what they should do when the authorities demand that they trample on the *fumie*? If they refuse, it isn't only they that will suffer. The authorities will return to the village and cross-examine everyone. Rodrigues, in his fourth letter home, describes the scene:

'Trample! Trample!' I shouted. But immediately I realized that I had uttered words that should never have been on my lips. Garrpe looked at me reproachfully.[24]

(Alas, although they follow his advice, only the treacherous Kichijiro can do so in a way that is convincing to Inoue, looking on.

He sees how Ichizo and Mokichi wince. And so, they're martyred, for the sake of deterrence, after all.)

Then, a second sign of Rodrigues's 'struggle with Christianity in his own heart': as he's watching, out of earshot, from the pine grove above, how Garrpe and the three Christian peasants are led out, and the peasants are trussed up and loaded onto boats to be tossed into the sea and drowned – all because Garrpe won't surrender – Rodrigues silently cries out.

'Apostatize! Apostatize!' He shouted out the words in his heart to Garrpe, who was listening to the officials, his back turned ...
'Apostatize! You must apostatize!' ...
I would apostatize. I would apostatize. The words rose up even to his throat, but clenching his teeth he tried to stop himself from uttering the words aloud.[25]

It's no longer, at this moment, for him, all about himself, or Garrpe, or the Jesuit Order. He has befriended these peasants, in the Nagasaki prison. His feelings for them really are the polar opposite of Inoue's utter instrumentalising contempt.

In the same situation, Ferreira argues, Christ himself would have trampled on the *fumie*!

'For love Christ would have apostatized. Even if it meant giving up everything he had.'[26]

Throughout the novel the theme of God's silence, which supplies the title, recurs. And yet, at the climax, that silence is finally broken. As Rodrigues gazes at the *fumie*, here a bronze image of Christ crucified –

'Ah,' he says trembling, 'the pain!'
'It is only a formality. What do formalities matter?' The interpreter urges him on excitedly. 'Only go through with the exterior form of trampling.'
The priest raises his foot. In it he feels a dull, heavy pain.

This is no mere formality. He will now trample on what he has considered the most beautiful thing in his life, on what he believed most pure, on what is filled with the ideals and the dreams of man. How his foot aches! And then the Christ in bronze speaks to the priest:

'Trample! Trample! I more than anyone know of the pain in your foot. Trample! It was to be trampled on by men that I was born into this world. It was to share men's pain that I carried my cross.'

The priest placed his foot on the *fumie*. Dawn broke. And far in the distance the cock crew.[27]

There's no indication that we are to take these words of Christ as anything other than genuine. Ferreira, it appears, isn't always wrong.

Only a novel could ever convey the full paradoxical inwardness of such a drama. Martin Scorsese made a film of *Silence*: a visually rich production, by a master film-maker. (And the Picador Classic edition from which I've been working has a brief introduction by Scorsese.[28]) Films may make one weep, *as a spectator*; they may make one admire, *as a spectator*. Scorsese's film does both, with great skill. But films can't do what good novels can: they can never take one so *directly* right into the mind of another person, *as an imaginative participant*. In order truly to show sublime virtue emergent, *that's* what's required. Endo's novel is entitled *Silence*. At its terrible climax, God-in-Christ breaks His silence. However, this can only really be *heard* by virtue of the long-drawn-out, preparatory silencing of Rodrigues's prayerful mind; and only insofar as the reader, also, communes with his plight in silent attentiveness. Gripping films, on the other hand, are intrinsically (more or less) noisy affairs. Sublime virtue doesn't manifest itself with a sound-track. Even music, here, even the most angelic music, becomes a distraction.

1. The Japanese text first appeared in 1966. Here I'm using the 1969 English translation by William Johnston (London: Picador Classic, 2015). Graham Greene, in particular, fulsomely admired it.

2. There had been earlier anti-Christian imperial Edicts, in 1565 and 1568, but these had no effective military power behind them, and were quite unenforceable.

3. Endo, *Silence*, 'Historical Note', p. xi.

4. See Jonathan Clements, *Christ's Samurai: The True Story of the Shimabara Rebellion* (London: Robinson, 2016). On the estimated numbers, see p. 191: perhaps 13,000 killed defending the castle; perhaps 23,000, chiefly women and children, then burnt, beheaded, or killed by throwing themselves from the battlements. Note the quasi-messianic Christian fervour of the rebel leader, a seventeen-year-old boy, Jerome Amakusa; also known as Amakusa Shirō Tokisada, Nirada Shirō, Masuda Shirō, or Ōyano Shirō.

5. See George Elison, *Deus Destroyed: The Image of Christianity in Early Modern Japan* (Cambridge MA: Harvard University Press, 1973). This includes translations of four early Japanese anti-Christian polemics; including Ferreira's own 'Deceit Disclosed'. (Shortly after his death, a rumour spread that he had at the last repented, and had, secretly, been put to death in 'the pit' as a result. However, the lack of corroborating Japanese, or Dutch, sources for this story renders it doubtful.)

6. Rodrigues and Garrpe are described as having been students of Ferreira back in Portugal. Chronologically, this doesn't fit with the actual historic fact that Ferreira was already in Japan before Rodrigues is said to have been born, in 1610. But, of course, it adds pathos to their quest.

7. *Silence*, p. 109. Inoue (1585 – 1662) was a native of Kyūshū; and is said himself to have been baptised as an infant. His rise as a courtier in Edo appears to have been largely thanks to a homosexual relationship with the Shōgun, Tokugawa Iemitsu. He wasn't equally hostile to all Europeans, but cultivated quite friendly relations with the Dutch, who unlike the Portuguese didn't sponsor missionaries; but who, in order to gain competitive favour, accepted the rigorous restrictions imposed by the Japanese authorities, without complaint. See Elison, *Deus Destroyed*.

8.   *Silence*, p. 144.

9.   Ibid. pp. 147—8.

10. Ibid. p. 166.

11. Ibid. p. 111.

12. Ibid. p. 180.

13. Ibid. p. 218.

14. Ibid. p. 223.

15. Ibid. pp. 202—03.

16. Ibid. p. 251.

17. A curious bit of evidence for this is a document dating from 1645. Here, under duress a husband and wife are submitting a signed oath of apostasy:

> We have been Christian believers for many years. Yet we have found out that the Christian religion is an evil religion ... We hereby witness this statement in writing before you, worshipful magistrate. Hereafter we shall never revoke our apostasy, not even in the secret places of the heart. Should we ever entertain the slightest thought thereof, then let us be punished by God the Father, God the Son and God the Holy Ghost, St. Mary, and all Apostles and Saints. Let us forfeit all God's mercy, and all hope like Judas Iscariot, becoming a laughing-stock to all men, without thereby arousing the slightest pity, and finally die a violent death and suffer the torments of Hell without hope of salvation. This is our Christian Oath.

> Cited in C. R. Boxer, *The Christian Century in Japan 1549 – 1650* (Manchester: Carcanet Press, 1993), p. 441.

18. *Silence* pp. 252—3. C.f. Clements, *Christ's Samurai*; pp. 204—12.

19. Earlier on, the Portuguese engagement with Japan had introduced not only Christianity but also an extensive slave trade: the export of Japanese slaves all around the Portuguese Empire. No unequivocal 'good news for the poor' to begin with, then! (Toyotomi Hideyoshi's revulsion against this actually appears to have been a major motive for

his initiating the persecution of the Church.) Once the persecution really got going, however, at least that obstacle to faith was removed.

See J. F. Moran, *The Japanese and the Jesuits: Alessandro Valignano in Sixteenth-Century Japan* (London: Routledge, 1993), pp. 106—10.

20. *Silence*, p. 38.

21. Ibid. p. 54.

22. Ibid. p. 251.

23. Ibid.

24. Ibid. p. 69.

25. Ibid. pp. 179—80.

26. Ibid. p. 229.

27. Ibid. p. 231.

28. This Introduction notably references Bernanos.

F.

'Our Lord was a Gentleman ...'

CHAPTER EIGHTEEN

Ford Madox Ford:
Parade's End

A s I've said: to admire a saint, in the primordial sense intended here, is by no means just to admire some great standard-bearer for a given notion of supposed truth-as-correctness.

What's at stake isn't, after all, ideological truth-as-correctness at all. It's, purely and simply, truth-as-openness. Novelistic depictions of primordial sainthood are, ideally, sacramental celebrations of that altogether more elusive phenomenon.

In other words, the point isn't for us, the readers, always to think the same thoughts as the characters in question. It isn't that they represent a particular brand of herd- or gang-morality with which we agree, over against particular others, which we deplore; that they're 'progressive', if we're 'progressive'; or that they're 'conservative', if we're 'conservative'. We may well doubt whether we ourselves would at all readily feel at ease with them, were we to meet them. But, nonetheless, we're invited to admire them – even where we most certainly don't agree, or even where we find them quite jarringly eccentric. Indeed, the more acute our cultural differences from them, mixed with perhaps reluctant admiration, the more thought-provoking the novel is liable to be; the more effective as a mind-opener.

Thus, consider for example the central figures of Ford Madox Ford's four-novel sequence, *Parade's End*: Christopher Tietjens and Valentine Wallop. We're invited to admire both alike; and yet they stand, in the first instance, for two very different worldviews!

~

The four novels that make up *Parade's End* are (i) *Some Do Not ...*, (ii) *No More Parades*, (iii) *A Man Could Stand Up –*, and (iv) *The Last Post*.[1] Ford wrote them in the mid-1920s. And the setting for much of the action here is the First World War.

In one war-time scene we see Christopher Tietjens's estranged wife Sylvia ensconced in a hotel lounge, a little way behind the front lines, where he's serving as a captain in charge of troop-transports. She has smuggled herself in, so as to make trouble for him; mischievously, to 'pull the strings of the shower-bath', as she likes to put it. And she's accompanied by another officer, Major Perowne; with whom, some four years earlier, she had an affair, which she made sure Christopher knew all about.

Christopher appears. Perowne, a jumpy individual, is immediately thrown into a panic. He exclaims,

'But what does he want? ... Good God! ... what does he want?'
'He wants,' Sylvia said, 'to play the part of Jesus Christ.'
Major Perowne exclaimed:
'Jesus Christ! But he's the most foul-mouthed officer in the general's command. ...'[2]

And then:

'But what are we going to do? What will *he* do?'
'I,' Sylvia answered, 'shall tell the page-boy when he comes with his card to say that I'm engaged. ... I don't know what *he'll* do. Hit you, very likely. He's looking at your back now. ....'
Perowne became rigid, sunk into his deep chair.
'But he *couldn't!*' he exclaimed agitatedly. 'You said that he was playing the part of Jesus Christ. Our Lord wouldn't hit people in a hotel lounge. ...'
'Our Lord!' Sylvia said contemptuously. 'What do

you know about our Lord? Our Lord was a gentleman. ...
Christopher is playing at being our Lord calling on the woman
taken in adultery. ... He's giving me the social backing that his
being my husband seems to him to call for.'[3]

She's infuriated.

Or, then, another scene: a wedding reception in the same town.
(The groom is one of Christopher's fellow-officers; he's marrying
a Frenchwoman.) And Sylvia is calumniating Christopher to his
godfather, General Campion, who's also his commanding officer.
She accuses Christopher, not because it's true but because of the
effect she knows it'll have, of being a Socialist. Campion is, at first,
duly outraged – he speaks of having Christopher drummed out of
the service! – then bewildered.

> 'Hang it all, what *is* at the bottom of that fellow's mind? ...'
>
> 'He desires,' Sylvia said, and she had no idea when she
> said it, 'to model himself upon our Lord ...'
>
> The general leant back in the sofa. He said almost
> indulgently:
>
> 'Who's that ... our *Lord*?'
>
> Sylvia said:
>
> 'Upon our Lord Jesus Christ ...'
>
> He sprang to his feet as if she had stabbed him with a
> hatpin.
>
> 'Our ...' he exclaimed. 'Good God! ... I always knew he
> had a screw loose ... But ...' he said briskly: 'Give all his goods
> to the poor! ... But He wasn't a ... Not a Socialist! What was
> it He said: Render unto Caesar ... It wouldn't be necessary to
> drum Him out of the army ...'[4]

The general is of course a good Anglican.

That night Sylvia successfully arranges a farcical scene, which
involves Christopher, with chivalrous intent, forcibly ejecting first
Major Perowne, and then another general, out of her bedroom;
before himself ending up under arrest. It's perhaps fortunate

that Campion was his father's best friend, and remains, after all, affectionately disposed towards him. Cleared from suspicion of being a Socialist, he isn't drummed out of the army; but is despatched, instead, to fresh duties on the front line, in a yet more hellish sector than before.

What motivates Sylvia? At one level: an impulsive delight in sheer irresponsible devilment. She has a very low boredom threshold. When she originally appears on the scene, in *Some Do Not ...*, almost the first words she utters are, 'I'm bored.'[5.] And later in the same novel, when Christopher is back in London on leave, and the two of them are about to have things out in a decisive conversation, once again her opening words are 'I'm bored! Bored! Bored!' Whereupon she abruptly chucks a plate full of two cold cutlets and some salad at him; leaving a conspicuous dribble of oil and vinegar down the front of his uniform.[6] She's always willing to risk the wildest mischief, for a laugh; for the hell of it. At the same time, she's coolly beautiful, and utterly self-assured. Possessed of all the talents proper to a natural predatory seductress, she sees herself relating to other women as a sea eagle to gulls.[7] A major part of her motivation is just a bully's cruel will to power. She loves Christopher in the sense of obsessively coveting his submission. But he's almost the only man she can neither bring to heel nor goad to fury. And this drives her wild.

Although Sylvia may often be bored, she's never boring. She behaves outrageously. The way however that Ford portrays her, the reader may certainly feel the tingle of her attractiveness. And, crucially, the reader may also sympathise with her recoil from Christopher's moral intransigence. She finds his 'playing the part of Jesus Christ' profoundly offensive. Her allergic reaction to his attempt at goodness brings to light the recalcitrant pettiness of her nature, her flirtatious superficiality, after all; the qualities she has in common with her giggling high-society friends. This is, so to speak, her basic role in the moral *argument* of the novel: to channel the resistant reader's own superficiality. So, she represents your, and my, all too natural recoil from the sort of challenge that Christopher stands for; and does so just as charmingly – just as glamorously, just as seductively – as possible. In Sylvia we see the primordial recoil of superficial-beauty-alone from the sublime; whereas in Christopher's redemptive love affair with Valentine Wannop we see the sublime answering the sublime. Yet, Ford does everything he can to embody this underlying dialectic in well-realised, vividly credible characters; all three of whom are, in different ways, essentially sympathetic.

∾

Christopher, for his part, isn't in superficial terms either beautiful or charming. He's repeatedly described as having 'a mealsack of a body'; and Sylvia deplores his scruffiness. By temperament taciturn, he can also be brusque – or even, as Perowne remarks, when under pressure 'foul-mouthed'. As an officer, interacting with the troops under his command, he's indulgent and generous. But, highly intelligent himself, he doesn't suffer fools *of his own privileged social class* gladly. One might well wonder how his 'playing the part of Jesus Christ' fits with such apparent arrogance. But, in a sense, it's surely a sublation of just that aspect of his character. Inasmuch as his arrogance liberates him to question the herd-morality of his class, as such, it's a necessary precondition for his exceptionally vivid sense of personal vocation. It's the raw material he's re-working.

Many readers may, on the other hand, still be alienated by his class identity. 'And again I tell you, it is easier for a camel to enter in through the eye of a needle than for a rich man to enter into the Kingdom of God': *Parade's End* is partly a meditation on that tight squeeze. Christopher is a 'Tietjens of Groby'; his ancestor came over with 'Dutch William' in 1689, the family had been rewarded with extensive land-holdings across Cleveland. Their ancestral mansion, Groby Hall, lies on the northern edge of the North York Moors. And they own coal mines.

Sylvia may accuse Christopher of being a Socialist but, as a Tietjens, he thinks of himself as being 'Tory'. Mind you, though, this is an *extremely* eccentric form of 'Toryism'. Thus he tells General

Campion: 'I've no politics that did not disappear in the eighteenth century'(!)[8] Notably, he completely rejects the identification of Toryism with 'Empire', the whole heritage of Disraeli. Musing to himself in the trenches, he thinks: 'Damn the Empire! It was England [that mattered]! ...'[9] Or, more particularly, Yorkshire.[10] Again, talking over dinner with the 'extreme Radical' government minister Mr Waterhouse, he finds that they agree, for example, on the need for a generous minimum wage; which was by no means Tory policy at the time.[11] When his round of golf with Waterhouse and others is disrupted by Valentine Wannop and one of her Suffragette colleagues, engaged in a direct-action protest (this is his first encounter with Valentine), he not only intervenes to help them escape arrest. But, in discussing the matter with Valentine subsequently, he also expresses the warmest approval of such militant Suffragette tactics as the firing of letter boxes. Although sceptical whether achieving women's suffrage will have all the beneficial effects Valentine hopes for, he wholeheartedly admires the insurgent courage of the movement; in quite un-Tory fashion.[12] In general he enjoys humorously playing with ideas, exploring extravagant views. Sylvia, trying to discredit him to Father Consett, a Roman Catholic priest, describes what she calls his 'immorality':

> 'Look here. Try and be just. Suppose I'm looking at the *Times* at breakfast and say, not having spoken to him for a week: "It's wonderful what the doctors are doing. Have you seen the latest?" And at once he'll be on his high-horse – he knows everything! – and he'll prove, *prove* that all unhealthy children must be lethal-chambered or the world will go to pieces. And it's like being hypnotised; you can't think of what to answer him. Or he'll reduce you to speechless rage by proving that murderers ought not to be executed.'[13]

Well, Sylvia is a highly unreliable witness, and there's no other mention of his holding eugenicist opinions. But, at all events, it's clear that he isn't always conventionally devout.

So, what's the actual substance of Christopher's Toryism?

Essentially, one might say: a set of tribal reflexes. *Parade's End* is a modernist novel, constantly dipping into stream-of-consciousness. One effect of this is to display the upsurge of prejudices in Christopher's mind, which, taciturn individual that he is, actually remain, for the most part, unexpressed. As his inheritance is old money, he has an instinctive mistrust of parvenus with their new money. Groby is just a few miles across Cleveland from Middlesbrough, and his uneasy relationship with the local Tory MP, Mr Sandbach, for instance, whose wealth comes from the Teesside steel industry, reflects this mistrust. For 'the feuds between the Cleveland landowners and the Cleveland plutocrats are very bitter'.[14] So, too, he distinguishes in his mind between the 'Ruling Class' proper, to which he belongs, and the 'Administrative Class': inasmuch as the former, he thinks, have a feudal duty to enlist, in time of war, whereas the latter don't.[15] He's a close friend of Vincent Macmaster. Yet, he disparagingly thinks of Macmaster as a 'Whig', not least because he's a social climber. And, ranking Yorkshiremen above all others, he also entertains a bantering disdain for Macmaster as a Scot. Is he antisemitic? At one point in *No More Parades* he's enraged by the meddling of a certain Lord Beichan, with regard to the army's use of horses, and curses that 'hog' Beichan 'whose real name was Stavropolides, formerly Nathan'.[16] There's certainly a whiff of Tory snobbery there. Ruggles, on the other hand, is a man who does him a great deal of personal mischief; yet he never curses Ruggles's Jewishness. He considers the Jewish Colonel Levin a bit of a 'popinjay', but is nevertheless fond of him; he responds to Private Eisenstein, alias Smith, the Jewish Socialist militant journalist, with serious respect. And in *The Last Post* we find that he has gone into business with an American Jew, Mr Schatzweiler: exporting antique furniture from Britain to the United States.

At the real heart of his Toryism, however, is his loyalty to the Church of England. (The often-quoted description of the Church of England as 'the Conservative Party at prayer' actually comes from a speech by the reformer Agnes Maude Royden in 1917. Her prayer that it should evolve away from that partisan identity has, as it happens, largely been fulfilled; but *Parade's End* reflects a period when the phrase was all too apt.) Christopher's mother is widely remembered as a saint; General Campion had greatly admired her. Interviewing Christopher, he suddenly enquires:

> 'How do you define Anglican sainthood? The other fellows have canonisations, all shipshape like Sandhurst examinations. But us Anglicans ... I've heard fifty people say your mother was a saint. She was. But why?'

It's a good question! (Sandhurst is the British Army's leading military academy.) Christopher replies:

> 'It's the quality of harmony, sir. The quality of being in harmony with your own soul. God having given you your own soul you are then in harmony with heaven.'[17]

At one point in 1914, we find him – not expecting Britain to join the war, and profoundly dissatisfied with his life – considering enlistment in the French Foreign Legion:

> His desire was to be a saint of the Anglican variety ... as his mother had been, without convent, ritual, vows, or miracles to be performed by your relics! That sainthood, truly, the Foreign Legion might give you ... A mysticism ...[18]

Later, we observe him crouching in a front-line trench, as the sun comes up, thinking of how it must also now be rising over 'the parsonage of George Herbert, author of *Sweet day, so cool, so calm, so bright, the bridal of the earth and sky!*' What's the name of the place?

> The name *Bemerton* suddenly came on to his tongue. Yes, Bemerton, Bemerton, Bemerton was George Herbert's parsonage. Bemerton, outside Salisbury ... The cradle of the race as far as our race was worth thinking about. He imagined himself standing up on a little hill, a lean contemplative

parson, looking at the land sloping down to Salisbury spire. A large, clumsily bound seventeenth-century testament, Greek, beneath his elbow ... Imagine standing up on a hill! It was the unthinkable thing there![19]

He wonders about being ordained an Anglican priest like George Herbert. But the complications of his marital life rule this out. He wants to live with Valentine Wannop, instead.[20]

Ford wasn't himself an Anglican; he was a (not very observant) Roman Catholic. However, he was already wondering about the distinction between Roman Catholic and Anglican sainthood well before he began writing *Parade's End*. In 1914 he published a little, light-hearted article, celebrating the most light-hearted, 'friendly', form of Roman Catholic folk-piety – with its candle-lighting, its muttering cult of Our Lady and the other Saints, and all its other fuss – as contrasted in particular with the sheer sublimity, the intense inwardness, of that version of classical Anglicanism which is so beautifully represented by Herbert's poetry. When he thinks of Anglican sainthood, he writes, in his mind's eye he sees

> at the end of an immense, serenely dark Jacobean room, an immensely tall square mirror, on a square table, between two very tall wax candles – thin wax candles in silver sticks. The mirror reflects nothing but the black serene emptiness of the room, and behind it is an immensely tall window, with square panes giving on to a perfectly black night ...
>
> Indeed, I am a little afraid; I recognize a goodness that, to me, is almost a wickedness and almost certainly a cruelty. It is so apparently austere, restrained, non-communicative.[21]

The article is in the first instance a review of the novel, *Initiation* by Mgr R. H. Benson. But these remarks bear almost no relation to Benson's work. In effect, they mark the first, as yet still unnamed, emergence of Christopher Tietjens into Ford's writing. Why, then, is Ford so interested in the notion of specifically *Anglican* sainthood, which, at first, he'd sought to fend off? Why this focus on General

Campion's question: how to *define* the phenomenon? That he sets the question in the mouth of such an essentially comic character is characteristic self-deprecation. It's Ford himself who is asking it, through Campion; and, indeed, essaying an answer in *Parade's End* as a whole.

From the days of Elizabeth I onwards – with the brief, and really quite mild, exception of the period of Oliver Cromwell's rule – the Church of England lacks any history of major conflict with the state establishment. Over the centuries its privileges have gradually eroded. But, after Mary's brief reign, it was never again engaged in the kind of struggle which originally gave rise to the early Church's cult of martyrs, and which, since then, has so often re-energised the Roman Catholic devotion to the Saints generally, envisaged in propagandist terms. The notion of sainthood according to which the Congregation for the Causes of Saints, in the Vatican, operates is largely designed for the propagandist purposes of a Church institution which sees itself as being, in many places quite intensely, embattled against the secular world. The Church of England – not having been, on the whole, engaged in any such struggle – was never motivated to replicate this particular aspect of Roman Catholic institutional practice. As the good general puts it, "The other fellows have canonisations, all shipshape like Sandhurst examinations"; part of their constant preparations for spiritual warfare. We Anglicans don't. Nevertheless, Anglicans still observe saints' days. We still allow fresh names to percolate into our calendar. It's just that the criteria by which this happens remain somewhat vague and indeterminate. The Church of England's history of complacent privilege is no doubt in many regards deplorable, but one may, I think, be quite glad of at least some of the knock-on consequences; not least, including the absence of anything quite like the propagandist Congregation for the Causes of Saints! For that leaves the question of how to (re-) define true sainthood wide open.

~

Anyhow, we aren't primarily invited to admire Christopher Tietjens, in an anti-ecumenical sense, for being a staunch Anglican; or for any of his other mere opinions, as such. But, far rather, he's presented to us as being admirable for the substantive virtues, *in themselves*, to which those opinions then help give contingent form. Ford indeed explicitly deplores the tendency of critics to misattribute the opinions of his hero to himself.[22] And, although I'm not exactly a member of Christopher's tribe, either, I don't find that that by any means hinders me from appreciating Ford's work as a convincing depiction of sainthood. The opinions, the personality: these are, so to speak, aspects of the 'flesh' in which a certain saintliness is here made more or less incarnate.

Note, moreover, that Christopher for his part has no interest in the reading of novels; this is one of the first things we learn about him.[23] Whatever else we may think of his various opinions, his disdainful attitude specifically towards novel-readers is calculated, straight away, to unite us all – as readers of the novel-sequence *Parade's End* – against him! Ford is teasing us, here, to make the point.

And yet, there can be no denying that Christopher's life is, in fact, quite a vivid amalgam of the *Amos* impulse with the Isaianic archetype. Unlike the prophet Amos, he doesn't have a public platform from which to hurl his thunderbolts. But he *is* a moral outsider, just as Amos was. That's the crucial point. His ethical outlook decisively transcends the herd-morality of his world. And the herd's initial response, largely orchestrated by Sylvia, is to repudiate him as a great sinner.

Here then are some of his eccentric virtues:

- His code notably exceeds any form of herd- or gang-morality, for instance, by virtue of its enshrining the most 'princely' commitment to *generosity*. 'Princely' is his older brother Mark's term for it. 'I suppose you don't give money to every fellow that asks for it?' Mark asks, wondering how Christopher appears to have run through so much money so quickly.

Christopher said:

'I do. It's a matter of principle.'

'It's lucky,' Mark said, 'that a lot of fellows don't know that. You wouldn't have much brass left for long.'

'I didn't have it for long,' Christopher said.

'You know,' Mark said, 'you couldn't have expected to do the princely patron on a younger son's portion. It's a matter of taste. I never gave a ha'penny to a beggar myself. But a lot of the Tietjens were princely. One generation to addle brass; one to keep; one to spend. That's all right …'[24]

Christopher lends especially large sums in particular to his friend Macmaster; with no expectation of being paid back, even after Macmaster has finally made good, and could no doubt well afford it. (Macmaster's wife, the half-crazed Edith Ethel, previously Mrs Duchemin, ensures that this never happens.[25]) So too later on, in 1918, by which time his financial affairs have actually become quite parlous, he still agrees to guarantee an overdraft for his commanding officer on the front line; and it reassures him to find that he remains 'the sort of man who automatically lent money'.[26]

- He has an exceptional regard for the imperatives of *truth-telling*. Before volunteering for military service, he works as a senior civil servant, engaged in the computation of statistics. His scrupulosity, however, wrecks his career. At the beginning of *Some Do Not …* we find him in a state of anguish over being commissioned by government politicians, as he sees it, to 'fake' figures. Macmaster remonstrates with him, in vain.[27] In the event, he does as he is ordered, under protest, although as courteously as he can; but is altogether mortified then to be congratulated on his excellent work.[28] And two years later, discussing with Valentine, who's a Pacifist and whose brother is a conscientious objector, why he's enlisting, he remarks that it's precisely because he too is another sort of conscientious objector: his conscience just won't allow him to go on doing such a dirty job.[29]

- He's also dedicated to *extravagant loyalty*, way beyond the norm. To Macmaster, despite everything, he is a loyal friend; to the troops he commands, a self-abnegating loyal pastor of sorts; to Sylvia, above all, a loyal husband. Why doesn't he divorce her? Again, Campion asks the question.[30] Isn't it driving her mad? And Christopher does wonder: '*Why* the devil am I so anxious to shield that whore? It's not reasonable. It is an obsession' ...[31] But Sylvia doesn't want a divorce. For one thing, she's Roman Catholic, so her religion forbids it. And then, perhaps more significantly, she herself is still obsessed with him; still, in that sense, loves him, albeit sadistically. And right from the outset Christopher has taken the principled position, announced to his father, that 'No one but a blackguard would ever submit a woman to the ordeal of divorce'.[32] Is it inconsistent of him that he then allows Valentine to submit to the still very considerable public shame of being an unmarried mother? No: in both cases alike, he's loyally acceding to the woman's free choice. Valentine, after all, is much less concerned than Sylvia is with maintaining a place in respectable society. True, Sylvia has given him the legal grounds for divorce, with her brazen adultery; and it's quite clear that their relationship has irretrievably broken down. Yet, Christopher persists in never publicly complaining; constantly covering for her; never retaliating, even as she spreads the most outrageous slander about him. His stubborn loyalty to her, as his wife, really is astonishing. It baffles her, defeats her. Try as she may, she just can't break him.

- The relationship between Christopher and Valentine emerges out of this tortuous situation as an unconventional paradigm of *chastity*. Early on, in conversation with Macmaster, Christopher declares, in characteristically gruff and abrasive fashion:

> 'I stand for monogamy and chastity. And for no talking about it. Of course, if a man who's a man wants to have a

275

woman he has her. And again, no talking about it. He'd no doubt be in the end better and better off, if he didn't. Just as it would probably be better for him if he didn't have the second glass of whisky and soda ...'[33]

'No talking about it' – the chastity in question here is distinctive, just by virtue of its radically un-puritanical nature. Unlike the puritan ideal which goes under the same name, it isn't at all envisaged as a code for other people, to restrain and control them; it precludes that sort of 'talk' altogether. It isn't censorious; has nothing to do with the mere maintenance of social order, binding together the herd as such; isn't just the flip-side of moralistic shaming and bullying. But, rather, it's purely and simply the *private* code according to which Christopher regulates his own sexuality: a maximum opening-up of impassioned *eros*, reciprocally delighting in what's received from the other person, to *agapé*, unconditional sheer self-giving.

Christopher's formulation offends Macmaster's more conventional, Pre-Raphaelite sensibility, as it's intended to. It's above all, in that context, a rejection of the sort of art that informs a clamorous erotic neediness; the artistic glamourising of such clamour. 'Chastity' here, in essence, surely means freedom from mere neediness. And so, it's the clearing of a space for *agapé*.

Edith Ethel – Macmaster's future wife – when first we encounter her, whilst she's still Mrs Duchemin, advocates a very different notion of chastity: as a 'thrilling' ideal, somewhat unnervingly, by her, associated with the memory of John Ruskin; lifelong fidelity, even in such a ghastly marriage as hers, at that time, in fact is. 'You mean like an egg and spoon race', says Valentine ...[34] The Revd Mr Duchemin, as a young man, had been a disciple of Ruskin's. But, alas, he has gone crazy. Presiding over breakfast, surrounded by a whole company of guests, he starts to rave:

> 'Chaste!' He shouted. 'Chaste, you observe! What a world of suggestion in the word ...'
>
> ...

He shouted three obscene words and went on in his Oxford Movement voice: 'But chastity ...'

...

'When my revered preceptor,' Mr Duchemin thundered on, 'drove away in the carriage on his wedding day he said to his bride: "We will live like the blessed angels!" How sublime! I, too, after my nuptials ...'

Mrs Duchemin suddenly screamed:

'Oh ... *no!*'[35]

Duchemin-style chastity is by no means freedom from neediness. On the contrary, it's a form of the most extreme neediness, locked however in sanctified frustration; frozen loveless-ness; 'sublime', only in the sense of being a blasphemy against proper beauty.

The sense in which Christopher and Valentine represent the virtue is pretty much the *exact* opposite. Thus, it takes them half a dozen years from first falling in love to finally sleeping together. But the delay isn't due to any inclination to 'live like the blessed angels.' It's due, in the first instance, to his failed attempt to patch up some sort of relationship with Sylvia; and, then, to the interruption of the War. They're by nature two equally strong and self-sufficient people. Valentine is Christopher's equal even in his famous brilliance as a scholar, home-schooled as she has been by her late father, a distinguished classicist. We see them right at the beginning of their relationship, in 1912, having just delivered Valentine's Suffragette comrade Gertie, who's wanted by the police for her subversive exploits, to a safe house; him driving a dog-cart through a moon-lit mist across Romney Marsh. And they're absurdly sparring over fragments of Latin verse.[36] Here we have a humorous token of the way in which their love is so securely grounded in mutual respect. Some five years later, in London, home on leave but due the next morning to return to France and possible death, he suddenly asks her, 'Will you be my mistress tonight?' To which she answers: 'Yes!' and bursts into tears. In the event, circumstances prevent it happening. This is at the end of the first novel in the sequence, *Some Do Not –*. That title phrase recurs in different contexts. But the most notable is to be found here, as we see an old tramp, watching the scene:

> 'That's women!' he said with the apparently imbecile enigmaticality of the old and hardened. 'Some do!' He spat into the grass; said: 'Ah!' then added: 'Some do not!'[37]

'Some do', out of neediness. 'Some do not': that is, they don't need to. Yet, then, of course, it counts for all the more, if and when those who don't need to eventually 'do'.

Parade's End is, to say the least, a paradoxical study of 'Anglican sainthood', inasmuch as it's a tale of sanctified adultery! Nevertheless, such is the magic of the novel that it somehow contrives to make perfect sense of that paradox.

∽

Meanwhile, as for the Isaianic archetype: the core pathos of *Parade's End* as a whole comes from the exposure of these two exceptionally free-spirited and resilient characters to such intensities of affliction, and what this shows us of their character. On the one hand, there's the vast collective affliction of the War; on the other hand, the affliction deriving from the malice of the offended herd. It's the latter which constitutes the specifically Isaianic element. But the War, as context, serves as a general intensifier.

Christopher and Valentine represent two very different attitudes towards the War; and Sylvia, notably, another. Sylvia's response is Pacifist, as Valentine's is, but of quite a different kind. She spends the War as a celebrity socialite, regularly appearing in the illustrated papers; defiantly befriends a group of aristocratic Austrian prisoners of war; looks upon the military world with contempt:

> She saw Christopher buried in this welter of fools, playing a schoolboy's game of make-believe. But of a make-believe that was infinitely formidable and infinitely sinister.[38]

Valentine, by contrast, doesn't *enjoy* being Pacifist, 'because it was the attitude of the superior and she did not like being superior'.[39] She is one, however, simply out of compassion.

Note that Christopher, in conversation with Valentine, by no means denies the monstrous cruel absurdity of the War. In fact, he tacitly concedes the absolute validity of her arguments, so far as they go. Only, given that it *is* taking place, he feels a moral compulsion to take part. No one was demanding that men of his age should enlist. But, as he sees it, *noblesse oblige*.

And then here he is in enigmatic conversation with Colonel Levin, in the winter of 1917, overlooking a battle-scarred landscape:

[Levin] remained looking at the view, drooping, in intense dejection. He said: 'This *beastly* war! This *beastly* war ... Look at all that view ...'

Tietjens said:

'It's an encouraging spectacle, really. The beastliness of human nature is always pretty normal. We lie and betray and are wanting in imagination and deceive ourselves, always, at about the same rate. In peace and in war! But, somewhere in that view there are enormous bodies of men ... If you got a still more extended range of view over this whole front you'd have still more enormous bodies of men. Seven to ten million ... All moving towards places towards which they desperately don't want to go. Desperately! Every one of them is desperately afraid. But they go on. An immense blind will forces them in the effort to consummate the one decent action that humanity has to its credit in the whole of recorded history; the one we are engaged in. That effort is the one certain creditable fact in all their lives ... But the *other* lives of all those men are dirty, potty and discreditable affairs ... Like yours ... Like mine ...'[40]

'The one decent action that humanity has to its credit'! I take it that by 'decency' in general, synecdochally represented by the concerted doings of all those millions – on both sides – he means *any* action inspired by a spirit of sublime self-sacrifice, in solidarity with one's comrades. He's by no means saying that the War, in itself, is justified because it so often makes just this sort of demand on those engaged in it; nor that that by any means nullifies the monstrous cruel absurdity of the whole affair. But, rather: that the fact, here revealed, of the sublime human capacity for 'decency' so defined may, nonetheless, go some way towards morally justifying our very existence as a species. In which case, adopting Valentine's point of view, one might well say: the true tragedy of the War is that it has taken the fundamental moral potential of humanity for 'decency', sublime virtue, and exploited it precisely in the service of, at a secondary level, such *indecent purposes*!

Thus, again: what constitutes sainthood, in the strict sense? In general, I'd argue, it's nothing other than this essential human 'decency', valued no longer as a mere instrument in the service of extraneous projects, military or otherwise, but purely and simply as a sublime ideal *in itself*. The authentic 'sublime of the warrior' is indeed sublime, just as the authentic 'sublime of the saint' is. But the point is: only the latter, by its very nature, ultimately transcends such instrumentalisation.

At any rate, Ford depicts the horror of war, full-on; entirely divested of any more superficial propaganda-justification. The account includes moments of rich sensuous description, like this hellish scene of a behind-the-frontline air raid at the beginning of *No More Parades*:

> An immense tea-tray, august, its voice filling the black circle of the horizon, thundered to the ground. Numerous pieces of sheet-iron said 'Pack. Pack. Pack.' In a minute the clay floor of the hut shook, the drums of ears were pressed inwards, solid noise showered about the universe, enormous echoes pressed these men – to the right, to the left, or down towards the tables, and crackling like that of flames among vast underwood became the settled condition of the night. Catching the light of the brazier as the head leaned over, the lips of one of the two men on the floor were incredibly red and full and went on talking and talking ...[41]

Then, sights and sounds are intercut with anxious dialogue, and anxious flickering thoughts. The multi-tasking of Ford's prose elegantly renders the high-stress multi-tasking of Christopher's mind. So, we find him sitting there in the hut. His job, administering the transfer of troops from the reserve to the trenches, involves a vast amount of paper-work; regulations to be complied with, decisions to be made; coping with fresh instructions from HQ. Plus: counselling garrulous soldiers with personal problems; supporting one fellow-officer in his love-life, and another who's suffering a nervous breakdown; whilst all the while he's haunted by thoughts of his own unresolved affairs back home. Partly in order to distract Captain McKechnie (*alias* 'Mackenzie'), the officer suffering a nervous breakdown – another who prides himself on his gifts as a scholar – he devises a game, a challenge. Let McKechnie give him the end-rhymes for a sonnet, and he'll compose one in less than two and a half minutes. McKechnie accepts the challenge, and further commits himself to then translating the result into Latin hexameters in less than three. A man has just been killed, and his remains laboriously cleared up, in that same hut. In the middle of Christopher's conversation with McKechnie, one of the two men we've just seen, sprawled on the floor by the brazier – a Welsh miner known as 'O Nine Morgan' – was hit by a stray bomb fragment. Christopher had lately refused Morgan permission to return home on leave. He'd done so on receipt of advice from the Pontardulais police that Morgan's wife was engaged in an affair with a local prize-fighter, and that it wouldn't be safe. Nevertheless, he feels the guilt of having, in effect, unwittingly helped cause the man's death. – All these different layers of concurrent preoccupation!

This is one of three moments in which violent death suddenly irrupts into the prevailing outer tedium of Christopher's military career; one in each of the three novels which cover it. In *A Man Could Stand Up –*, at the end of Part Two, an explosion buries him in mud. It kills Lance-Corporal Duckett – a boy from Teesside, with ambitions to be a chef, who knows all about the Tietjens of Groby Hall – and leaves 'little Aranjuez', a young Portuguese who hero-worships Tietjens, blinded in one eye. This is in 1918. And in *Some Do Not ...*, at some earlier point in the War, he tells Sylvia about his experience of being hospitalised with shell-shock: how, in his bewilderment, he'd been left wondering, 'What is my name?'.

'I lay and worried and worried and thought how discreditable it would appear if a nurse came along and asked me and I didn't know. Of course my name was on a luggage label tied to my collar; but I'd forgotten they did that to casualties ...

Then a lot of people carried pieces of a nurse down the hut; the Germans' bombs had done that of course. They were still dropping about the place ...

'The poor dear wasn't dead ... I wish she had been. Her name was Beatrice Carmichael ... the first name I learnt after my collapse. She's dead now of course ... That seemed to wake up a fellow on the other side of the room with a lot of blood coming through the bandages on his head ... He rolled out of his bed and, without a word, walked across the hut and began to strangle me ...

He let out a number of ear-piercing shrieks and lots of orderlies came and pulled him off me and sat all over him. Then he began to shout, '*Faith!*' He shouted: 'Faith! ... Faith! ... Faith! ...' at intervals of two seconds, as far as I could tell by my pulse, until four in the morning, when he died. ... I don't know whether it was a religious exhortation or a woman's name, but I disliked him a good deal because he started my tortures, such as they were.'[42]

Here begins his 'dark night of the soul'.

Eventually, he recovers from the worst of his shell-shock, well enough to take up fresh duties. In *A Man Could Stand Up* –, we see him nonchalantly strolling through the trenches under his command, according to 'his conviction that he must show the men his mealsack of a body, mooning along; but attentive'.[43] A few months later, however, when Valentine arrives at his apartment on Armistice Day – before she can ring the bell – all of a sudden, the door opens, and he comes running out, another figure entirely:

> He charged upon her. There in the open ... He came, grey all over, his grey hair – or the grey patches of his hair – shining, charging down the steps, having slammed the hall door. And lopsided. He was carrying under his arm a diminutive piece of furniture. A cabinet.
>
> It was so quick. It was like having a fit. The houses tottered. He regarded her. He had presumably checked violently in his clumsy stride. She hadn't seen because of the tottering of the houses. His stone-blue eyes came fishily into place in his wooden countenance ...
>
> What was he doing? Fumbling in the pocket of his clumsy trousers. He exclaimed – she shook at the sound of his slightly grating, slightly gasping voice –:
>
> 'I'm going to sell this thing ... Stay here.' He had produced a latchkey. He was panting fiercely beside her. Up the steps. He was beside her.
>
> Beside her. It was infinitely sad to be beside this madman. It was infinitely glad ...[44]

As the 'madman' has indicated she should, she goes inside. The apartment is empty. Except that in the middle of a large room upstairs

> As if set down in a field ... there camped ... A camp bed for the use of officers, G.S. one, as the saying is. And implements of green canvas, supported on crossed wooden staves: a chair, a bucket with a rope handle, a washing basin, a table. The bed was covered over with a flea-bag of brown wool.[45]

A typewritten document is lying on the floor. She reads the words: *'Mrs Tietjens is leaving the model cabinet by Barker of Bath which she believes you claim ...'*[46] The apartment is empty because Sylvia has emptied it; yet another act of war against Christopher. And he's engaged in selling the one item she has left him, a particular treasure, just so as to get through the next few days.

~

This is, in retrospect the moment of Sylvia's decisive defeat. But it really has been a formidable campaign; and she's determined to persist with it to the last. That night the streets are filled with revellers celebrating Peace, and the apartment is invaded by a group of Christopher's comrades. *A Man Could Stand Up* – concludes with a carnivalesque scene in that upper room. The memory of what happens afterwards, however, emerges only gradually in *The Last Post*: how they hire a horse-drawn cab to transport a man dying of cancer to his home, and the raving McKechnie to an asylum, with an escort of some sixteen revellers – how the sick man dies on the way – and how Christopher and Valentine then return to the dark apartment, only to find Sylvia waiting for them, lamp-lit and clad all in white, at the head of the stairs. She declares herself to be sick with cancer. And then, melodramatically, collapses when they approach. It's a lie: *she* doesn't have cancer. She keeps up the act for some months. But fortunately, neither Christopher nor Valentine is deceived.[47]

Largely, though not exclusively, due to Sylvia's campaign against them, Christopher and Valentine are victims of endless hurtful gossip. She slanders him shamelessly, both to her fashionable women friends and, notably, to General Campion, who's fond of her. Is Christopher truly the father of her son? She's unsure; it may be Major Drake, a military intelligence officer. Either way, Drake loathes Christopher, and is in a position to do him damage by adding some highly critical comments to his military file: alleging excessive Francophilia and a degree of poverty, liable to render him vulnerable to bribery. Earlier in the War Christopher, as a fluent French-speaker, had enjoyed working as a liaison officer with the French; but when he returns after his recovery from shell-shock, he's no longer allowed to continue in that role.[48] And then another man whose hatred of

Christopher derives from an infatuation with Sylvia is 'Brownie', Mr Brownlie, a banker, who engineers a situation in which two of Christopher's cheques bounce; leading to Christopher's resignation from his club. However, Sylvia doesn't reciprocate Brownie's passion, and in this case unmasks his discreditable manoeuvre.[49]

Sylvia herself insists that, regardless of his refusal to believe it, Christopher's mother 'died of a broken heart' as a result of her affair with Perowne.[50] His father's death, meanwhile, looks suspiciously like suicide. If so, was that also due to a broken heart? A little while previously, Mr Tietjens had commissioned Christopher's older brother Mark to find out whether Christopher was in particular need of money. Mark had delegated the task to his room-mate, Ruggles, a dedicated lover of gossip for gossip's sake. And Ruggles had come up with all sorts of salacious story, doing the rounds, which he'd diligently passed on.[51]

Christopher is rumoured to be Edith Ethel, Mrs Duchemin's lover, both before and after her second marriage, to Macmaster. This is chiefly the result of her having been seen, on the eve of war being declared, by a number of society people travelling back down to London from their holidays in the north, in a railway carriage, weeping on his shoulder. Actually, she was in acute distress, finding herself pregnant with Macmaster's child, which she then aborted.[52] Sylvia actually suggests to Valentine that Christopher was the father.[53] He's also rumoured to be Valentine's lover, long before that's actually the case. Again, Sylvia spreads this lie. And Edith Ethel, after she has turned against Christopher, directly confronts Valentine with it: 'Seven people', she says, 'in the past five weeks have told me you have had a child by that brute beast.'[54] Ruggles is another conduit for the same rumour. In addition, he speculates on Christopher's reasons for marrying Sylvia when she was, supposedly, with child by Drake; and his reasons for taking her back after her adultery with Perowne. Was it, he wonders, in order to make money by pimping her out, for instance to a wealthy banker like Lord Port Scatho?[55] (Port Scatho is, as it happens, an eminently respectable, evangelical gentleman.)

In short, Christopher acquires an entirely unmerited reputation for 'drunkenness and debaucheries' of every kind.[56]

The sheer swirl of it!

Such is the extent of all this slander that one may perhaps wonder: is *Parade's End* the work of a positively *paranoid* imagination? There's nothing paranoid about either Christopher or Valentine, as Ford presents them. That's to say, there's nothing delusional about their world-view. But the charge has nevertheless been levelled against *Ford* himself. Melvin Seiden for example (as I understand him) argues that their plight as individual victims of calumny is, essentially, the analogical expression of a whole paranoid political world-view on Ford's own part; the microcosm corresponding to the macrocosm.[57]

In my view, however, Seiden has fundamentally missed the real point here. Indeed, he has missed the point just because he fails to see the way in which Ford is tacitly following the logic of the Isaianic archetype. True, there's political paranoia in the air, amongst the troops in France; which Ford refers to.[58] Nor is it surprising that the troops are often bitter about the civilians in Westminster and Whitehall: is politics, after all, *ever* driven by the sort of generous empathy these men, in the extremity of their plight, ideally need? And, moreover, there may be a number of good reasons for mistrust here. Christopher, who's well informed, does think so.[59] But I don't find this to be such a primary theme of the work, generally, as Seiden suggests. Ford's real reason for depicting all the accumulation of slanderous gossip around his two central characters is not, I think, displaced political paranoia. On the contrary: the true rationale of his writing here is, on the contrary, *the exact opposite* of paranoid! He's depicting two individuals who – whilst, yes, they have every reason to respond to their plight in paranoid fashion – nevertheless, to a quite remarkable degree, don't. Paranoia, surely, is an impulse of self-pity, run out of control. Ford wants us to feel all the potential moral justification that Christopher and Valentine might have for self-pity. And he certainly lays it on thick. Yet, the point is for us to be all the more aware of how well they overcome that temptation. We're privy to their inmost thoughts. Christopher is by no means immune to 'the luxury of self-pity', if only for an occasional brief moment:

> He considered that he was dull-minded, heavy, ruined, and so calumniated that at times he believed in his own infamy, for it is impossible to stand up for ever against the obloquy of your kind and remain unhurt in the mind.[60]

He also confides to Valentine his bitter sense of being scapegoated, by the herd:

> 'You see in such a world as this, an idealist – or perhaps it's only a sentimentalist – must be stoned to death. He makes the others so uncomfortable. He haunts them at their golf … No, they'll get me, one way or the other.'[61]

But note: he confides this *only* to Valentine. True, at one point he does resign from his club, in justified fury. But, notwithstanding so much provocation, he never returns spite for spite. Is he just masking his resentment? Well, yes, but then how else is resentment ever to be overcome? Isn't the masking of it a necessary first step? Christopher's bitterness remains absolutely reined in; there isn't even a hint of his desiring vengeance. And neither does Valentine.

Again, compare Isaiah's description of the Suffering Servant:

> He was oppressed, and he was afflicted,
> yet he did not open his mouth;
> like a lamb that is led to the slaughter,
> and like a sheep that before its shearers is silent,
> so he did not open his mouth.
>
> > (*Isaiah* 53:7)

Ford's supreme achievement is, in effect, to have translated the moral energy encapsulated in that archetypal image of restraint, into extended novelistic form.

Thus: above all, consider for instance Christopher's really quite extravagant chivalry face to face with Sylvia:

'As I hope to stand before my Redeemer,' Sylvia said 'I believe [that you never did a dishonourable action] ... But, in the name of the Almighty, how could any woman live beside you ... and be for ever forgiven? Or no: not forgiven; ignored! ... Don't you know, Christopher Tietjens, that there is only one man from whom a woman could take *"Neither I condemn thee"* and not hate him more than she hates the fiend! ...'

Tietjens so looked at her that he contrived to hold her attention.

'I'd like you to let me ask you,' he said, 'how I could throw stones at you? I have never disapproved of your actions.'

Her hands dropped dispiritedly to her sides.

'Oh, Christopher,' she said, 'don't carry on that old play-acting ...'

'As you said just now,' he exclaimed slowly, 'as I hope to meet my Redeemer I believe you to be a good woman. One that never did a dishonourable thing.'

She recoiled a little in her chair.

'Then!' she said, 'you're the wicked man I've always made believe to think you, though I didn't.'

Tietjens said:

'No! ... Let me try and put it to you as I see it.'

She exclaimed:

'No! I've been a wicked woman. I have ruined you. I am not going to listen to you.'

He said:

'I daresay you have ruined me. That's nothing to me. I am completely indifferent.'[62]

Is he, truly, 'play-acting', as she alleges? *She* has certainly been playing a game, from the beginning of their relationship, one she has every intention of continuing: a game of endless cruelty, constant provocation. So how *can* he say that he considers her never to have done a 'dishonourable' thing? Clearly, he's using the word 'dishonourable' in a very particular sense! I take his meaning to be that she too is someone who, whatever her faults, has at any rate never sought to justify them in terms of self-pity. Just as he refuses to indulge self-pity in his own life, so he respects her, inasmuch as she follows that same principle. And my guess is that this is how he's able to say he has never 'disapproved' of her actions. Of course, he has constantly disagreed with them, regretted them. But he has never 'disapproved' of them to the extent of altogether losing his respect for her, as a person with too much self-respect herself ever wilfully to surrender to self-pity.

In the *Last Post*, which is set some years after the end of the War, we find that Sylvia has after all finally initiated divorce proceedings against Christopher; or, at any rate taken the first preparatory step, in the form of a petition for the restitution of conjugal rights. Not that she was really looking for divorce even now, but just for yet another way to harass him. And her lawyer, Mr Hatt, an aspiring radical politician, 'had cast as much mud as an enthusiastic terrier with its hind legs out of a fox's hole', in the hope of publicity.

> It had embarrassed Sylvia herself, sitting brilliantly in Court. And it had roused the judge, who knew something of the case having, like half London of his class, taken tea with the dying Sylvia beneath the crucifix and amongst the lilies of the nursing home which was also a convent.[63]

Against her will, Mr Hatt invokes her pretend-cancer. She can't bear it. The whole affair turns out to be so mortifying!

> She had precipitately left the court when Mr Hatt had for the second time appealed for pity for her – but she had not been able to stop him … Pity! She appeal for pity! She had regarded herself as – she had certainly desired to be regarded as – the sword of the Lord smiting the craven and the traitor to Beauty![64]

Self-pity – a self-righteous revelling in a sense of victimhood – is perhaps the innermost latent energy of herd-morality, as such; herd-morality's most basic defence-stratagem against criticism. Inasmuch as she refuses self-pity, Sylvia is just as much an outsider to herd-morality, albeit in a different way, as Christopher and Valentine are.[65] The difference is just the response, in each case, to the outsider-nature of the other: as Christopher responds to Sylvia's lack of self-pity with fundamental respect, but she finds *his* resistance to self-pity simply exasperating. It's this resistance which she seeks to break: not least, by manipulating her friends' love of titillating gossip, or in other words the herd-nature of high society.

Christopher's response to Sylvia isn't, exactly, 'forgiveness'. She doesn't ask to be forgiven; in fact, it seems that she's incapable of the repentance that full forgiveness requires. But, in their relationship, what we see is 'Beauty' confronted by the Sublime: a beautiful cruelty, a sublime magnanimity, the latter subjected to Suffering Servant affliction, no less. We're shown the most radical drive towards truth-as-openness, prevailing through even the most extreme of stress-tests.

∾

Considered in the context of Ford's writing as a whole, the four constituent novels of *Parade's End* actually represent something of a miracle! As an often-struggling full-time professional writer, Ford published some eighty works, large and small, during his lifetime (1873—1939); plus, a great number of articles, notably in reviews that he himself edited. He wrote volumes of poetry; literary history and cultural criticism; biography and autobiography; local history and travel books; as well as political commentary; and some thirty-one novels, including two co-authored with Joseph Conrad. His novels are of many diverse kinds. By general consent, they're of very uneven quality. He himself also considered them so. Besides *Parade's End*, the one indisputably great one is *The Good Soldier*, which first appeared in 1915.[66] But that's quite a different sort of work from *Parade's End*: a first-person narrative of adultery and deception, the narrator being the long-time deceived husband, surveying the past in bemusement. In it, Ford achieves a certain sort of technical perfection; only, however, by working on a very much more confined scale, and at very much lesser intensity, than he does in the later work.

Parade's End is an altogether more ambitious work than *The Good Soldier* or than any of Ford's other novels: both because of its context in the vast world-historic trauma of the First World War, and also by virtue of the way he rises here to the ethical challenge of this trauma. He pours substantial elements of his own experience into the work. The character of Christopher Tietjens is, for instance, in numerous details based upon that of his one-time friend Arthur Marwood, who'd died in 1916. Aspects of Sylvia's campaign against Christopher resemble incidents in the break-up of Ford's own love-affair with Violet Hunt. In writing of Valentine, as a Suffragette, he does so as one who had himself, in 1913, been commissioned by the Women's Freedom League to write a pamphlet helping to promote the cause. When it comes to the tension between Valentine and Christopher due to the former's Pacifism, he's no doubt drawing upon conversations with his own partner during the writing of *Parade's End*, Stella Bowen who was likewise a Pacifist. And, above all, the description of life as a soldier on, or just behind, the front line is directly drawn from his own experience. Aged forty-one, he volunteered for military service in 1915; went out to France the following year, to fight in the Battle of the Somme; was blown up there, suffered concussion, lost his memory for three weeks, and was discharged from hospital still suffering from shell-shock; then returned to the front in the Ypres Salient; before finally being withdrawn, and sent back to hospital with pneumonia, probably complicated by the after-effects of poison gas. There's evidence, notably in some of his unpublished fiction-writing of 1919—20, that, at that point, he remained psychologically very fragile; haunted, even if never altogether overwhelmed, by paranoid impulses. But *Parade's End* marks his full recovery: the difference being precisely that, as

Ford's biographer Max Saunders puts it, 'the earlier works endorse their heroes' imputations of universal victimisation, whereas the hero of *Parade's End* himself achieves enough detachment from his anxieties – his gut feelings of persecution and victimization – not to impute conspiracies'; at any rate, not to any unrealistic degree.[67] Thus, once again: *Parade's End* is surely the outcome of a decisive imaginative triumph over potential paranoia – albeit the triumph of an imagination that has been seared by what it overcomes.

Ford was clearly not a perfect saint, himself. He was a novelist through and through; perhaps too much so, in fact, ever fully to emulate the virtues that he seeks to celebrate. Thus, he was notoriously inclined to tell lies, in the form of tall stories about his own past; not, on the whole it would seem, out of conceit, but rather in simple pursuit of story-teller entertainment. And, evidently a loveable and loving man – who loved love at its aesthetically most intense – he was, in consequence, also somewhat fickle in his love-affairs, once the initial spark had died; not altogether a man to rely on. Well, the ethical sense informing *Parade's End* is far more than just veiled self-justification, self-affirmation! And (fortunately!) one doesn't have to be a saint to write about saints.

I've called this work a 'miracle'. The abundance of richly delineated characters; the multi-layered complexity of the plot, largely unfolding in retrospect; the sharp attention to sensory detail: all of these factors, working together, make it a slow read. At the same time, it's also remarkable for its emotional range. It depicts scenes of infernal horror; yet is often very funny, sometimes even slapstick-farcical. The prevailing mood runs from anguish to jubilation, caustic irony to wistful poignancy.

Most 'miraculous' of all, however, is just the way it rises, at its core, to such a sustained intensity of religious concern. For there's nothing quite like this in any of Ford's other writing.

Parade's End, although widely acclaimed, has never properly attained the classic status it may be said to deserve. It's, not least, without doubt the best-written, most ambitious, and most thought-provoking study of genuine sainthood that I've yet seen, in novelistic form.

⌇

Ford's work indeed vividly illustrates the great potential advantages that novelists have, over the purveyors of standard hagiography. Thus, in the first place, they're free to explore the concept of sainthood with reference to a far wider range of exemplary figures. In *Parade's End* there are in fact two other minor characters, besides Christopher, actually referred to as 'saintly': his mother, and the Roman Catholic Father Consett. And Valentine is another major figure who surely has to be considered, more or less, in the same light; such is Christopher's own unstinting admiration for her.

Of the four, Christopher's mother is the one who most nearly conforms to an abstract conventional model. But that's just because we never see her direct, but only as she's remembered, by Christopher himself, by Christopher's brother Mark, and by General Campion.

Father Consett we encounter early in *Some Do Not* …: 'out to have an uproarious good time during his three weeks' holiday from the slums of Liverpool', which he's spending as one of the company gathered around Sylvia's mother, in a German resort-hotel.[68] He too is immediately introduced as a 'saint'. We see him then as he confronts and scolds Sylvia, for her scandalous behaviour towards her husband. He's notably another man, besides Christopher, who shows no fear of her. Subsequently, we learn that he has, in a sense, been martyred: as an Irish Republican, executed by the British authorities, an associate of Roger Casement.[69] Sylvia is haunted by her memories of him. He becomes, as it were, a heavenly embodiment of her conscience, such as it is.[70] Yet, he's also a somewhat unconventional saint; swigging whisky and, whilst on holiday, obsessed with playing bridge.

Another advantage which the novelist has, with regard to the depiction of heroic virtue, is in being able to show how such virtue *arises*, out of the sublimation of cruder, pre-moral impulses. In other words: how it still remains rooted in the fallibility, and vulnerability, of the flesh. Ford's portrayal of both Christopher and Valentine – probing beneath the surface of their public personas – illustrates the point here with especial boldness. For, the admirable freedom from mere herd-morality characteristic of them both is energised by a tremendous intensity of basic animal spirits, which *in itself* is simply anarchic. Take for example the scene, shortly after they have first met, when they're out for a walk together, across fields not far from Valentine's home in Kent. It's mid-day, in summer. Christopher, having eaten a sumptuous breakfast, and lit a pipe, is at ease. Valentine is walking ahead of him.

> On the left [was] a ten-foot, untrimmed quicken hedge, the hawthorn blossoms just beginning to blacken at the edges and small green haws to show. On the right the grass was above knee high and bowed to those that passed. The sun was exactly vertical; the chaffinches said: 'Pink! pink!' The young woman had an agreeable back.
>
> This, Tietjens thought, is England! ...[71]

In his mind he runs, luxuriantly, through the names of all the likely local birds; all the grasses of this landscape; all the wildflowers and the weeds. He imagines a great orchestra, launching out into 'Land of Hope and Glory'. Whereupon:

> [he] paused and aimed with his hazel stick an immense blow at a tall spike of yellow mullein with its undecided, buttony, unripe lemon-coloured flower. The structure collapsed, gracefully, like a woman killed among crinolines!
>
> 'Now I'm a bloody murderer!' Tietjens said. 'Not gory! Green-stained with vital fluid of innocent plant ... And, by God! Not a woman in the country who wouldn't let you rape her after an hour's acquaintance!' He slew two more mulleins and a sow-thistle! A shadow, but not from the sun, a gloom, lay across the sixty acres of purple grass bloom and marguerites, white: like petticoats of lace over the grass!
>
> 'By God', he said, 'Church! State! Army! H. M. Ministry:

H. M. Opposition: H. M. City Man ... all the governing class!
All rotten!'[72\]

These somewhat shockingly anarchic, dreamy half-thoughts of
murder and consensual (!) 'rape' constitute a first moment in the
dialectic of overcoming herd-morality, a moment of pure negation
(also negating the gang-morality of the 'governing class')
which will then be transformed, as it were in a second moment,
negating *that* negation, into the absolute moral integrity of the
Amos impulse. The second moment: the moment of the 'shadow',
a sudden tempering of sensual exhilaration with subversive
seriousness ...

What is it that attracts Valentine to Christopher; and Christopher
to Valentine? Each, in effect, recognises in the other a resolute
devotee of the primordial *Amos* impulse. For both of them, thus,
intense sexual passion fuses with, and is very much subordinated
to, moral passion. Never mind that herd-morality frowns upon
the irregularity of their relationship. Valentine has been brought
up 'amongst rather "advanced" young people'. Without thinking
much about the matter, her immediate inclination is to repudiate
the official, puritan sexual mores of her parents' generation. At
a deeper level, observation of life has instilled in her a fierce,
aesthetic appreciation of freely chosen chastity.[73] Nevertheless, in
A Man Could Stand Up – we find her on Armistice Day looking back
over the War years that have finally ended, and considering how,
for her, everything has changed. Again, the moral that she draws
is, in the first instance, quite anarchic:

> Now ... She was never going to show respect for anyone ever
> again. She had been through the mill: the whole world had
> been through the mill! No more respect![74]

She is, at this point, working as a Physical Instructress at a
Protestant girls' public school. The prospect of Armistice Day poses
a particular challenge to those in charge of discipline at the school,
as it does for all those concerned to maintain social discipline:

Undoubtedly what the Mistresses with the Head at their head had feared was that if they, Headmistresses, Mistresses, Masters, Pastors ... should cease to be respected because saturnalia broke out on the sounding of a maroon the world would go to pieces! An awful thought! The Girls no longer sitting silent in the nonconformist hall while the Head addressed repressive speeches to them. ....[75]

A couple of days before, a false alarm had – 'horribly' – led to a mass chorus of

'Hang Kaiser Bill from the hoar apple tree
And Glory, Glory, Glory till it's tea-time!'

Accordingly, to prevent any repetition of that, the Head has asked Valentine to keep the girls in the playground right through the morning, all six hundred of them tidily lined up in rows, doing Physical Jerks and the like. Valentine senses a great fear in the air:

If, at this parting of the ways, at this crack across the table of History, the School – the World, the future mothers of Europe – got out of hand, would they ever come back? The Authorities – Authority all over the world – was afraid of that; more afraid of that than of any other thing. Wasn't it a possibility that there was to be no more Respect? None for constituted Authority and consecrated Experience?[76]

She does as the Head instructs her. But she herself is less and less inclined to show respect for what herd-morality envisages as Authority. And therefore – even though she has heard nothing from Christopher – why not take the initiative and, in the midst of the saturnalia, go seek him out?

Again, though, the *Amos* impulse as an alternative, and now genuine, basis for authority requires mediation through at any rate some rough approximation to the Isaianic archetype. The whole narrative of the first three novels enacts this mediation.

Christopher's share in the affliction of the Suffering Servant is of course horrifically accentuated by what he undergoes in the War. Valentine's is partly shaped by her anxiety at not having heard any news of him; and partly, also, by the consequences of poverty. Her father, the distinguished Oxford academic, died long ago; her mother, being a novelist, is consequently (as Ford sees it!) always on the verge of penury. Much of Valentine's rebelliousness is attributable to her experience – highly educated though she is – of having been obliged, before gaining employment at the school, to work as a domestic servant. She has been a 'tweeny': a between maid, the lowest rank of all, charged with serving at table in the Servants' Hall. Never brought up to be subservient, she has nevertheless learnt from experience what humiliating subservience feels like – and quietly, yet with all her youthful energy, recoils in dissident solidarity with the humiliated, everywhere.

~

It's a singular feature of *Parade's End* that the same primary characters appear in two very different narrative contexts. First, in *Some Do Not ...*, *No More Parades* and *A Man Could Stand Up* –: framed in an epic progression of events, that culminates on Armistice Day. Then, in *The Last Post*: coming together for a single hour, a decade or so after the War's end, one summer's afternoon, out on a steep, rural West Sussex hillside, where Christopher and Valentine have settled with his brother Mark and French sister-in-law Marie-Léonie.

There has been much critical controversy over the status of *The Last Post*. Ford himself had an ambivalent attitude towards it. When an omnibus edition of *Parade's End* was planned in 1930, he wrote: 'I strongly wish to omit *The Last Post* from the edition. I do not like the book, and have never liked it, and always intended the series to end with *A Man Could Stand Up* –'.[77] But then he back-tracked and left the matter up to the publishers, who decided to include it. Graham Greene, as editor of the Bodley Head edition (1962—63), *did* omit it. Greene deplored *The Last Post* in the strongest terms. He accused it of being sentimental – which I certainly think is unfair. It's true that the relationship between *The Last Post* and the previous three novels is asymmetrical: it depends on them; they don't depend on it. Specifically with regard to the depiction of sainthood in *Parade's End*, it's the first three which do all the heavy lifting. *The Last Post* has a different role; but still, I think, a very interesting one. And it builds towards a wonderfully lyrical conclusion.

Christopher, for his part, only appears on the scene in *The Last Post* right at the very end: he has been up in an aeroplane, visiting the Tietjens' ancestral home at Groby, in Cleveland. As the older brother, Mark has offered to give him Groby, plus all the agricultural rents and coal-mine income linked with it. Christopher has refused the offer: for one thing, it doesn't seem proper to him whilst he remains married to Sylvia, yet living with Valentine. Let Sylvia have the place instead, with their son, as the Tietjens' heir! However, he has flown there, vainly hoping to forestall Sylvia's latest great act of spite. There's a Great Tree at Groby, a cedar, planted too close to the house and therefore darkening some of the rooms, but a magnificent specimen, regarded by Christopher as a treasure. Acting in league with an entirely ludicrous but extremely rich American, Mrs de Bray Pape who's renting the place, Sylvia schemes to have the Great Tree felled. Christopher has in fact arrived too late to stop this happening; indeed, the felling of the tree has brought down half a wall of the house itself.

Valentine, meanwhile, is also absent for the greater part of the book. She's pregnant and resting in her room. Outside in a leafy garden bower, Mark Tietjens lies, largely paralysed. Having suffered a stroke at the end of the War, he has retreated into silence; and now he's dying. The book ends with his death. We follow his ruminations; and the flickering thoughts of Marie-Léonie as she cares for him. Meanwhile, the cast assembles. On the one hand, there are the local peasants. On the other hand: a troupe of visitors on horseback, the guests of the local aristocrat

Lord Fittleworth, with Sylvia amongst them; also, her son Michael, a. k. a. (young) Mark and an American woman with whom Michael/Mark is besotted; General Campion; and Mrs de Bray Pape. Finally, Edith Ethel arrives, as well, accompanied by Mr Ruggles. Sylvia has organised it all, as part of her ongoing campaign against Christopher. But, finding Valentine pregnant, she's suddenly shocked into recognising the actual reality of the situation! Now that her defeat is final, it all seems so futile. The Great Tree having been felled, has a curse perhaps been lifted from the Tietjens family? She's superstitious enough to think so: 'The thought suddenly recurred, sweeping over with immense force: God had changed sides at the cutting down of Groby Great Tree'![78] Weeping, she repents; disgusted with herself. And so, she sets to work, at once: shooing her people back, away again.

After all the drama and dynamism of the previous books, there's a quality of wistfulness about *The Last Post*. Groby without the Great Tree – that great symbol of Christopher's romantic nostalgia – is diminished. Sylvia, repentant, is still magnificent; yet, for the first time, seems truly pitiable. Christopher, observed as it were from a distance, is a much fainter figure than before; and, apart from her brief appearance, so too is Valentine. Replacing them centre-stage, Mark and Marie-Léonie, his long-time companion and now at last wife, are two curious, charming, but essentially comic characters.

What's Ford showing us in this extended, deflationary epilogue?

The preceding trilogy has portrayed, at length, the *Amos* impulse mediated through the Isaianic archetype: sainthood, in short. In the *Last Post*, on the other hand, we're being brought to see the fundamental *contingency of the conditions for the possibility of any truly effective manifestation of such virtue*. The point is: everything depends on the witness's angle of vision; and on the general context. Christopher and Valentine are still who they were. Yet, it took a particular mode of narration, and the circumstances of the War, to reveal the deeper truth of their being, which here has largely ceased to appear. (Somewhat, as the Teresa-potential of Dorothea Brooke in *Middlemarch*, for instance, remains half-hidden ...)

And this prompts the further thought: how much other saintliness is, no doubt, all around us at this very moment – but unrevealed – obscure to us! So, Mark, breathing his last, and dreaming of Noah's Flood, ushers us towards the Last Judgement, when all will, after all, be clear:

> 'Do you remember the Yorkshireman who stood with his chin just out of the water on Ararat Top as Noah approached. And: "It's boon to tak oop!" said the Yorkshireman. ... It's bound to clear up!'[79]

---

1. *Some Do Not ...* was first published in 1924; *No More Parades* in 1925; *A Man Could Stand Up –* in 1926; *The Last Post* in 1928. In what follows I shall be quoting from the Penguin Classics edition of *Parade's End* as a whole, published in 2012.

2. *No More Parades*, Part II, §1, p. 379.

3. Ibid., p. 380.

4. Ibid. §2, p. 412.

5. *Some Do Not ...*, Part I, §2, p. 28.

6. Ibid. Part II, §1, p. 156.

7. Ibid. pp. 145—6.

8. *No More Parades*, Part III, §2, p. 489.

9. *A Man Could Stand Up –*, Part II, §3, p. 591.

10. *No More Parades*, Part I, §4, p. 363.

11. *Some Do Not ...*, Part I, §4, pp. 78—9.

12. Ibid. §6, pp. 114—16.

13. Ibid, §2, pp. 39—40.

14. Ibid. §4, p. 64.

15. Ibid., Part II, §2, p. 182.

16. *No More Parades*, Part I, §4, p. 372. Ford's own outlook (notwithstanding his longstanding friendship with Ezra Pound) was quite unequivocally philosemitic.

17. Ibid., Part III, §2, p. 496.

18. *Some Do Not ...*, Part II, §2, p. 187.

19. *A Man Could Stand Up –*, Part II, §2, pp. 566—7; and, before that, §3, p. 586, quoting the first two lines of Herbert's poem 'Vertue'. Bemerton also acquires symbolic meaning for Valentine: *The Last Post*, Part II, §3, pp. 813—14.

20. *A Man Could Stand Up – ,* §4, p. 603.

21. 'Monsignor Benson and *Initiation'*, *Outlook*, Feb. 28th 1914; in Ford, *Critical Essays*, ed. Max Saunders and Richard Stang (Manchester: Carcanet, 2002); p. 130.

    Ford had actually been received into the Roman Catholic Church at the age of eighteen, in 1892. In the crisis of 1893 – 94, however, which culminated in his elopement with Elsie Martindale, we find him, in his letters to her, decidedly hostile to religion in general; or, at any rate, to the all too conventional religion of her parents, who were determined to try and prevent the marriage. (She was legally under-age.) Here he denounces 'God almighty who is a plaguing beast'. And again: 'that stupid creature called God almighty who sits grinning & says in dreary platitude: "Wait, wait, all things in the fitness of time".' See Max Saunders, *Ford Madox Ford: A Dual Life*, Vol. 1 (Oxford University Press, 1996), p. 64

22. See the original Preface to *No More Parades* (London: Duckworth, 1925), p. v: 'State, underline and emphasize the fact how you will it is impossible to get into the heads of even intelligent public critics the fact that the opinions of a novelist's characters as stated in any novel are not of necessity the opinions of the novelists. It cannot be done.'

23. *Some Do Not ...*, Part I, §1, pp. 18—19.

24. Ibid., Part II, §3, p. 215.

25. Ibid. §, pp. 242—4. She goes on manoeuvring to evade the obligation, also, after Macmaster has died: *The Last Post*, Part II, §1, pp. 787—8.

26. *A Man Could Stand Up –*, Part II, §5, p. 615. (Note that the officer in question, a colonel, has previously been quite hostile.)

27. *Some Do Not ...*, Part I, §3, pp. 46—7. And c.f. General Campion's indignation: *No More Parades*, Part III, §2, p. 481.

28. *Some Do Not...*, Part I, §3, pp. 59—62. A conversation involving the left-wing government minister Mr Waterhouse, with Christopher and Macmaster, then also General Campion and Mr Sandbach.

29. Ibid., Part II, §4, pp. 235—7. Nor is it only in this context that he's incorruptible: c.f. §1, p. 158, his response to Valentine's own mother, in her role as a journalist, asking for spurious statistical assistance in the writing of a sensationalist article. He's fond of Mrs Wannop, and she needs the money. But he's unbending.

30. *No More Parades*, Part III, §2, p. 492.

31. Ibid., p. 495.

32. *Some Do Not ...*, Part I, §1, p. 6.

33. Ibid. p. 18. And c.f. Part II, §6, p. 281.

34. Ibid. §5, p. 85.

35. Ibid. p. 99.

36. Ibid. §7.

37. Ibid., Part II, §5, p. 280.

38. *No More Parades*, Part II, §2, p. 437.

39. *A Man Could Stand Up –*, Part I, §1, p. 514.

40. *No More Parades*, Part III, §1, pp. 453—4.

41. Ibid., Part I, §1, p. 291.

42. *Some Do Not* ...Part II, §1, pp. 169—70.

43. *A Man Could Stand Up –*, Part II, §5, p. 617.

44. Ibid., Part III, §1, pp. 645—6.

45. Ibid. p. 650.

46. Ibid. p. 652.

47. *The Last Post*, Part I, §7, pp. 776—7; Part II, §1, p. 782; §2, pp. 804—5; §3, p. 820—21.

48. *Some Do Not* ..., Part II, §3, pp. 207—8. (And Sylvia's befriending of aristocratic Austrian prisoners of war also counts against him, with regard to his military career.)

49. Ibid. §2. Sylvia's attitude towards Christopher does, after all, fluctuate: for all her mischief, there are also moments when she finds all the falsehoods circulating about him (at any rate those not started by herself) quite nauseating. C.f. Ibid. §1, p. 166: a few minutes after having chucked a plateful of food at him, she has dug her nails into the palms of her hands, in anguish. And then: 'she looked at Tietjens ... with a sort of gloating curiosity. How was it possible that the most honourable man she knew should be so overwhelmed by foul and baseless rumours? It made you suspect that honour had, in itself, a quality of the evil eye ...'

50. Ibid., §1, pp. 171—2.

51. Ibid., §3, pp. 204—11.

52. Ibid., §2, pp. 184, 188—90; §4, pp. 229—31; §5, p. 265.

53. Ibid., §3, p. 222; §5, p. 270.

54. Ibid., §4, p. 260.

55. Ibid., §3, pp. 206—7.

56. Ibid. §4. p. 257.

57. Seiden, 'Persecution and Paranoia in *Parade's End*', in *Criticism*, 8. 3, Summer 1966; pp. 246—62.

58. McKechnie is notably infected by it: *No More Parades*, Part I, §1, pp. 304—5.

59. The politicians are variously accused of heartless sheer indifference to the sufferings of the army; of egoistic meddling in military affairs; of plotting, in particular, to starve a general nicknamed 'Puffles' of the troops he needs; and of scheming to betray the French. Here's Christopher, in the midst of an artillery barrage, musing to himself:

> Intense dejection, endless muddles, endless follies, endless villainies. All these men given into the hands of the most cynically care-free intriguers in long corridors who made plots that harrowed the heart of the world. All these men toys, all these agonies mere occasions for picturesque phrases to be put into politicians' speeches without heart or even intelligence. Hundreds of thousands of men tossed here and there in that sordid and gigantic mud-brownness of midwinter ... by God, exactly as if they were nuts wilfully picked up and thrown over the shoulder by magpies ... But men.

No More Parades Part I, §1, pp. 296—7. The prose is violent; but quite understandably so, given the violence of the immediate context to which he's responding!

60. *Some Do Not ...*, Part II, §2, p. 188.

61. Ibid. §4, p. 237; and c.f. Part I, §7, p. 128, Christopher pondering: 'Why was he born to be a sort of lonely buffalo outside the herd?'

62. Ibid. Part II, §1, pp. 173—4.

63. *The Last Post*, Part II, §2, p. 804.

64. Ibid. p. 805.

65. C.f. *Some Do Not ...*, Part I, §7, pp. 127—8.

66. *The Good Soldier* was initially published in London by John Lane, at The Bodley Head.

67. Max Saunders, *Ford Madox Ford: A Dual Life* (Oxford University Press, 1996), Vol. 2, p. 236. The two unpublished narrative texts in question are 'True Love & a G.C.M.' and (especially) 'Mr Croyd'.

68. *Some Do Not ...* Part I, §2, p. 22.

69. Ford, a long-time advocate of Irish Home Rule, had known Casement personally; and regarded the British government's refusal of clemency, after Casement's capture in 1916, as scandalous.

70. *No More Parades*, Part II, §1, pp. 394—5; §2, pp. 413—6; *The Last Post*, Part II, §2, pp. 805—7, 827

71. *Some Do Not ...*, Part I, §6, pp. 104—5.

72. Ibid. p. 106

73. Ibid. Part II, §5, pp. 264—5.

74. *A Man Could Stand Up –*, Part I, §1 p. 506.

75. Ibid. p. 509.

76. Ibid. pp. 511—12.

77. Letter to Eric Pinker, 17 Aug. 1930. Ford, *Letters*, ed. Richard Ludwig (Princeton University Press, 2019), pp. 196—7. And see Saunders, *Ford Madox Ford: A Dual Life*, Vol. 2, pp. 254—5.

78. *The Last Post*, Part II, §2, p. 805.

79. Ibid. §3, p. 833.

G.

Coda:
'Why write if you can feel?'

*W*here *Reasons End*, by Yiyun Li, is a searing little book. Written in the immediate aftermath of Li's sixteen-year-old son's suicide, it's a dialogue between bereaved mother and dead son; a dialogue occurring within the mother's head; the mother unnamed, but clearly conceived as a self-portrait; the son re-named as 'Nikolai', but clearly modelled on her boy. The son is unrepentant; strikingly precocious; fondly teasing his mother. The mother is unreproachful; reticent. But it's she who has conjured him up, refusing after all to let him go. They spar with each other, playing word games; wit sparking against wit.

At one point, Nikolai teases his mother about her role as a writer:

Why write, he said, if you can feel?
What do you mean?
I always imagine writing is for people who don't want to feel, or don't know how to.
And reading? I asked. Nikolai was a good reader.
For those who do.[1]

In what sense?

∽

'Why write, if you can feel?' In the same way that Hegel spoke of 'speculative propositions', one might well call this a 'speculative question'. That's to say: a nagging, enigmatic, multi-layered, irresolvable one.

In 2017 Li published a collection of essays, written just before her son died, entitled *Dear Friend, from My Life I Write to You in Your Life*. (The title is a quotation from Katherine Mansfield.) These essays constitute a memoir, or perhaps better an anti-memoir; a set of reflections in part prompted by Li's own experience of acute depression, which had recently led to two suicide attempts, on her part, anticipating her son's. She meditates here, not least, on her yearning to erase the self that she's portraying; the way in which that yearning also paradoxically informs her impulse to write. 'But for those who wish to erase their selves by writing: Why write at all?' she asks. When she first came to the USA, Li had been a scientist. 'When I gave up science,' she goes on,

> I had a blind confidence that in writing I could will myself into a nonentity. I had for a few years relished that status, living among the characters who did not know my existence. But how does one remain forever an emotional hanger-on when one wants the characters to live, if not better, or more honestly, or more wisely, at least more fully? Uncharitably one writes in order to stop oneself from feeling too much; uncharitably one writes to become closer to that feeling self.[2]

In the essay, she's simply concerned with a civil war inside her self. In the equivalent passage from the dialogue, by contrast, the struggle is between herself as a representative writer – provocatively charged with 'not wanting to feel, or not knowing how to' – and Nikolai as a representative 'good reader', unhampered either by that recoil or by that inability. But otherwise the basic, probing thought is the same in both cases.

～

'Uncharitably one writes in order to stop oneself from feeling too much.' This assessment is 'uncharitable' inasmuch as it's a harsh confession of weakness. There are truth-laden feelings that one finds oneself too weak to bear.

What are the feelings, the truths, in question here?

I take it that they'd include:

- all that's evoked by the pain of unruly painful memory, in general;

310

- more particularly, all that leads to, and follows from, the attainment of truly honest self-knowledge; and then above all, precisely, all that's generated, in one's soul, by the challenge of sublime virtue.

Li's own idiosyncratic term for these pressures, as a whole, is *'melodrama'*.[3] 'If a tragedy makes us weep out of compassion and a comedy makes us laugh out of appreciation,' she writes, 'a melodrama alienates and discomfits'.[4] Unlike tragedy and comedy, therefore, 'melodrama is never political'; that is, it's never exploitable by manipulative propaganda.[5] For how, after all, can one manipulate by 'alienating' and 'discomfiting'? On the other hand: putting the content of 'melodrama', so defined, into words is part of the necessary process of civilising it, keeping it within safe bounds, harnessing its raw power. And this, she intimates, is for her the supreme form of literary ambition.

By contrast, most imaginative literature with broad appeal is clearly more or less a spiritual narcotic; 'opium of the people'.

Let me indeed straight away confess the quite unalloyed pleasure that I myself derive from reading, say, P. G. Wodehouse or R. K. Narayan – to give just two random examples – writers whose work, delightfully, helps make the world a brighter place! And, of course, there are many, many such, working in all different genres. To appreciate the ethically most challenging forms of literature is by no means to denigrate unpretentious others.

Nevertheless, the admittedly 'uncharitable' twofold thrust of Li's 'uncharitable' thought, lit up by her fierce melancholy, puts me in mind of *Pascal*. That's to say: Pascal's sardonic observation of the universal human, all too human craving for *divertissement* ('diversion'). Thus, Pascal writes:

> When I have occasionally set myself to consider the different distractions of men, the pains and perils to which they expose themselves at court or in war, whence arise so many quarrels, passions, bold and often bad ventures, etc., I have discovered

that all the unhappiness of men arises from one simple fact,
that they cannot stay quietly in their own chamber.[6]

For Pascal, in this passage, 'staying quietly in one's chamber' is
synecdoche for the ideal contemplative life in general: meditating
upon difficult reality; cultivating honest self-knowledge; fully
acknowledging the imperatives of sublime virtue.

Again, Pascal is unsparing:

> Man is obviously made to think. It is his whole dignity and
> his whole merit; and his whole duty is to think as he ought.
> Now, the order of thought is to begin with self, and with
> its Author and its end. Now, of what does the world think?
> Never of this, but of dancing, playing the lute, singing, making
> verses, running at the ring, etc., fighting, making oneself king,
> without thinking what it is to be a king and what to be a man.[7]

He also cites such other typical *divertissements* of aristocratic
seventeenth-century men as going to sea; womanising; gambling;
hunting hare or boar; playing 'real' tennis, or other ball games.
And, in our day, one might surely very well add to the list, amongst
much else, the writing, and the reading, of spiritual-narcotic
narrative literature. (Except that, in this case, one is driven out of
one's chamber only in one's imagination!)

There's an element of puritanical evangelistic impatience in
Pascal's critique of *divertissement* that may perhaps rather get in
the way of its actual truth. So, he frames it as a depiction of 'the
misery of man without God'. A life reduced to mere survival plus
divertissement, alone, is certainly, in a radical sense, incomplete. But
to equate the incompleteness in question, as Pascal does, to '*misery*'
– isn't that a bit strained? Isn't it a bit glittery-eyed?

And if we're to say that a life reduced in this way is a
life 'without God' – which, well yes, it surely is – then let's
nevertheless immediately add that that isn't an advertisement
for any *preconceived* notion of the divine. But, on the contrary, the
transcendence of addictive *divertissement* is precisely a refocussing

of one's search for the *hidden*, true divine essence. Which isn't only present where explicitly named, but may sometimes be revealed to far greater practical effect in anonymity.

I come back, then, to Li's reflections on her, as it happens, not at all overtly religious inspiration as a writer. 'Why write if you can feel?' By her own account, Li began her literary career very much as an addict to the sheer spiritual-narcotic pleasure of the process. But then (as she tells the tale) she started to grow discontented, chafing at the constraints of that limited ambition. More and more, she found herself writing *out of* that discontent. Her purpose had swung around to more or less the opposite of what it had been at first.

∽

'Uncharitably one writes to grow closer to [one's] feeling self.' This second assessment is, again, 'uncharitable' inasmuch as it's a frank admission of being disconnected – dulled, because trapped by one's neurotic defences. Now, though – ('Why write?') – the writer's whole desire is to escape their entrapment in superficiality.

Karen Blixen ('Isak Dinesen') once famously said:

All sorrows can be borne if you put them into a story or tell a story about them.[8]

The real sorrows behind a story may perhaps be transformed, by it, out of all immediate recognition. But if they're genuinely in there – not just fabricated for entertainment's sake, but in there, somehow, as coming from the very core of the story-teller's 'alienated' and 'discomfited' soul – they become a salutary gift. A gift of pathos, decisively exceeding the limitations of the spiritually narcotic: *pathos of shakenness*, at work in the most abrasive fashion, helping dislodge the callous thoughtless prejudices of gang and mob, the stubborn thoughtless prejudices of the herd.

In the end, Li's dialogue with her dead son culminates thus:

313

You write fiction, Nikolai said.

Yes.

Then you can make up whatever you want.

One never makes up things in fiction. One has to live there as one has to live here.

Here is where you are, not where I am. I am in fiction, he said. I am fiction now.

Then where you are is there, which is also where I live...[9]

Nothing is just 'made up' in fiction truly *written in pursuit of a vocation*; but only in fiction of the spiritual-narcotic kind, written for fun or as a job.

One never just 'makes things up' in *fiction-at-full-stretch*. For such writing is essentially responsive to the most difficult (or 'melodramatic') of realities.

---

1. Yiyun Li, *Where Reasons End* (London: Penguin, 2019), p. 56.

2. Li, *Dear Friend, from My Life I Write to You in Your Life* (London: Penguin, 2017), p. 46.

3. Ibid. pp. 51—81. This discussion emerges out of a consideration of suicide: specifically, the widespread tendency to *dismiss* suicide 'as a drama gone awry and entering the realm of melodrama', in an altogether derogatory sense (pp. 51—52).

4. Ibid. p. 52. 'Tragedy and comedy,' she goes on, 'involve an audience, so they must give – sharing themselves to elicit tears and laughter. Melodrama is not such a strategist. It meets no one's expectation but its internal need to feel.'

5. Ibid. p. 65

6. Pascal, *Pensées*, trans. William Finlayson Trotter, § 139.

7. Ibid. §146.

8. From an interview with Bent Mohn in the *New York Times Book Review*,

3rd Nov. 1957; quoted by Hannah Arendt, in *Men in Dark Times* (London: Penguin, 1973), p. 106. To give the quote more fully:

> 'I am not a novelist, really not even a writer. One of my friends said about me that I think all sorrows can be borne if you put them into a story or tell a story about them, and perhaps this is not entirely untrue.'

(In claiming to be a 'story-teller' but not really a 'writer', is Blixen perhaps reserving the latter category for the professional purveyors of what I'm calling 'spiritual narcotics'?)

9. Li, *Where Reasons End*, p. 168.